DATA ANALYSIS FOR SOCIAL SCIENCE

DATA ANALYSIS FOR SOCIAL SCIENCE

A FRIENDLY AND PRACTICAL INTRODUCTION

ELENA LLAUDET AND KOSUKE IMAI

PRINCETON UNIVERSITY PRESS

Princeton and Oxford

Published by Princeton University Press
41 William Street, Princeton, New Jersey 08540
99 Banbury Road, Oxford OX2 6JX

press.princeton.edu

All Rights Reserved

ISBN 9780691199429
ISBN (pbk.) 9780691199436
ISBN (e-book) 9780691229348

British Library Cataloging-in-Publication Data is available

Editorial: Bridget Flannery-McCoy and Alena Chekanov
Production Editorial: Mark Bellis
Cover Design: Wanda España
Production: Erin Suydam
Publicity: Kate Hensley and Charlotte Coyne
Copyeditor: Melanie Mallon

Cover Credit: Human Alphabets by Sudarsan Thobias / Shutterstock

This book has been composed in Iwona

Printed on acid-free paper. ∞

Printed in the United States of America

10 9 8 7 6 5 4 3 2 1

To my students,
        Elena Llaudet

To Christina, Keiji, and Misaki,
        Kosuke Imai

CONTENTS

PREFACE

With this book, we hope to make data analysis for the social sciences accessible to everyone. Drawing conclusions from data and being able to evaluate the strengths and weaknesses of social scientific studies are critical skills that should be available to all. Not only can these skills lead to a job as a data scientist, but they also help us better understand and address important issues and problems facing society.

This book project was born when Elena suggested to Kosuke several ways to make more accessible the materials covered in *Quantitative Social Science: An Introduction* (Princeton University Press, 2017; aka QSS). Like QSS, this book teaches the fundamentals of data analysis for social science while analyzing real-world data from published research. This book, however, focuses on a smaller set of essential concepts with an emphasis on reaching students with no prior knowledge of statistics and coding and with minimal background in math. Our goals are to lower the barriers to becoming a data scientist and to share more broadly the excitement of quantitative social science research.

Many people have contributed their knowledge and talents to the production of this book. First and foremost, we would like to thank Kathryn Sargent for the countless hours she spent improving our writing and helping us bring our vision to reality. She has been an integral part of the project from the very beginning, and this book has greatly benefited from her attention to detail, editorial expertise, and good cheer. We are also grateful to all those who have given us feedback, especially our students, early adopters, and reviewers. In particular, we want to thank Alicia Cooperman, Michael Denly, Max Goplerud, Florian Hollenbach, Justin Leinaweaver, Emilee Martichenko, Davi Cordeiro Moreira, Leonid Peisakhin, Sheila Scheuerman, Tyler Simko, Robert Smith, Omar Wasow, and Hye Young You. Our thanks also go to Eric Crahan at Princeton University, who encouraged us to take on this project, and to Bridget Flannery-McCoy and Alena Chekanov, who made sure that the review and production process was as smooth as possible. In addition, Elena would like to offer special thanks to Harvard professor Stephen Ansolabehere for being a constant source of advice, support, and friendship.

Finally, we would like to thank our families and friends for their love and patience throughout this project. Elena thanks her mom, Didi, and brother, Jorge, for always being there for her, despite being on the other side of the Atlantic. She also thanks her friends, especially Bulbul, Baptiste, and Émile, for keeping her fed, sane, and high-spirited during all these years. Kosuke thanks Christina for a lifelong partnership that has made everything, both personal and professional, possible. He also thanks Keiji and Misaki for making sure that their family had many fun moments together, even during the pandemic.

Elena Llaudet and Kosuke Imai
Cambridge, Massachusetts
January 2022

DATA ANALYSIS FOR SOCIAL SCIENCE

1. INTRODUCTION

This book provides a friendly introduction to data analysis for the social sciences. It covers the fundamental methods of quantitative social science research, using plain language and assuming absolutely no prior knowledge of the subject matter.

Proceeding step by step, we show how to analyze real-world data using the statistical program R for the purpose of answering a wide range of substantive questions. Along the way, we teach the statistical concepts and programming skills needed to conduct and evaluate social scientific studies. We explain not only how to perform the analyses but also how to interpret the results and identify the analyses' strengths and potential limitations.

Through this book, you will learn how to *measure*, *predict*, and *explain* quantities of interest based on data. These are the three fundamental goals of quantitative social science research. (See outline 1.1.)

R symbols, operators, and functions introduced in this chapter: $+$, $-$, $*$, $/$, $<-$, $*$, (), sqrt(), #, setwd(), read.csv(), View(), head(), dim(), $, and mean().

WHY DO WE ANALYZE DATA IN THE SOCIAL SCIENCES?

In the social sciences we analyze data to:

- *measure* a quantity of interest, such as the proportion of eligible voters in favor of a particular policy

- *predict* a quantity of interest, such as the likely winner of an upcoming election

- *explain* a quantity of interest, such as the causal effect of attending a private school on student test scores.

OUTLINE 1.1. The three goals of quantitative social science research.

Figuring out whether you aim to measure, predict, and/or explain a quantity of interest should always precede the analysis and often also precede the data collection. As you will learn, the goals of your research will determine (i) what data you need to collect and how, (ii) the statistical methods you use, and (iii) what you pay attention to in the analysis. As you read this book and learn about each goal in detail, the distinctions will become clearer. Here we provide a brief preview.

To measure a quantity of interest such as a population characteristic, we often use survey data, that is, information collected on a sample of individuals from the target population. To analyze the data, we may compute various descriptive statistics, such as mean and median, and create visualizations like histograms and scatter plots. The validity of our conclusions depends on whether the sample is representative of the target population. To measure the proportion of eligible voters in favor of a particular policy, for example, our conclusions will be valid if the sample of voters surveyed is representative of *all* eligible voters.

To predict a quantity of interest, we typically use a statistical model such as a linear regression model to summarize the relationship between the predictors and the outcome variable of interest. The stronger the association between the predictors and the outcome variable, the better the predictive model will usually be. To predict the likely winner of an upcoming election, for example, if economic conditions are strongly associated with the electoral outcomes of candidates from the incumbent party, we may be able to use the current unemployment rate as our predictor.

To explain a quantity of interest such as the causal effect of a treatment on an outcome, we need to find or create a situation in which the group of individuals who received the treatment is comparable, in the aggregate, to the group of individuals who did not. In other words, we need to eliminate or control for all confounding variables, which are variables that affect both (i) the likelihood of receiving the treatment and (ii) the outcome variable. For example, when estimating the causal effect of attending a private school on student test scores, family wealth is a potential confounding variable. Students from wealthier families are more likely to attend a private school and also more likely to receive after-school tutoring, which might have a positive impact on their test scores. To produce valid estimates of causal effects, we may conduct a randomized experiment, which eliminates all confounding variables by assigning the treatment at random. In the current example, we would achieve this by using a lottery to determine which students attend private schools and which do not. Alternatively, if we cannot conduct a randomized experiment and need to rely on observational data instead, we would need to use statistical methods to control for all confounding variables such as family wealth. Otherwise, we would not know what portion of the difference in average test scores between private and public school students was the result of the type of school attended and what portion was the result of family background.

1.1 BOOK OVERVIEW

The book consists of seven chapters.

Chapter 1 is the introductory chapter, which lays the groundwork for the forthcoming data analyses.

Chapters 2 through 5 each introduce one or two published social scientific studies. In these chapters, we show how to analyze real-world datasets to answer different kinds of substantive questions. Specifically, we teach how to use several quantitative methods to measure, predict, and explain quantities of interest. (See outline 1.2, which indicates how each chapter relates to the three goals of quantitative social science research.)

BOOK OUTLINE	
Chapter	Goal
1. Introduction	
2. Estimating Causal Effects with Randomized Experiments	Explain
3. Inferring Population Characteristics via Survey Research	Measure
4. Predicting Outcomes Using Linear Regression	Predict
5. Estimating Causal Effects with Observational Data	Explain
6. Probability	
7. Quantifying Uncertainty	All Three

OUTLINE 1.2. Book outline showing how each chapter relates to the three goals of quantitative social science research.

As you can see, chapters 2 and 5 are both about explanation, also known as causal inference. They teach how to estimate causal effects using different types of data. Since the methods differ, they are presented in separate chapters.

The book progresses from simple to more complex methods. Chapter 2 shows how to estimate causal effects using data from a randomized experiment. Chapter 3 is about measurement and teaches how to infer the characteristics of an entire population from a sample of survey respondents. Chapter 4 is about prediction and demonstrates how to use simple linear regression. Chapter 5 shows how to estimate causal effects with observational data and teaches multiple linear regression, the most complicated method we see in the book.

In chapter 6, we cover basic probability, and in chapter 7 we complete some of the analyses from chapters 2 through 5 by quantifying the uncertainty of our empirical findings. A more detailed description of each chapter is below.

1.2 CHAPTER SUMMARIES

In the current introductory chapter, we discuss why data analysis is a required skill among social scientists. We also explain how to get our computers ready, and we familiarize ourselves with RStudio and R, the two programs we will use. Then, we learn to load and make sense of data and practice computing and interpreting means.

In chapter 2, we define and learn how to estimate causal effects using data from a randomized experiment. As the working example, we analyze data from one of the largest experiments in U.S. education policy research, Project STAR, to determine whether attending a small class improves student performance.

In chapter 3, we use survey research to measure population characteristics. In addition, we learn how to visualize and summarize the distribution of single variables as well as the relationship between two variables. To illustrate these concepts, we analyze data related to the 2016 British referendum on withdrawing from the European Union, a decision popularly known as Brexit.

In chapter 4, we learn how to predict outcomes using simple linear regression models. For practice, we analyze data from 170 countries in order to predict growth in gross domestic product (GDP) using night-time light emissions as measured from space.

In chapter 5, we return to estimating causal effects, but this time using observational data. We define confounding variables, examine how their presence complicates the estimation of causal effects, and learn how to use multiple linear regression models to help mitigate the potential bias these variables introduce. To illustrate how this works step by step, we estimate the effects of Russian TV reception on the 2014 Ukrainian parliamentary elections. In this context, we introduce the concepts of internal and external validity. We then discuss the pros and cons of randomized experiments and of observational studies.

In chapter 6, we shift our focus away from data analysis to cover basic probability. We learn about random variables and their distributions as well as the distinction between population parameters and sample statistics. We then discuss the two large sample theorems that enable us to measure statistical uncertainty.

In chapter 7, we use everything we have learned in the preceding chapters and show how to quantify the uncertainty in our empirical findings in order to draw conclusions at the population level. In particular, we show how to quantify the uncertainty in (i) population inferences, (ii) predictions, and (iii) causal effect estimates. As illustrations, we complete some of the analyses we started in chapters 2 through 5.

1.3 HOW TO USE THIS BOOK

This is no ordinary textbook on data analysis. It is intentionally designed to accommodate readers with a variety of math and programming backgrounds.

The book uses a two-column layout: a main column and a side column or margin.

The main column contains the essential material and code, which are intended for all readers, except for the sections labeled FORMULA IN DETAIL. These contain more advanced material and are clearly identified so that you can easily skip them if you so choose.

In the margin are various types of notes and figures, each with a different purpose:

- At the beginning of each chapter, we list the R functions, symbols, and operators that will be introduced. You can look through the list to get a sense of what will be covered. (See, for example, the list for this chapter shown on the first page, and note that we always display code in cyan.)
- TIPs include supplemental material, such as additional explanations, answers to common questions, notes on best practices, and recommendations.
- RECALLs remind you of relevant information mentioned earlier in the book. These reminders are particularly helpful when the book is read only a few pages at a time, such as over the course of a semester.
- To help you review the core concepts, which are shown in **bold red** in the main text, we repeat their definitions in the margin. These notes are displayed in red.
- To help you with R functions, symbols, and operators, the first time these are introduced, we include in the margin an explanation of how they work and provide an example. These explanations are displayed in a cyan-colored frame.

At the end of each chapter, in place of the usual list of supplementary exercises, we include CHEATSHEETS to help you review the core concepts as well as the R functions, symbols, and operators covered.

Supplementary chapter-specific exercises, categorized by degree of difficulty, are available at http://press.princeton.edu/dss.

Finally, at the end of the book, we include three separate indexes for concepts, mathematical notation, and R-related topics.

1.4 WHY LEARN TO ANALYZE DATA?

As a social scientist, sooner or later you will need to rely on data to (i) measure the characteristics of a certain population of interest, (ii) make predictions, and/or (iii) make or evaluate decisions involving cause-and-effect relationships. What proportion of a population is in favor of a particular policy? Who is the candidate most likely to win an upcoming election? Shall we implement a particular policy to boost economic growth? You will want to be able to answer these types of questions either by analyzing data yourself or by understanding and assessing someone else's data analysis.

Even if you are not planning to become a social scientist, it is useful for you to know how to analyze data and/or how to distinguish a good quantitative study from a poorly conducted one. These are highly marketable skills. Recent advancements in computing power and the proliferation of data have increased the demand for data analysts who can inform decision makers in the public and private sectors alike.

The analytical skills you will learn by making your way through this book can also be used to improve everyday decisions, from choosing a candidate to vote for to determining the best way to increase your productivity. Perhaps most importantly, by learning the strengths and limitations of different quantitative methods, you will become less vulnerable to arguments based on faulty inferences from data. In the era of big data, we all stand to benefit from becoming savvy consumers of quantitative research, even if we do not all become skilled researchers ourselves.

1.4.1 LEARNING TO CODE

For the purpose of analyzing data, we write and run code. Code contains instructions that a computer can implement. These instructions consist of sequences of clearly defined steps written in a particular programming language. In this book, we code in R, which is a programming language used by many data analysts.

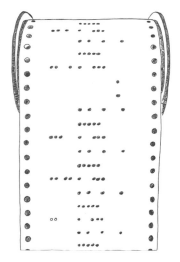

Don't worry if you have never done any coding before. Learning to code is not as difficult as one might think. You may even find it fun. Back in 1944, when the first programmable computer in the United States was built, only highly trained mathematicians were able to code. At that time, coding required punching paper tape in specific sequences that the machine could read. (See a rendition of what this tape looked like in the margin.) Today, anyone with access to a computer, some spare time, and a little patience can learn how to code.

1.5 GETTING READY

To perform the analyses in this book, we first need to download and install the necessary files and programs. We should also familiarize ourselves with RStudio, which is the interface we use throughout.

❶ DOWNLOAD AND SAVE FILES

All the files we will use are in a folder named DSS, which is available at http://press.princeton.edu/dss. For easy access, we recommend saving the folder on your Desktop. This is where the code used throughout the book assumes the DSS folder is located. In case you choose to save the folder elsewhere, we also provide instructions for making the necessary changes to the code.

TIP: By default, your computer will likely save the DSS folder to your Downloads. To move it, you can copy and paste it or drag it to the new location.

❷ DOWNLOAD AND INSTALL R AND RSTUDIO

We will use two programs: R and RStudio. R is the statistical program, the engine if you will, that will perform the calculations and create the graphics for us. RStudio is the user-friendly interface we will use to communicate with R. While we could use R directly, going through RStudio makes writing and running code much easier.

Why do we use R as our statistical program? Because it is free, open-source (anyone can see the underlying code and improve it), powerful, and flexible. It is also widely used. Indeed, many jobs these days require knowledge of R.

Unfortunately, these programs are compatible only with Linux, Mac, and Windows operating systems. They cannot be used on tablets or phones. We provide instructions for using these two programs on a Mac or a Windows computer.

To download and install R, go to http://cran.r-project.org, select the link that matches your operating system, and follow the instructions.

To download and install RStudio, go to http://rstudio.com, select the link that matches your operating system, and follow the instructions.

❸ BECOME FAMILIAR WITH RSTUDIO

To analyze data, we always operate R through RStudio. Let's take a moment to become acquainted with RStudio's layout.

After installing both programs, go ahead and start RStudio. Then, from within RStudio, open a new R script, which is the type of file we use to store the code we write to analyze data. Instructions are shown in the margin.

TIP: How do we open a new R script? In the RStudio dropdown menu, click on File > New File > R Script. A new "Untitled" file will open. The extension of this type of file is ".R", which is why R scripts are also called R files.

After opening a new R script, RStudio's interface should look like figure 1.1.

- The upper-left window is the *R script*, which is where we write and run code, giving R commands to execute.
- The lower-left window is the *R console*, where R provides either the results of successfully executed code (known as outputs) or any error messages.
- The upper-right window is the *environment*, which is the storage room of the current R session. It lists all the objects we have created. (We will soon explain what objects are and provide examples showing how the environment works.)
- The lower-right window is where we find the *help* and *plots tabs*, which we will learn how to use later on.

FIGURE 1.1. Layout of RStudio after opening a new R script. The upper-left window is the R script. The lower-left window is the R console. The upper-right window is the environment of the R session. The plots and help tabs appear in the lower-right window.

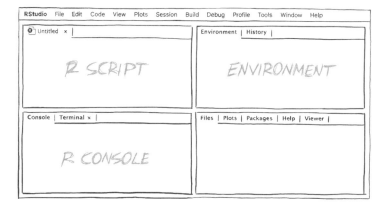

1.6 INTRODUCTION TO R

To use R, we need to learn the R programming language. (R is the name of both the statistical program and the programming language.) Learning a programming language is like learning a foreign language. It is not easy, and it takes a lot of practice and patience. The exercises in this book will help you learn to code in R, so be sure to follow along. Practice is everything!

Let's begin. R can be used to do many things. In our case, we will use R (i) as a calculator; (ii) to create objects, which is how R stores data; and (iii) to interact with data using functions.

WE WILL USE THE STATISTICAL PROGRAM R TO:
(i)   do calculations
(ii)   create objects
(iii) use functions.

1.6.1 DOING CALCULATIONS IN R

We can use R as a calculator. R can do summation ($+$), subtraction ($-$), multiplication (*), and division ($/$), as well as other more complicated mathematical operations. For example, the code to ask R to calculate 1 plus 3 is:

```
1 + 3
```

$+$, $-$, *, and $/$ are some of the arithmetic operators recognized by R. Example: $(4 - 1 + 3)^*(2 / 3)$

To run this or any other code, we first type it in the R script (the upper-left window of RStudio). Then, we highlight as much of it as we want to run and either (a) manually hit the run icon (shown in the margin) or (b) use the shortcut *command+enter* in Mac or *ctrl+enter* in Windows. The result, or output, of the executed code will show up in the R console (the lower-left window of RStudio). (Instead, we could type the code directly in the R console and hit enter, but we should avoid doing it that way. It is best to run code through an R script so that you can save it, re-run it, tweak it, expand it, and share it.)

After running the code above, we should see the following in the R console: first, the executed code shown in blue, indicating that R was able to run it without problems, and then the output shown in black. In this case, the output is:

```
4
```

Indeed, one plus three equals four.

Congratulations! You just wrote and ran your first line of code in R. Notice that now that you have written some code in the R script, RStudio shows the name of the file in red. This is to remind you that you have some unsaved changes. Once you save the file, the file name will return to black.

TIP: To save any changes you make to the R script, either (a) use the shortcut *command+S* in Mac or *ctrl+S* in Windows or (b) click on File > Save or Save As...

Throughout the book, we show the output that you should see in the R console right after the code that produces it. To distinguish the output from the code, we display the output with the symbol ## at the beginning of the line. For example, we display the code and output above as follows:

```
1 + 3
## [1] 4
```

TIP: Adding spaces around operators makes the code easier to read. R ignores these spaces. Example: 1+3 produces the same output as 1 + 3.

The first line, shown in cyan, is the code to be typed and run in the R script. The second line, which begins with ## and is shown in gray, is what should appear in the R console after running the code.

What does the number in brackets before the 4 mean? It indicates the position of the output immediately to its right. In this instance, [1] indicates that 4 is the first output of the code we ran. Later in the chapter, we will see examples of code that produce multiple outputs, which will clarify how this works.

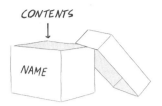

CONTENTS

NAME

<- is the assignment operator. It creates new objects in R (unless one with the same name already exists, in which case R overwrites its contents). To its left, we specify the name of the object (without quotes). To its right, we specify the contents of the object. Example: four <- 4.

TIP: We would accomplish the same thing by running: four <- 4.

TIP: RStudio continues to work in the same R session until you quit the program. At that time, R will ask whether you want to save the workspace image, which contains all the objects you created during the R session. We recommend that you do not save it. If you need to continue to work with those objects, you can always re-create them by re-running your code.

1.6.2 CREATING OBJECTS IN R

In order to manipulate and analyze data, we need to load and store datasets. R stores information in what are known as objects, and so we need to learn how to create objects in R.

Think of an object as a box that can contain anything. All we need to do is give it a name, so that we know how to refer to it, and specify its contents.

To create an object in R, we use the assignment operator <-:

- To its left, we specify the name we want to give the object. This name can be anything as long as it does not begin with a number or contain spaces or special symbols like $ or % that are reserved for other purposes. Underscores _ are permitted and are good substitutes for spaces.

- To its right, we specify the contents of the object, that is, the data we want to store.

CREATING OBJECTS: To store data as an object in R, we run code using this format:

object_name <- object_contents

where:

- object_name is the name we want to give the object
- <- is the assignment operator, which creates an object by assigning contents to a name
- object_contents is the data we want to store in the object.

For example, if we want to create an object called *four* containing the output of the calculation 1+3, we run:

```
four <- 1 + 3
```

Notice that after running the code above, the object will show up in the environment (the upper-right window in RStudio). As mentioned earlier, the environment is the storage room of the current R session. It shows the objects that we have created and that are available for us to use.

If we want to know the contents of the object *four*, we can type and run the name of the object in the R script. Its contents will appear in the R console. This is equivalent to asking R, what is inside the object named *four*?

```
four
## [1] 4
```

Not surprisingly, the object *four* contains the number 4.

Objects can contain text as well as numbers. For example, to create an object called *hello* containing the text "hi" we run:

```
hello <- "hi"
```

After running the code above, the environment should contain two objects: *four* and *hello*.

Let's stop here to learn something important about R. Look at the code above. Why did we use quotation marks around the content of the object "hi" but not around the name of the object hello? In other words, when do we use quotes " when coding in R? Here is the rule: When writing code, the names of objects, names of functions, and names of arguments as well as special values such as TRUE, FALSE, NA, and NULL should *not* be in quotes; all other text should be in quotes. (In the next subsection, we will see what we mean by functions and arguments. We will learn the meaning and usage of TRUE and FALSE in chapter 2 and of NA and NULL in chapter 3.)

What would have happened had we tried to run the code above without quotes around *hi*? Go ahead and try it:

```
hello <- hi
## Error: object 'hi' not found
```

In the R console, you will see an error message (in red) that reads, "Error: object 'hi' not found". Indeed, by typing *hi* without quotes, you are telling R that *hi* is the name of an object. Because there is no object named *hi* in the environment, R gives you an error message. Encountering programming errors is part of the coding process. Try not to be discouraged by them.

A word of caution: R overwrites (replaces) old objects if we use the same name when creating a new object. For example, go ahead and run the following:

```
hello <- "hi, nice to meet you"
```

You should see that you still have only two objects in the environment: *four* and *hello*, but now *hello* contains the text "hi, nice to meet you" instead of simply "hi". To confirm this, we run:

```
hello
## [1] "hi, nice to meet you"
```

Note also that R is case-sensitive. It will treat *Hello* as a completely different object name than *hello*. If we run the name *Hello* by mistake, R will not be able to find the object because there is no object in the environment called *Hello* with an uppercase H at the beginning. To avoid this problem, we recommend using all lowercase letters when naming objects.

" when writing code, the names of objects, names of functions, and names of arguments as well as special values such as TRUE, FALSE, NA, and NULL should not be in quotes; all other text should be in quotes. Examples: "this is just text", object_name. Never use quotes around a number unless you want R to treat it as text, in which case you will not be able to use it to perform arithmetic operations.

TIP: If you have problems figuring out what a particular error means, Google it. Lots of data analysts participate in Q&A sites, such as Stack Overflow, which can be very helpful for this sort of thing.

1.6.3 USING FUNCTIONS IN R

Finally, we use R to interact with data, which requires using functions.

Think of a function as an action that you request R to perform with a particular piece of data, such as calculating the square root of four. A function takes one or more inputs, such as the number four; performs one or more actions with the inputs, such as calculating the square root of the inputs; and produces one or more outputs, such as the number two, which is the result of taking the square root of four.

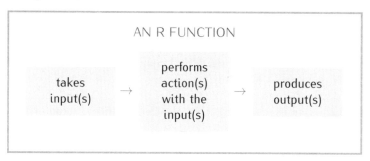

AN R FUNCTION

takes input(s) → performs action(s) with the input(s) → produces output(s)

R functions in this book: sqrt(), setwd(), read.csv(), View(), head(), dim(), mean(), ifelse(), table(), prop.table(), na.omit(), hist(), median(), sd(), var(), plot(), abline(), cor(), lm(), log(), c(), sample(), rnorm(), pnorm(), print(), nrow(), predict(), abs(), and summary().

> () the names of functions are always followed by parentheses. Inside the parentheses, we write the argument(s) of the function, separated by commas if there is more than one argument. Example: function_name(arg1, arg2).

TIP: There are two types of arguments: required and optional. Required arguments are the inputs that we must specify in order to use a particular function. Optional arguments are the inputs that we could specify if we wanted to modify the function's default settings.

Throughout the book, we will learn how to use the functions listed in the margin, which come automatically loaded with R. In time, we will learn their names, the actions they perform, the inputs they require, and the outputs they produce. Meanwhile, here are some important things to know about functions:

- The name of a function (without quotes) is always followed by parentheses: function_name()

- Inside the parentheses, we specify the inputs to be used by the function, which we refer to as arguments: function_name(arguments)

- Most functions require that we specify at least one argument but can take many optional arguments. When multiple arguments are specified inside the parentheses, they are separated by commas: function_name(argument1, argument2)

- To identify the type of argument that we are specifying, we either enter the arguments in a particular order or include their names (without quotes) in our specification: function_name(argument1, argument2) or function_name(argument1_name = argument1, argument2_name = argument2)

- In this book, we follow the most common practices. We always specify required arguments first. If there is more than one required argument, we enter them in the order expected by R. We specify any optional arguments we want next and include their names so that R knows how to interpret them: function_name(required_argument, optional_argument_name = optional_argument)

USING R FUNCTIONS: To use a function in R, we typically write code in one of these two formats:

(a) *function_name(required_argument)*

(b) *function_name(required_argument, optional_argument_name = optional_argument)*

where:

- *function_name* is the name of the function; for example, "mean" is the name of the function that computes the mean of a set of values
- *required_argument* is the argument the function requires, such as the values we want to calculate the mean of; we typically do not include the names of required arguments; we enter the required arguments first, and if there is more than one, we enter them in the order expected by R
- , is a comma, which we use to separate different arguments
- *optional_argument_name* is the name of the optional argument we want to use, such as the argument that enables us to eliminate missing values before calculating a mean
- *optional_argument* is what we set the optional argument to be.

We will see some complex R functions in the next section. For now, let's look at a simple one. The function sqrt(), which stands for "square root," calculates the square root of the argument specified inside the parentheses. For example, to calculate the square root of 4, we run:

```
sqrt(4)
## [1] 2
```

The output here is the number 2. Alternatively, given that the object *four* currently contains the number 4, we can run:

```
sqrt(four)
## [1] 2
```

Note that R will be able to execute the code above only after we have created the object *four*. If we start a new R session and attempt to run this code without having first created the object *four*, R will not be able to find the object in the environment and will give us an error message. This is just to say that one must run code in order. When returning to work on an R script, it is a good idea to run all the code from the beginning of the file up to the line that we are working on.

sqrt() calculates the square root of the argument specified inside the parentheses. Example: sqrt(4).

TIP: Here, the name of the function is sqrt, which, as with all function names, is followed by parentheses (). Inside the parentheses, we need to specify the required argument, which is 4, in this case. The output of the executed code is 2. Indeed, the square root of four is two.

One of the major advantages of writing code using an R script (instead of writing it directly into the R console) is that we can always replicate our results by re-running the code we have written previously. Using an R script, we are able to work on complex problems that might require running hundreds or thousands of lines of code. As long as we save the code in an R script, we can keep tweaking and expanding it. Writing code in R scripts also means we can share our work and collaborate with others. Anyone with access to our R script will be able to replicate our analyses, which leads us to our next topic: the importance of annotating, or commenting, code.

It is good practice to comment code, that is, to include short notes to ourselves or to our collaborators explaining what the code does. This will make reading and understanding our code easier. To write comments in the R script, we use #. R ignores everything that follows this character until the end of the line and will not execute it. For example, running the following code produces exactly the same output as the code above:

```
sqrt(four) # calculates square root of four
## [1] 2
```

> # is the character used to comment code. R ignores everything that follows this character until the end of the line. Example: # this is a comment.

After seeing the # character, R stopped reading until the end of the line. Had we inserted the comment at the beginning of the line, before the code, R would not have executed the function sqrt() at all. Go ahead, run:

```
# calculates square root of four sqrt(four)
```

R will not produce an output. R thinks the whole line is a comment because it starts with #.

RStudio helps us write and read code by color coding it in the R script. For example, comments are shown in light green, while executable code is shown in black, gray, blue, and dark green. Becoming familiar with this color scheme will help you detect errors in your code. (In this book, we use only two colors when displaying code: cyan for executable code and gray for comments.)

1.7 LOADING AND MAKING SENSE OF DATA

Before starting any analysis, we must load the dataset. Then, we must understand what the observations represent and what each of the variables means. In this section, we show how to do all of this for the data from the Project Student-Teacher Achievement Ratio (Project STAR) in preparation for the analysis in chapter 2. The goal of Project STAR was to examine the causal effects of small classes on student performance. While exploring the

> TIP: We recommend that when you start a new study, you either (a) start a new R session (Session > New Session) or (b) remove all objects from the environment (Session > Clear Workspace > Yes) to avoid operating with objects from previous studies by mistake.

data from Project STAR, we learn what variables are and how to distinguish between different types of variables based on their contents.

To follow along, you can create a new R script (as shown in the previous section) and practice typing the code yourself. Alternatively, you can open the "Introduction.R" file, which contains the code used in the remainder of this chapter.

Here are the steps we recommend you follow before starting a data analysis:

TIP: How do we open an existing R script? In the RStudio dropdown menu, click on File > Open File... and then click on the ".R" file you want to open.

❶ SET THE WORKING DIRECTORY

Before we can load a dataset, we need to direct R to the working directory, that is, the name and location of the folder containing the data. If you followed the advice from the earlier section, all the files necessary for the exercises in this book will be in the DSS folder on your Desktop.

The easiest way to set the working directory is to first save the R script to the folder that contains the dataset, the DSS folder, in this case. Then, you can use the dropdown menu to set the working directory manually: Session > Set Working Directory > To Source File Location. After your last click, you will see a line of code appear in the R console. Every time you start a new R session and want to work with a dataset saved in the DSS folder, you will need to run this line of code. You may, therefore, want to copy and paste it in the R script as your first line of code.

TIP: To save an R script to the DSS folder, either (a) click on File > Save As ... and select the DSS folder, or (b) manually drag the corresponding ".R" file from its current location to the DSS folder.

The code to set the working directory uses the function setwd(), which stands for "<u>set</u> <u>w</u>orking <u>d</u>irectory." The only required argument is the path to the folder, which should be in quotes because it is text and not the name of an object, the name of a function, the name of an argument, or a special value such as TRUE, FALSE, NA, and NULL. The path differs depending on whether you have a Mac or a Windows computer. The code to set the working directory to the DSS folder on your Desktop should resemble one of these (where *user* is your own username):

setwd() sets the working directory, that is, directs R to the folder on your computer where the dataset is saved. The only required argument is the path to the folder in quotes. Examples: setwd("~/Desktop/*folder*") for Mac, setwd("C:/*user*/Desktop/*folder*") for Windows (where *user* is your own username).

```
setwd("~/Desktop/DSS") # example of setwd() for Mac
setwd("C:/user/Desktop/DSS") # example for Windows
```

❷ LOAD THE DATASET

Now we are ready to load the dataset. R can read a variety of data formats. In this book, datasets are always provided in comma-separated values files, known as CSV files. As the name indicates, CSV files contain data separated by commas. (See figure 1.2 for a rendition of a CSV file.)

TIP: Resist the temptation to double-click on a CSV file. If you open a CSV file directly, you risk inadvertently changing or losing data.

FIGURE 1.2. CSV files contain data separated by commas.

```
○ ○ ○                    STAR.csv
"classtype","reading","math","graduated"
"small",578,610,1
"regular",612,612,1
"regular",583,606,1
"small",661,648,1
"small",614,636,1
"regular",610,603,0
```

read.csv() reads CSV files. The only required argument is the name of the CSV file in quotes. Example: read.csv("file.csv").

To read the contents of a CSV file in R, we use the read.csv() function, which requires that we specify inside the parentheses the name of the CSV file in quotes. (We need to use quotes around the name of the CSV file because it is text and not the name of an object, the name of a function, the name of an argument, or a special value such as TRUE, FALSE, NA, and NULL.)

To store the dataset so that we can analyze it later, we need to not only read the CSV file but also save its contents as an object. We can do so by using the assignment operator <-. As we saw earlier, to the left of the assignment operator, we specify the name of the object. To its right, we specify the contents, which in this case are produced by reading the CSV file using the function read.csv().

Here, the dataset is in a file called "STAR.csv", and we choose to name the object where we store the dataset *star*. Putting it all together, the code to read and store the dataset is:

```
star <- read.csv("STAR.csv") # reads and stores data
```

After running the line of code above, the name of the object, *star*, should appear in the environment (the upper-right window in RStudio). If R gives you an error message instead, make sure that (i) you have set the working directory to the folder where the CSV file is saved, (ii) the name of the CSV file you are using in the code is exactly the same as the name of the CSV file saved in the working directory, and (iii) the extension of the CSV file in the working directory is indeed ".csv".

❸ UNDERSTAND THE DATA

To make sense of the dataset, we should start by looking at its contents.

To look at the data, we could type the name of the object, *star*, in the R script and run it. R will show the entire contents of the dataset in the R console, which might be hard to read unless the dataset is small.

A better option is to use the function View(), which requires that we specify inside the parentheses the name of the object where the dataset is stored (without quotes). Alternatively, you can manually click on the object name in the environment. Both of these actions open a new tab in the upper-left window of RStudio with the dataset in spreadsheet form. We can then easily scroll up, down, left, and right to look at the data in an organized manner. Figure 1.3 shows how the data will be displayed if we run:

```
View(star)  # opens a new tab with contents of dataset
```

▲	classtype ⇕	reading ⇕	math ⇕	graduated ⇕
1	small	578	610	1
2	regular	612	612	1
3	regular	583	606	1
4	small	661	648	1
5	small	614	636	1
6	regular	610	603	0

Tabs: Introduction.R ×   star ×

> View() opens a new tab in the upper-left window of RStudio with the contents of a dataset. The only required argument is the name of the object where the dataset is stored (without quotes). Example: View(data). Note that R is case-sensitive and the name of this function starts with uppercase V. The good news is this is the only function we will see in this book that uses any uppercase letters; all others are written in all lowercase letters.

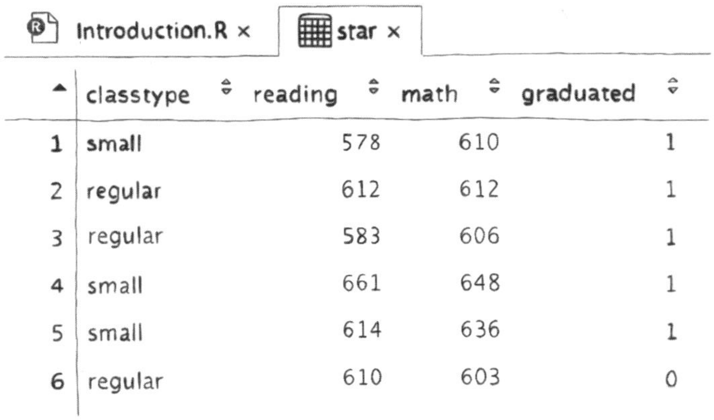

FIGURE 1.3. Tab that opens in the upper-left window of RStudio with entire contents of the *star* dataset as a result of either (a) running View(star) in the R script or (b) clicking on the object *star* in the environment. (To return to the R script, we can either close this tab by clicking on the gray X next to the name or by clicking on the R script tab.)

Sometimes it might be enough for us to see only the first few rows of data. For this purpose, we use the function head(), which requires that we specify inside the parentheses the name of the object where the dataset is stored (without quotes):

```
head(star)  # shows the first  six rows
##  classtype reading math graduated
## 1     small   578 610         1
## 2   regular   612 612         1
## 3   regular   583 606         1
## 4     small   661 648         1
## 5     small   614 636         1
## 6   regular   610 603         0
```

> head() shows the first six rows or observations in a dataset. The only required argument is the name of the object where the dataset is stored (without quotes). To change the number of observations displayed, we use the optional argument n. Examples: head(data) shows the first six rows and head(data, n=3) shows the first three. In the output, the first column identifies the position of the observations, and the first row identifies the names of the variables.

By default, the function head() displays the first six lines of data. If we want R to display a different number of lines, we specify an optional argument inside the parentheses. In particular, we specify the argument named n and set it to equal the number of lines we want R to show. For example, to ask R to display the first three lines of *star*, we run:

```
head(star, n=3)  # shows the first  three rows
##  classtype reading math graduated
## 1     small   578 610         1
## 2   regular   612 612         1
## 3   regular   583 606         1
```

RECALL: In R functions, multiple arguments are separated by commas, and the names of arguments should not be in quotes. Failing to follow these instructions will prevent R from executing the code and result in an error message.

How do we make sense of the data inside the dataset? Knowing the following common features of datasets should help:

- Datasets capture the characteristics of a particular set of individuals or entities: citizens, organizations, countries, and so on. As we will soon learn, this dataset contains information about students who participated in Project STAR.

- Datasets are typically organized as **dataframes**, where rows are observations and columns are variables.

  - What is an **observation**?

    - An observation is the information collected from a particular individual or entity in the study.

    - The **unit of observation** of the dataset defines the individuals or the entities that each observation in the dataframe represents. The unit of observation in the STAR dataset is students. Hence, every row of data in the *star* dataframe represents a different student in the study.

    - We usually refer to an observation by the row number in the dataframe, which we denote as i. See, for example, that in the output of head(), the rows are labeled by their position, i. When R displays the first six observations of a dataframe, the values of i range from 1 to 6.

  - What is a **variable**?

    - A variable captures the values of a changing characteristic for the multiple individuals or entities in the study.

    - Every column of data in the *star* dataframe is a variable; each variable captures a specific feature of the students, for all the students in the study.

    - We usually refer to a variable by its name. See, for example, that in the output of head(), the columns are labeled with the variable names: *classtype*, *reading*, *math*, and *graduated*. (Note that, for easy recognition, we italicize the names of variables in the text.)

    - From time to time, in this book we define new variables for the purpose of illustrating concepts. We represent a variable and its contents using the following mathematical notation:

$$X = \{10, 5, 8\}$$

    - On the left-hand side of the equal sign, we identify the name of the variable: X, in this case.

    - On the right-hand side of the equal sign and inside curly brackets, we have the contents of the variable: multiple observations, separated by commas. In the simple example above, the variable contains three observations: 10, 5, and 8.

In a **dataframe**, each row is an observation, and each column is a variable. An **observation** is the information collected from a particular individual or entity in the study. The **unit of observation** of a dataset defines what each observation represents. The **notation** i identifies the position of the observation; the observation for which $i=1$ is the first observation. A **variable** captures the values of a changing characteristic for multiple individuals or entities.

TIP: In this book, we are also going to teach you mathematical notation, a system of symbols and expressions that represent mathematical concepts. To help you keep track of the meaning of these symbols and expressions, at the end of the book we have included an index of all the mathematical notation we use.

- To represent each individual observation of the variable X, we use X_i (pronounced X sub i) where i stands for the observation number. The subscript i means that we have a different value of X for each value of i. Here, because there are only three observations, i can equal only 1, 2, or 3. For example, we represent the second observation (the observation for which $i=2$) as X_2, which in this case equals 5.

Now that we have looked at the data, we should read the description of the variables provided in table 1.1.

variable	description
classtype	class size the student attended: "small" or "regular"
reading	student's third-grade reading test scores (in points)
math	student's third-grade math test scores (in points)
graduated	identifies whether the student graduated from high school: 1=graduated or 0=did not graduate

TABLE 1.1. Description of the variables in the STAR dataset, where the unit of observation is students.

Reading table 1.1, we learn that:

- *classtype* captures the size of the class the student attended, which was either "small" or "regular"
- *reading* records the scores, measured in points, the student earned on the third-grade reading test
- *math* records the scores, measured in points, the student earned on the third-grade math test
- *graduated* indicates whether the student graduated from high school (it equals 1 if the student graduated and 0 if the student did not graduate).

Now we can look at the first few lines of data again and substantively interpret them. For example, the first observation represents a student who attended a small class, earned 578 points on the third-grade reading test and 610 points on the third-grade math test, and graduated from high school.

❹ IDENTIFY THE TYPES OF VARIABLES INCLUDED

At this point, we should learn the typology of the variables included in the dataset. This information will be especially helpful when we need to interpret the results of the analysis.

Based on the contents of the variables, we can distinguish between the types listed in outline 1.3.

OUTLINE 1.3. Types of variables based on their contents.

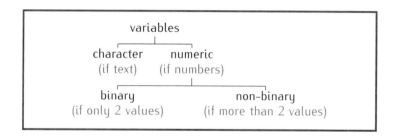

A **character variable** contains text, such as *names*={Elena, Kosuke, Kathryn}. A **numeric variable** contains numbers, such as *rank*={2, 1, 3}. A **binary variable** can take only two values; in this book, we define binary variables as taking only 1s and 0s, such as *voted*={1, 0, 1}. A **non-binary variable** can take more than two values, such as *distance*={1.452, 2.345, 0.298} and *dice_roll*={2, 4, 6}.

$$graduated_i = \begin{cases} 1 \text{ if student } i \\ \quad \text{graduated} \\ 0 \text{ if student } i \\ \quad \text{didn't graduate} \end{cases}$$

- The first distinction we make is between character and numeric variables. While **character variables** contain text, **numeric variables** contain numbers. For example, in the STAR dataset, *classtype* is a character variable, and *reading*, *math*, and *graduated* are numeric variables.

- Among numeric variables, we differentiate between binary and non-binary. A **binary variable** can take only two values ("bi" means two). In this book, all binary variables take only 1s and 0s to represent the presence or absence of a particular trait. In this type of binary variable, also known as a dummy variable, you may think of the 1s as capturing the positive responses to simple yes or no questions and of the 0s as capturing the negative responses. For example, in the STAR dataset, *graduated* is a binary variable that captures responses to the question, did the student graduate? The variable takes the value of 1 when the answer is yes (the student graduated) and 0 when the answer is no (the student did not graduate). (See mathematical definition in the margin.)

- In contrast, we categorize as **non-binary** all other numeric variables, that is, those that can take more than two values. For example, in the STAR dataset, both *reading* and *math* are non-binary variables because they each contain more than two different numbers.

❺ IDENTIFY THE NUMBER OF OBSERVATIONS

dim() provides the dimensions of a dataframe. The only required argument is the name of the object where the dataframe is stored (without quotes). The output is two values: the first indicates the number of observations in the dataframe; the second indicates the number of variables. Example: dim(*data*).

Finally, we should find out how many observations the dataset contains. For this purpose, we use the function dim(), which stands for "<u>dim</u>ensions" and requires that we specify inside the parentheses the name of the object where the dataframe is stored (without quotes). This function returns two values because dataframes have two dimensions: rows and columns. The first corresponds to the number of rows, which is equivalent to the number of observations. The second corresponds to the number of columns, which is equivalent to the number of variables.

```
dim(star)  # provides dimensions of dataframe: rows, columns
## [1] 1274    4
```

Given the output above, we learn that the STAR dataset contains 1,274 observations. And, as we already knew by looking at the data directly, it contains four variables. Given that each observation represents a student, we now know that we have information for 1,274 students in Project STAR. In mathematical notation, we represent the number of observations in a dataframe as n. In this case, we can state that $n=1,274$.

The **notation** n stands for the total number of observations in a dataframe or in a variable.

1.8 COMPUTING AND INTERPRETING MEANS

The mean, or average, of a variable is one of the foundational concepts of data analysis. In this section, we first show how to access a variable inside a dataframe in R so that we can operate with its values. Then, we explain in detail how to calculate and interpret the mean of a variable.

TIP: In chapter 3, we will see how to calculate and interpret other statistics, such as the median, standard deviation, and variance of a variable.

1.8.1 ACCESSING VARIABLES INSIDE DATAFRAMES

Suppose we want to operate with the variable *reading* inside the dataframe *star*. How do we access the values within this variable?

If we run the name of the variable, *reading*, R will give us an error message informing us that the object *reading* cannot be found. Indeed, there is no object called *reading* in the environment. If instead we run the name of the object that contains the dataframe, *star*, R will show all the values in the dataframe, not just those of the variable *reading*.

To access the values of a single variable, we use the $ character. To its left, we specify the name of the object where the dataframe is stored (without quotes). To its right, we specify the name of the variable (without quotes). In this case, *star$reading* is the code that instructs R to select the variable *reading* from within the object named *star*. It is equivalent to saying to R: look inside of *star* and find the variable called *reading*. (Note that when writing code, we do not use quotes around the names of elements within an object, such as the names of variables within a dataframe.) Go ahead and run:

$ is the character used to access an element inside an object, such as a variable inside a dataframe. To its left, we specify the name of the object where the dataframe is stored (without quotes). To its right, we specify the name of the variable (without quotes). Example: *data$variable* accesses the variable named *variable* inside the dataframe stored in the object named *data*.

```
star$reading
##   [1] 578 612 583 661 614 610 595 665 616 624
##  [11] 593 599 693 545 565 654 686 570 529 582
##  ...
```

In your R console (the lower-left window), you should see all the observations of *reading*. Here, we show you only the first 20. We use an ellipsis—three dots—to signify that more observations should appear after those displayed here.

TIP: The number in brackets shown on the second line in your R console might not be 11 because the size of your lower-left window might be different than ours. The larger the window, the more observations R will be able to display per line, and the higher the number in brackets shown on the second line will be.

What are the numbers in brackets at the beginning of each line? They indicate the position of the observation immediately to the right. The [1] on the first line indicates that the number 578 is the first observation of the variable *reading* ($reading_1$=578). The [11] on the second line indicates that the number 593 is the 11th observation of *reading* ($reading_{11}$=593), and so on.

Now that we know how to access the contents of a variable, we can learn how to compute and interpret the mean of a variable.

1.8.2 MEANS

The **mean**, or **average**, of a variable equals the sum of the values across all observations divided by the number of observations.

The **mean**, or **average**, of a variable characterizes its central tendency. It equals the sum of the values across all observations divided by the number of observations. In mathematical notation, the mean of a variable is often represented by the name of the variable with a bar on top, like so:

$$\overline{name\ of\ the\ variable}$$

TIP: The mean of a variable is a single number, which does not vary by observation. As a result, the mean of X ($\overline{X}$) is not subscripted by i.

The formula to compute the mean of X is:

$$\overline{X} = \frac{\sum_{i=1}^{n} X_i}{n} = \frac{X_1 + X_2 + \cdots + X_n}{n}$$

where:

- $\overline{X}$ (pronounced X-bar) stands for the mean of X
- X_i (pronounced X sub i) stands for a particular observation of X, where i denotes the position of the observation
- n is the number of observations in the variable
- the symbol $\sum$ (the Greek letter Sigma) is the mathematical notation for summation; $\sum_{i=1}^{n} X_i$ stands for the sum of all X_i (observations of X) from i=1 to i=n, meaning from the first observation of the variable X to the last one.

For example, if X={10, 4, 6, 8, 22}, then n=5 because the variable has five observations, and the mean of X is:

$$\overline{X} = \frac{\sum_{i=1}^{n} X_i}{n} = \frac{X_1 + X_2 + X_3 + X_4 + X_5}{5}$$

$$= \frac{10 + 4 + 6 + 8 + 22}{5} = \frac{50}{5} = 10$$

mean() computes the mean of a variable. The only required argument is the code identifying the variable. Example: mean(*data$variable*).

To calculate the mean of a variable in R, we can use the function mean(). The only required argument is the code identifying the variable. For example, to calculate the mean of the reading test scores of the students in the STAR dataset, we run:

```
mean(star$reading) # calculates the mean of reading
## [1] 628.803
```

How shall we interpret this output? First, we need to figure out the quantity in which the value is measured. This is called the **unit of measurement**. When interpreting numeric results, you should make it clear whether the number is measured in points, percentages, miles, or kilometers, for example.

The unit of measurement of the mean of a variable depends on whether the variable is non-binary or binary. Outline 1.4 summarizes how to interpret the mean of a variable (including units of measurement) based on this distinction. (We exclude from this discussion categorical variables, whose means generally have no straightforward substantive interpretation.)

> The **unit of measurement** is the quantity in which a value is measured. For example, depending on where you live, you might measure temperature in °F or °C and distance in miles or kilometers.

> TIP: Categorical, or factor, variables take a fixed number of values, where each value represents a qualitative outcome. For example, we can capture adult education levels in a categorical variable where 1=no qualifications, 2=high school diploma, and 3=undergraduate degree.

---

interpretation of the mean of a variable

if variable is non-binary:	if variable is binary:
as an average, in the same unit of measurement as the variable	as a proportion, in % after multiplying the result by 100

> OUTLINE 1.4. Interpretation of the mean of a variable based on the type of variable.

When the variable is non-binary, the mean should be interpreted in the same unit of measurement as the values in the variable. For example, in the output above, because *reading* is a non-binary variable measured in points, the mean of *reading* is also in points. We can, therefore, interpret the output as meaning that the students in Project STAR scored 629 points, on average, on the third-grade reading test.

> TIP: It is good practice to round numeric results to meaningful decimal places. This usually means no more than two decimals, but often one or none.

When the variable is binary, the mean should be interpreted as a percentage, after multiplying the result by 100. Why? Because the mean of a binary variable is equivalent to the proportion of the observations that are 1s (that have the characteristic identified by the variable). Let's go over a simple example to see how this works. Suppose we want to calculate the mean of the first six observations of the binary variable *graduated*. As we saw earlier in the output of head(), these are {1, 1, 1, 1, 1, 0}. The average of these six observations would be:

> TIP: The proportion of observations that meet a criterion is calculated as:
>
> $$\frac{\text{number of observations that meet criterion}}{\text{total number of observations}}$$

> To interpret the resulting decimal as a percentage, we multiply it by 100. For example, if X={1, 1, 1, 1, 1, 0}, the proportion of observations in X that are 1s is 83% ($5/6 = 0.8333...$ and $0.83 \times 100 = 83\%$).

$$\frac{\text{sum of observations}}{\text{number of observations}} = \frac{1+1+1+1+1+0}{6} = \frac{5}{6} = 0.8333...$$

> When the variable is binary, the numerator of the mean, the sum of the 1s and 0s, is equivalent to the number of observations that meet the criterion. As a result, the mean is equivalent to the proportion of observations in the variable that are 1s.

Notice that the fraction 5/6 is equivalent to the proportion of the observations that are 1s. (See TIP in the margin.) Now, to convert the result from decimal form (0.83) into a percentage, we multiply it by 100 ($0.83 \times 100 = 83\%$).

Putting it all together, we interpret the average of the first six observations of *graduated* as indicating that about 83% of the first six students in the STAR dataset graduated.

Now, let's compute the mean of all the observations within the binary variable *graduated* (rather than just the first six). We do so by running:

```
mean(star$graduated) # calculates the mean of graduated
## [1] 0.8697017
```

How shall we interpret this output? Since the variable is binary, the output means that about 87% of all the students in Project STAR received a high school diploma (0.87×100=87%).

1.9 SUMMARY

We began this chapter by providing an overview of the book and its main features. We then argued that knowing how to perform and evaluate data analyses is particularly useful for studying society and human behavior but can be helpful to anyone. These skills are also highly marketable in the current era of big data. We then got our computers ready and became acquainted with R and RStudio, the two programs we use. Finally, in preparation for the next chapter's data analysis, we learned how to load and make sense of data and how to compute and interpret means.

1.10 CHEATSHEETS

1.10.1 CONCEPTS AND NOTATION

concept/notation	description	example(s)
dataframe	structure of data in which each row is an observation and each column is a variable	variables *classtype* and *reading* in dataframe form:

i	*classtype*	*reading*
1	small	725
2	regular	692
3	small	725
. . .	. . .	. . .

concept/notation	description	example(s)
observation	information collected from a particular individual or entity in the study; each row in a dataframe is an observation	the first observation in the dataframe above represents a student who attended a small class and scored 725 points on the reading test
unit of observation	defines what each observation represents	students, schools, states, countries, . . .
i	identifies the position of the observation	the observation for which $i=3$ is the third observation in a dataframe or in a variable
variable (X)	captures the values of a changing characteristic for multiple individuals or entities; each column in a dataframe is a variable	$X=\{10, 8, 12\}$
character variable	variable that contains text	*names* = {Elena, Kosuke, Kathryn}
numeric variable	variable that contains numbers	*rank* = {2, 1, 3, 5, 4}
binary variable	variable that can take only two values, in this book 1s and 0s	*voted* = {0, 1, 1, 0, 1}
non-binary variable	variable that can take more than two values	*distance* = {2.568, 5.367, 7.235} *dice_roll* = {2, 5, 4, 3, 1}
n	stands for the total number of observations in a dataframe or in a variable	in the variable *dice_roll* above, $n=5$
$\sum$	Greek letter Sigma; mathematical notation for summation; $\sum_{i=1}^{n}$ means "sum what follows for all the observations, from $i=1$ to $i=n$" (the first to the last)	if $X=\{10, 8, 12\}$, then: $$\sum_{i=1}^{n} X_i = X_1 + X_2 + X_3$$ $$= 10 + 8 + 12 = 30$$
unit of measurement	quantity in which a value is measured	°F, °C, miles, kilometers, points, percentages, percentage points, . . .
mean or average of a variable ($\overline{X}$)	characterizes the central tendency of the variable; equals the sum of the values across all observations divided by the number of observations: $$\text{mean of } X = \overline{X} = \frac{\sum_{i=1}^{n} X_i}{n}$$ unit of measurement of $\overline{X}$: - if X is non-binary: in the same unit of measurement as X - if X is binary: in percentages, after multiplying the result by 100	if $X=\{10, 8, 12\}$, then: $$\overline{X} = \frac{\sum_{i=1}^{n} X_i}{n} = (X_1 + X_2 + X_3)/3$$ $$= (10 + 8 + 12)/3 = 30/3 = 10$$

1.10.2 R SYMBOLS AND OPERATORS

code	description	example(s)
+ − ° /	some of the arithmetic operators recognized by R	(4 − 1 + 3) ° (2 / 3)
<-	assignment operator; creates new objects or overwrites existing ones (if an object with the same name already exists); to its left, we specify the name of the object (without quotes); to its right, we specify the contents of the object; the name of an object cannot begin with a number or contain spaces, $, or %	object_name <- object_contents
"	when writing code, the names of objects, names of functions, and names of arguments as well as special values such as TRUE, FALSE, NA, and NULL should not be in quotes; all other text should be in quotes; numbers should not be in quotes	"this is text" object_name
()	the names of functions are always followed by parentheses; inside the parentheses, we write the argument(s) of the function, separated by commas if there is more than one argument; we enter required arguments first and in the order expected by R; we specify optional arguments by including their names in the specification (without quotes)	function_name(required_argument) function_name(required_argument, optional_argument_name = optional_argument)
#	character used to comment code; R ignores everything that follows this character until the end of the line	executable_code # comment
$	character used to access an element inside an object, such as a variable inside a dataframe; to its left, we specify the name of the object where the dataframe is stored (without quotes); to its right, we specify the name of the variable (without quotes)	data$variable # accesses the variable named variable inside the dataframe stored in the object named data

1.10.3 R FUNCTIONS

function	description	required argument(s)	example(s)
sqrt()	calculates the square root	what we want to compute the square root of	sqrt(4)
setwd()	sets the working directory, that is, directs R to the folder on your computer where the dataset is saved	path to folder in quotes	setwd("~/Desktop/folder") # for Mac setwd("C:/user/Desktop/folder") # for Windows, where user is your own username
read.csv()	reads CSV files	name of CSV file containing the dataset in quotes	read.csv("file.csv")
View()	opens a tab with the entire contents of a dataframe	name of object where the dataframe is stored	View(data)
head()	shows the first six observations in a dataframe; in the output, observations are identified by their position, i, and variables by their names	name of object where the dataframe is stored optional argument n: changes the number of observations displayed	head(data) # shows first six observations head(data, n=2) # shows first two observations
dim()	provides the dimensions of a dataframe; output is: [1] number of rows or observations [2] number of columns or variables	name of object where the dataframe is stored	dim(data)
mean()	calculates the mean of a variable	code identifying the variable (see $)	mean(data$variable)

2. ESTIMATING CAUSAL EFFECTS WITH RANDOMIZED EXPERIMENTS

One of the main purposes of data analysis in the social sciences is the estimation of causal effects, also known as causal inference. What are causal effects? And how can we best estimate them? These are the main questions we answer in this chapter. To illustrate the concepts covered, we analyze data from a real-world experiment. Specifically, we estimate the causal effect of small classes on student performance using data from Project STAR.

R symbols, operators, and functions introduced in this chapter: ==, ifelse(), and [].

2.1 PROJECT STAR

In the 1980s, Tennessee legislators began to consider reducing class size in the state's schools in an effort to improve student performance. Some studies had suggested that smaller classes are more conducive to learning than regular-size classes, especially in the early schooling years. Reducing class size, however, would require additional funds to pay for the extra teachers and classroom space. Before moving forward with the new policy, the legislature decided to commission a thorough investigation of the causal effects of small classes on student performance. The result was a multimillion-dollar study called Project Student-Teacher Achievement Ratio (Project STAR).

In this chapter, we analyze a portion of the data from Project STAR. The aim of the project was to examine the effects of class size on student performance in both the short and long term. The project consisted of an experiment in which kindergartners were randomly assigned to attend either small classes, with 13 to 17 students, or regular-size classes, with 22 to 25 students, until the end of third grade. Researchers followed student progress over time. As the outcome variables of interest, we have student scores on third-grade standardized tests in reading and math as well as high school graduation rates.

Based on Frederick Mosteller, "The Tennessee Study of Class Size in the Early School Grades," *Future of Children* 5, no. 2 (1995): 113–27. We study the effects of small classes as compared to regular-size classes (without aides), disregarding data from students who were assigned to regular-size classes with aides. We focus on the initial group of participants who were randomly assigned to different class types before entering kindergarten and exclude observations with any missing data in the variables used in the analysis.

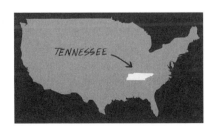

2.2 TREATMENT AND OUTCOME VARIABLES

Tennessee legislators wanted researchers to estimate the causal effects of small classes on educational outcomes. Specifically, they wanted to know whether student performance improves as a direct result of attending a small class and not just as a result of other factors that may accompany small class sizes, such as better teachers, higher-performing classmates, or greater resources.

Causal relationships refer to the cause-and-effect connection between two variables. In this case, the two variables are (i) small class and (ii) student performance.

In this book, we study causal relationships in which there is clear directionality in how the two variables relate to each other: changes in one variable may cause changes in the other. We use this directionality to distinguish between the variables. We refer to the variable where the change originates as the **treatment variable**. We refer to the variable that may change in response to the change in the treatment variable as the **outcome variable**. Here, small class is the treatment variable, and student performance is the outcome variable.

A **causal relationship** refers to the cause-and-effect connection between:
- the **treatment variable** (X): variable whose change may produce a change in the outcome variable
- the **outcome variable** (Y): variable that may change as a result of a change in the treatment variable.

TIP: At some point, you might have learned about dependent and independent variables. Treatment variables are a type of independent variable, and outcome variables are the same as dependent variables.

In mathematical notation, we represent the treatment variable as X and the outcome variable as Y. We represent the causal relationship between them visually with an arrow from X to Y. The direction of the arrow indicates that changes in X may produce changes in Y but not the other way around:

$$X \rightarrow Y$$

In Project STAR, we are interested in the following causal link:

$$small\ class\ \rightarrow\ student\ performance$$

The distinction between treatment and outcome variables depends on the nature of the causal relationship between them as well as on the research question. The same variable might be the outcome in one study but be the treatment in another. For example, in one study we may be interested in the effect of attending a small class on the probability of graduating from high school. Here, the variable that indicates whether a student graduated from high school, *graduated*, is the outcome variable (diagram A below). In another study, we may be interested in the effect of graduating from high school on future wages. In that case, *graduated* would be the treatment variable (diagram B).

(A)   *small class → graduated*
(B)   *graduated → future wages*

2.2.1 TREATMENT VARIABLES

In this book, for the sake of simplicity, we focus on treatment variables that are binary, that is, that indicate whether the treatment is present or absent. We define the treatment variable for each individual i as:

$$X_i = \begin{cases} 1 \text{ if individual } i \text{ receives the treatment} \\ 0 \text{ if individual } i \text{ does not receive the treatment} \end{cases}$$

RECALL: A binary variable takes only two values, in this book 1s and 0s, and the notation i identifies the position of the observation in a dataframe or in a variable.

Based on whether the individual receives the treatment, we speak of two different conditions:

- **treatment** is the condition with the treatment (X_i=1)
- **control** is the condition without the treatment (X_i=0).

Two conditions:
- **treatment**: when X_i=1
- **control**: when X_i=0.

We describe the observations that receive the treatment as being *under treatment* or *treated* and those that do not as being *under control* or *untreated*.

For example, in the analysis of the STAR dataset, we are interested in examining the effects of attending a small class on student performance. The treatment variable, which we name *small*, is a binary variable that equals 1 if the student attended a small class and 0 otherwise. Formally, we define *small* as:

RECALL: In the STAR dataset, each observation i represents a different student because the unit of observation is students.

$$small_i = \begin{cases} 1 \text{ if student } i \text{ attended a small class} \\ 0 \text{ if student } i \text{ did not attend a small class} \end{cases}$$

2.2.2 OUTCOME VARIABLES

We will see different types of outcome variables. For example, in the STAR dataset, we will analyze the effect of attending a small class on three different measures of student performance: *reading*, *math*, and *graduated*. While the first two outcome variables are non-binary, the third is binary. As we will see later in the chapter, the interpretation of the results depends on the type of outcome variable used in the analysis.

2.3 INDIVIDUAL CAUSAL EFFECTS

When estimating the **causal effect of** X **on** Y, we attempt to quantify the change in the outcome variable Y that is caused by a change in the treatment variable X. For example, if interested in the effect of *small* on *reading*, we aim to measure the extent to which student performance on the reading test improves or worsens as a result of attending a small class, as opposed to a regular-size class.

The **causal effect of** X **on** Y is the change in the outcome variable Y caused by a change in the treatment variable X.

Note that when estimating a causal effect, we are trying to measure a *change* in Y, specifically the change in Y caused by a change in X. In mathematical notation, we represent change with $\triangle$ (the Greek letter Delta), and thus, we represent a change in the outcome as $\triangle Y$.

To measure this change in the outcome Y, ideally we would compare two potential outcomes: the outcome when the treatment is present and the outcome when the treatment is absent. In mathematical notation, we represent these two potential outcomes as follows:

- $Y_i(X_i=1)$ represents the **potential outcome under the treatment condition** for individual i (the value of Y_i if $X_i=1$)
- $Y_i(X_i=0)$ represents the **potential outcome under the control condition** for individual i (the value of Y_i if $X_i=0$).

Two potential outcomes:

- **potential outcome under the treatment condition** (the value of Y_i if $X_i=1$)
- **potential outcome under the control condition** (the value of Y_i if $X_i=0$).

If, for each individual i, we could observe both potential outcomes, then computing the change in the outcome Y caused by the treatment X would be simple. We would just compute the difference between these two potential outcomes. Mathematically, the individual causal effects of receiving the treatment X on the outcome Y would be computed as shown in formula 2.1.

FORMULA 2.1. Definition of the individual causal effects of a treatment on an outcome.

IF WE COULD OBSERVE BOTH POTENTIAL OUTCOMES

$$individual\_effects_i = \triangle Y_i = Y_i(X_i=1) - Y_i(X_i=0)$$

where:

- $\triangle Y_i$ is the change in the outcome individual i would have experienced by receiving the treatment, as compared to not receiving the treatment
- $Y_i(X_i=1)$ and $Y_i(X_i=0)$ are the two potential outcomes for the same individual i, under the treatment and the control conditions, respectively.

For example, if we are estimating the effect of attending a small class on reading test scores using the data from Project STAR, the treatment variable X would be *small* and the outcome variable Y would be *reading*. In this case, for each student i, we would like to observe third-grade reading test scores both (i) after attending a small class from kindergarten to third grade and (ii) after attending a regular-size class from kindergarten to third grade. If this were possible, we could directly measure the causal effect that attending a small class had on each student's reading performance by calculating:

$$\triangle reading_i = reading_i(small_i{=}1) - reading_i(small_i{=}0)$$

where:

- $\triangle reading_i$ is the change in reading test scores student i would have experienced by attending a small class, as compared to a regular-size class
- $reading_i(small_i{=}1)$ is the third-grade reading test score of student i after attending a small class (the value of $reading_i$ if $small_i{=}1$)
- $reading_i(small_i{=}0)$ is the third-grade reading test score of the same student i after attending a regular-size class (the value of $reading_i$ if $small_i{=}0$).

Let's imagine, for a moment, that we *could* observe both potential outcomes for each of the first six students in the STAR dataset. See the first two columns of table 2.1 below. For illustration purposes, we made up the values of the potential outcomes that were not observed (shown in gray). If these were indeed the true potential outcomes, then the individual causal effects of *small* on *reading* for these six students would be the values shown in the third column of table 2.1.

i	$reading(small{=}1)$	$reading(small{=}0)$	$\triangle reading$
1	578	571	7
2	611	612	-1
3	586	583	3
4	661	661	0
5	614	602	12
6	607	610	-3

Based on table 2.1, we would conclude that attending a small class as opposed to a regular-size one:

- increased the reading score of the first student by 7 points, the score of the third student by 3 points, and the score of the fifth student by 12 points
- decreased the reading score of the second student by 1 point, and the score of the sixth student by 3 points
- had no effect on the reading score of the fourth student.

Notice that the same treatment might have different effects for different individuals. In addition, note that since a causal effect is a measure of change, we should interpret a causal effect as an increase if positive, as a decrease if negative, and as having no effect if zero. (See TIP in the margin.)

TIP: This is formula 2.1 with *reading* as the Y variable and *small* as the X variable. If we could observe both potential outcomes for every student, we could use this formula to compute the individual causal effects of attending a small class on reading test scores.

TABLE 2.1. If for each student i, we could observe both potential outcomes, then we could measure the causal effects of *small* on *reading* at the individual level. (Warning: Here we made up the values of the unobserved potential outcomes, shown in gray, for the sake of illustrating individual causal effects.)

TIP: When interpreting the sign of causal effects, we should interpret:

- a positive effect as the treatment causing an *increase* in the outcome variable
- a negative effect as the treatment causing a *decrease* in the outcome variable
- an effect of zero as the treatment causing *no change* in the outcome variable.

A different way of expressing the two potential outcomes:

- **the factual outcome**: potential outcome under whichever condition (treatment or control) was received in reality
- **the counterfactual outcome**: potential outcome under whichever condition (treatment or control) was not received in reality.

Unfortunately, this kind of analysis is not possible. In the real world, we never observe both potential outcomes for the same individual. Instead, we observe only the **factual outcome**, which is the potential outcome under whichever condition (treatment or control) was received in reality. We can never observe the **counterfactual outcome**, which is the potential outcome that would have occurred under whichever condition (treatment or control) was not received in reality. As a result, we cannot compute causal effects at the individual level. In our example, a student attends either a small or a regular-size class during the early schooling years but cannot enter a parallel universe to attend both at the same time. (See figure 2.1.)

FIGURE 2.1. If an individual could split into two identical beings, and each one of them could receive a different condition, then we could observe the outcome under the treatment condition and the outcome under the control condition for the same individual. We could then calculate the causal effect of the treatment on the outcome for this specific individual by simply measuring the difference between the two outcomes.

For each student in Project STAR, for instance, we observe only one third-grade reading test score, the score earned after the student actually attended one of the two types of classes. As a result, we cannot measure how class size affected each student's performance on the reading test. (See table 2.2, where the counterfactual outcomes for the first six observations are indicated as ??? because they were unobserved.)

TABLE 2.2. Values of *small, reading, reading(small=1),* and *reading(small=0)* for the first six observations in the STAR dataset. Unobserved potential outcomes, or counterfactuals, are indicated as ???.

i	small	reading	reading(small=1)	reading(small=0)
1	1	578	578	???
2	0	612	???	612
3	0	583	???	583
4	1	661	661	???
5	1	614	614	???
6	0	610	???	610

Take the first student, the observation when $i=1$. The value of $small_1$ is 1, which means this student attended a small class. The value of $reading_1$, then, indicates the performance of this student on the reading test after attending a small class ($reading_1(small_1=1)=578$). The score of 578 points is this student's factual outcome because we did observe it. What we did not observe is the counterfactual outcome, that is, how this student would have performed on the reading test after attending a regular-size class ($reading_1(small_1=0)=???$). Consequently, we cannot measure the effect attending a small class had on this student's reading test score:

$$\triangle reading_1 = reading_1(small_1=1) - reading_1(small_1=0)$$
$$= 578 - ??? = ???$$

The fundamental problem we face when inferring causal effects is that we never observe the same individual both receiving the treatment and not receiving the treatment at the same time.

We observe only what happens in reality (the factual outcome). We can never observe what would have happened had we made different decisions (the counterfactual outcome).

FUNDAMENTAL PROBLEM OF CAUSAL INFERENCE:
To measure causal effects, we need to compare the factual outcome with the counterfactual outcome, but we can never observe the counterfactual outcome.

2.4 AVERAGE CAUSAL EFFECTS

To get around the fundamental problem of causal inference, we must find good approximations for the counterfactual outcomes. To accomplish this, we move away from individual-level effects and focus on the *average* causal effect *across a group of individuals*.

The **average causal effect** of the treatment X on the outcome Y, also known as the **average treatment effect**, is the average of all the individual causal effects of X on Y within a group. Since each individual causal effect is the change in Y caused by a change in X for a particular individual, the average causal effect of X on Y is the *average* change in Y caused by a change in X *for a group of individuals*.

If we could observe both potential outcomes for each individual in the group, then we could measure individual causal effects (using formula 2.1) and compute the average causal effect as shown in formula 2.2.

RECALL: The average of a variable equals the sum of the values across all observations divided by the number of observations. It is often represented by the name of the variable with a bar on top.

The **average causal effect** of X on Y, also known as the **average treatment effect**, is defined as the average of the individual causal effects of X on Y across a group of individuals. It is the average change in Y caused by a change in X for a group of individuals.

FORMULA 2.2. Definition of the average causal effect of a treatment on an outcome, or the average treatment effect.

IF WE COULD OBSERVE
BOTH POTENTIAL OUTCOMES

$$\overline{individual\_effects} = \frac{\sum_{i=1}^{n} individual\_effects_i}{n}$$

where:

- $\overline{individual\_effects}$ is the average causal effect for the observations in the study, and $individual\_effects_i$ is the individual causal effect for observation i
- $\sum_{i=1}^{n} individual\_effects_i$ stands for the sum of all $individual\_effects_i$ from $i=1$ to $i=n$, meaning from the first observation of $individual\_effects$ to the last one
- n is the number of observations in the study.

Let's return to the idealized scenario where we could observe both potential outcomes for each of the first six students in the STAR dataset. As we saw earlier, if the potential outcomes were those shown in table 2.1, the individual causal effects of *small* on *reading* for these students would be:

$$individual\_effects = \{7, -1, 3, 0, 12, -3\}$$

Then, the average causal effect of *small* on *reading* would be:

$$\overline{individual\_effects} \quad - \quad \frac{\sum_{i=1}^{n} individual\_effects_i}{number\ of\ students}$$

$$= \frac{7 + (-1) + 3 + 0 + 12 + (-3)}{6} = \frac{18}{6} = 3$$

We would conclude that, among the first six students in Project STAR, attending a small class, as opposed to a regular-size one, improved student performance on the reading test by 3 points, on average. Remember, though, this kind of analysis is not possible because we never observe both potential outcomes for the same individual. Therefore, we are not going to be able to compute average causal effects directly, either.

How can we obtain good approximations for the counterfactual outcomes, which by definition cannot be observed? As we will see in detail soon, we must find or create a situation in which the treated observations and the untreated observations are similar with respect to all the variables that might affect the outcome other than the treatment variable itself. The best way to accomplish this is by conducting a randomized experiment.

2.4.1 RANDOMIZED EXPERIMENTS AND THE DIFFERENCE-IN-MEANS ESTIMATOR

In a **randomized experiment**, also known as a randomized controlled trial (RCT), researchers decide who receives the treatment based on a random process.

A **randomized experiment** is a type of study design in which treatment assignment is randomized.

For example, in Project STAR, researchers could have flipped a coin to decide whether a student would attend a small or a regular-size class. If the coin landed on heads, the student would be assigned to a small class. If tails, the student would be assigned to a regular-size class. (See figure 2.2.)

FIGURE 2.2. One way of assigning treatment at random is to flip a coin for every individual in the study. If the coin lands on heads, the individual is assigned to the treatment group. If tails, the individual is assigned to the control group.

Heads   Tails

In practice, researchers do not flip coins but instead use a computer program like R to assign at random a 1 or a 0 to each individual. Individuals who are assigned a 1 are given the treatment, and individuals who are assigned a 0 are not given the treatment.

Once the treatment is assigned, we can differentiate between two groups of observations:

- the **treatment group** consists of the individuals who received the treatment (the group of observations for which $X_i=1$)
- the **control group** consists of the individuals who did not receive the treatment (the group of observations for which $X_i=0$).

Two **groups**:
- **treatment group**: observations that received the treatment
- **control group**: observations that did not receive the treatment.

In Project STAR, the students who attended a small class are the treatment group. The students who attended a regular-size class are the control group.

When treatment assignment is randomized, the only thing that distinguishes the treatment group from the control group, besides the reception of the treatment, is chance. This means that although the treatment and control groups consist of different individuals, the two groups are comparable to each other, *on average*, in all respects other than whether or not they received the treatment.

Random treatment assignment makes the treatment and control groups *on average* identical to each other in all observed and unobserved pre-treatment characteristics. **Pre-treatment characteristics** are the characteristics of the individuals in a study before the treatment is administered. (By definition, pre-treatment characteristics cannot be affected by the treatment.)

Pre-treatment characteristics are the characteristics of the individuals in a study before the treatment is administered.

TIP: An unobserved characteristic is a characteristic that we have not measured.

For example, in Project STAR, since the treatment was randomly assigned, the average age of the treatment group—the students who attended a small class—should be comparable to the average age of the control group—the students who attended a regular-size class.

> RANDOMIZATION OF TREATMENT ASSIGNMENT:
> By randomly assigning treatment, we ensure that treatment and control groups are, on average, identical to each other in all observed and unobserved pre-treatment characteristics.

Let's return to the formula of the average treatment effect. If we could observe both potential outcomes for each individual, we could compute individual causal effects (using formula 2.1), and the average treatment effect would equal the average difference between the two potential outcomes:

$$\text{average\_effect} = \overline{\textit{individual\_effects}} = \overline{Y(X=1) - Y(X=0)}$$

By the rules of summation, the average of a difference is equal to the difference of averages. (For an example, see the TIP in the margin.) This allows us to rewrite the average treatment effect:

$$\text{average\_effect} = \overline{Y(X=1) - Y(X=0)} = \overline{Y(X=1)} - \overline{Y(X=0)}$$

where:

- $\overline{Y(X=1)}$ is the average outcome under the treatment condition across all observations
- $\overline{Y(X=0)}$ is the average outcome under the control condition across all observations.

TIP: Using the values in the table below, we can confirm that the average of the difference between X and Y equals the difference between the average of X and the average of Y:

i	X	Y	X−Y
1	4	2	2
2	10	4	6
averages	7	3	4

$\overline{X-Y} = 4$ and $\overline{X}-\overline{Y} = 7-3 = 4$

Unfortunately, we cannot compute the average treatment effect this way because, as you may recall, we never observe both potential outcomes for each individual. Therefore, we cannot compute either the average outcome under the treatment condition *across all observations* or the average outcome under the control condition *across all observations*. All we can observe is the average outcome for the treatment group after receiving the treatment and the average outcome for the control group after not receiving the treatment.

If the treatment and control groups were comparable before the treatment was administered, however, then we can use the factual outcome of one group as an approximation for the counterfactual outcome of the other. In other words, we can assume that the average outcome of the treatment group is a good estimate of the average outcome of the control group, had the control group received the treatment. Similarly, we can assume that the average outcome of the control group is a good estimate of the average outcome of the treatment group, had the treatment group not received the treatment. As a result, we can approximate the average treatment effect by computing the difference in the average outcomes between the treatment and control groups. Since both of these average outcomes *are* observed, this is an analysis we *are* able to perform.

To summarize, if the treatment and control groups were comparable before the treatment was administered, we can estimate the average causal effect of treatment X on outcome Y with formula 2.3, which is known as the **difference-in-means estimator**.

IF GROUPS WERE COMPARABLE BEFORE
THE TREATMENT WAS ADMINISTERED

$$\widehat{average\_effect} = \overline{Y}_{treatment\ group} - \overline{Y}_{control\ group}$$

where:

- $\widehat{average\_effect}$ stands for the estimated average treatment effect (the "hat" on top of the name denotes that this is an estimate or approximation)
- $\overline{Y}_{treatment\ group}$ is the average outcome for the treatment group and $\overline{Y}_{control\ group}$ is the average outcome for the control group (both of which are observed).

FORMULA 2.3. The right-hand side of the equation is the formula for the **difference-in-means estimator**, which produces a valid estimate of the average treatment effect when the treatment and control groups are comparable with respect to all the variables that might affect the outcome other than the treatment variable itself.

TIP: To estimate causal effects, it is necessary to have both a treatment group and a control group. In other words, it is not sufficient to observe a group of individuals who received the treatment; we also need to observe a group of individuals who did not receive the treatment.

Note that the "hat" on top of the name denotes that this is an estimate, that is, a calculation based on approximations. All estimates, including this one, contain some uncertainty. (We will see how to quantify this uncertainty in chapter 7.)

It is worth repeating that the difference-in-means is a valid estimator of the average causal effect of a treatment on an outcome only when the treatment and control groups are comparable with respect to all the variables that might affect the outcome other than the treatment variable itself. As stated earlier, this is best achieved in experiments such as Project STAR, in which the treatment is randomly assigned. The randomization of treatment assignment enables researchers to isolate the effect of the treatment from the effects of other factors.

> ESTIMATING AVERAGE CAUSAL EFFECTS USING RANDOMIZED EXPERIMENTS AND THE DIFFERENCE-IN-MEANS ESTIMATOR: By using random treatment assignment, we can assume that the treatment and control groups were comparable before the administration of the treatment. As a result, we can rely on the difference-in-means estimator to provide a valid estimate of the average treatment effect.

Unfortunately, we are not always able to conduct an experiment. Three types of obstacles might prevent us from running one:

- Ethical: It would not be ethical to randomize certain treatments, such as a potentially lethal drug.
- Logistical: Some treatments, such as height or race, cannot be easily manipulated.
- Financial: Experiments are often expensive. Project STAR cost many millions of dollars, for example.

Experimental data are data collected from a randomized experiment, whereas **observational data** are data collected about naturally occurring events. Studies that use observational data are called **observational studies**.

Given that we cannot always run experiments, we need to learn how to estimate causal effects in non-experimental settings, using what is called **observational data**. Unlike **experimental data**, which refers to data collected from a randomized experiment, observational data are collected about naturally occurring events. Treatment assignment is out of the control of the researchers and is often the result of individual choices. For example, we may want to estimate the average causal effect of small classes on student performance by collecting data from school districts where the size of the classes varies as a result of factors such as school budgets, student enrollment, or the physical limitations of the school buildings. In these types of studies, known as **observational studies**, we have to find a statistical way to make treatment and control groups comparable without relying on the randomization of treatment assignment. We will learn how to do this in chapter 5.

Now that we know that when analyzing the STAR dataset, we can use the difference-in-means estimator to estimate the average causal effect of small classes on student performance, it is time to perform the analysis.

2.5 DO SMALL CLASSES IMPROVE STUDENT PERFORMANCE?

To follow along with this chapter's analysis, you may create a new R script in RStudio and practice typing the code yourself. Alternatively, you may open "Experimental.R" in RStudio, which contains all the code for this chapter. We begin the analysis by running the following code from the previous chapter:

```
setwd("~/Desktop/DSS") # setwd() if Mac
setwd("C:/user/Desktop/DSS") # setwd() if Windows

star <- read.csv("STAR.csv") # reads and stores data

head(star) # shows first observations
##   classtype reading math graduated
## 1     small     578  610         1
## 2   regular     612  612         1
## 3   regular     583  606         1
## 4     small     661  648         1
## 5     small     614  636         1
## 6   regular     610  603         0
```

Here, we are interested in using this dataset to estimate the average causal effect of attending a small class on three different measures of student performance: *reading*, *math*, and *graduated*. For each outcome variable, we need to perform a separate analysis. Since Project STAR was a randomized experiment, we can use the difference-in-means estimator to estimate each of the three average treatment effects.

Before we can compute the difference-in-means estimators, we need to learn to use relational operators, which enable us to create and subset variables.

2.5.1 RELATIONAL OPERATORS IN R

There are many relational operators in R that can be used to set a logical test. In this book, we use only the operator ==, which evaluates whether two values are equal to each other. If they are, R returns the logical value TRUE. If they are not, R returns the logical value FALSE. (TRUE and FALSE are not character values. They are special values in R, with a specific meaning, and therefore are not written in quotes.) For example, if we run:

```
3==3
## [1] TRUE
```

R lets us know that indeed 3 equals 3. If we instead run:

TIP: If you are starting a new R session, to operate with the data, you need to re-run some of the code we wrote in the previous chapter, specifically the lines of code that:

- set the working directory to the folder containing the dataset using the function setwd()
- read the dataset using read.csv() and store it as an object called *star* using the assignment operator <-.

We provide here the code to set the working directory if the DSS folder is saved directly on your Desktop. (Note that in the code for Windows computers, you must substitute your own username for *user*.) If the DSS folder is saved elsewhere, please see subsection 1.7.1 for instructions on how to set the working directory.

== is the relational operator that evaluates whether two values are equal to each other. The output is a logical value: TRUE or FALSE. Example: 3==3.

RECALL: In the STAR dataset, the variable *classtype* identifies the class the student attended. In R, we use the $ character to access a variable inside a dataframe. To its left, we specify the name of the object where the dataframe is stored (without quotes). To its right, we specify the name of the variable (without quotes). Example: *data$variable*. We use quotes around values that are text but not around values that are numbers. In the output, the numbers in brackets at the beginning of each line indicate the position of the observation immediately to the right.

```
3==4
## [1] FALSE
```

R returns a FALSE, indicating that 3 is not equal to 4.

We can apply relational operators to all the values in a variable at once. In this case, R considers the value of each observation one by one and returns a TRUE or a FALSE for each of them. For instance, if we wanted to determine which students in the STAR dataset attended a small class, we run:

```
star$classtype=="small"
## [1]    TRUE FALSE FALSE TRUE TRUE FALSE
## [7]    TRUE TRUE FALSE FALSE FALSE FALSE
## ...
```

After running the code above, R returns as many logical values as observations in the variable *classtype*. (Here we show you only the first 12.) For students who attended a small class, R returns TRUE because the value of *classtype* equals "small". For students who did not, R returns FALSE. For example, as we saw in the output of head() above, the value of *classtype* for the first observation is "small", and therefore, here R returns TRUE as the first output.

Now we can ask R to perform a different action depending on the results from a logical test (the TRUE or FALSE returned from applying the == operator). For example, we can ask R to produce values for a new variable or to extract specific values from an existing variable based on the results of the logical test.

ifelse() creates the contents of a new variable based on the values of an existing one. It requires three arguments in the following order, separated by commas: (1) the logical test, (2) return value if test is true, and (3) return value if test is false.

== is the relational operator we use to set the logical test that evaluates whether the observations of a variable are equal to a particular value. We write values in quotes " if text but not if numbers.

Example: ifelse(*data$var*=="yes", 1, 0) returns a 1 when *var* equals "yes" and a 0 otherwise, creating the contents of a binary variable using the existing character variable *var*.

2.5.2 CREATING NEW VARIABLES

Using the function ifelse(), which stands for "if logical test is true, return this, else return that," we can create the contents of a new variable based on whether the values of an existing variable pass a logical test. For example, we can create the contents of a new binary variable based on the values of *classtype*. For the students whose value of *classtype* equals "small", we ask R to return a 1, and for all other students a 0.

The function ifelse() requires three arguments:

- The first is the logical test, which specifies the true/false question that serves as the criterion for creating the contents of the new variable. In the current application, for every student, we want to evaluate whether the value of *classtype* equals "small". As shown above, the code star$classtype=="small" accomplishes this.
- The second argument is the value we want the function to return when the logical test is true. In this case, we want the return value to be a 1 whenever *classtype* equals "small".

- The third argument is the value we want the function to return when the logical test is false. In this case, we want the return value to be a 0 whenever *classtype* does not equal "small".

Go ahead and run the following code:

```
ifelse ( star $ classtype =="small", 1, 0)
## [1] 1 0 0 1 1 0 1 1 0 0 0 0
## ...
```

The function returns a 1 or a 0 for every student in the STAR dataset depending on the type of class they attended. (Here again, we show you only the first 12 values.)

To store these values as a new variable, we use the assignment operator <-. To its left, we need to specify the name of the new variable. Here, we chose to name the variable *small*. To store it as a variable inside the dataframe and not just as a new object by itself, we need to identify the name of the dataframe before the name of the variable with the $ character in between. (Note that the $ character allows us to create a new variable, and not just access an existing one as we saw in chapter 1.)

Putting it all together, to create the new variable *small* we run:

```
star$small <- ifelse ( star $ classtype == "small", 1, 0)
```

Whenever you create a new variable, it is good practice to check its contents. Doing so can save you a lot of trouble down the road. For example, here we can take a quick look at the first few observations of the dataframe using head() to ensure that the new binary variable was created correctly.

```
head(star) # shows first observations
##   classtype reading math graduated small
## 1     small     578  610         1     1
## 2   regular     612  612         1     0
## 3   regular     583  606         1     0
## 4     small     661  648         1     1
## 5     small     614  636         1     1
## 6   regular     610  603         0     0
```

Looking at the output, we can see that we have a new variable called *small*. Comparing the values of *small* to the values of *classtype*, we can confirm that whenever *classtype* equals "small", *small* equals 1 and that whenever *classtype* equals "regular", *small* equals 0. Indeed, in the first, fourth, and fifth observations, the value of *classtype* is "small" and the value of *small* is 1. In the second, third, and sixth observations, the value of *classtype* is "regular" and the value of *small* is 0.

TIP: Here, the first return value is a 1 and the second is a 0. Why? In the first observation of the STAR dataset, *classtype* equals "small", and so the logical test is TRUE, and therefore, the ifelse() function returns a 1. In the second observation, *classtype* equals "regular", and so the logical test is FALSE, and therefore, the ifelse() function returns a 0.

$ is the character used to identify a variable inside a dataframe, either to access it or to create it. To its left, we specify the name of the object where the dataframe is stored (without quotes). To its right, we specify the name of the variable (without quotes). Example: *data$variable*.

TIP: Recall that the name of an object or variable can be anything as long as it does not begin with a number or contain spaces or special symbols like $ or %. For practical reasons, the name of an object or variable should reflect the meaning of its contents, be short, and be written in all lowercase letters.

RECALL: mean() calculates the mean of a variable. The only required argument is the code identifying the variable. Example: mean(*data$variable*).

2.5.3 SUBSETTING VARIABLES

Using square brackets [], we can extract the selection of observations for which a logical test is true. This is useful in a variety of situations. For example, to estimate the average causal effect of *small* on *reading*, we need to compute the following difference-in-means estimator:

$$
\begin{pmatrix} \text{average reading} \\ \text{test scores among} \\ \text{students in} \\ \text{small classes} \end{pmatrix} - \begin{pmatrix} \text{average reading} \\ \text{test scores among} \\ \text{students in} \\ \text{regular-size classes} \end{pmatrix}
$$

This formula requires calculating the averages of two subsets of observations of *reading* for which a certain criterion is met. To subset a variable, we use the [] operator. To its left, we specify the variable we want to subset, star$reading in this case. Inside the square brackets, we specify the criterion of selection. The examples below should clarify how this works.

As stated in the previous chapter, we can use the function mean() to compute the mean of a variable in R. To calculate the average reading scores among all students in the STAR dataset, we run:

```
mean(star$reading)  # calculates the mean of reading
## [1] 628.803
```

To calculate average reading scores among *only* the students who attended a small class, we need to include in the average *only* the observations of *reading* for which *small* equals 1. The following code accomplishes this:

```
mean(star$reading[star$small==1])  # for treatment group
## [1] 632.7026
```

Values of *small* and *reading* for the first six observations in the STAR dataset. Observations from students who attended a small class (*small*=1) are in black, and observations from students who attended a regular-size class (*small*=0) are in gray.

i	small	reading
1	1	578
2	0	612
3	0	583
4	1	661
5	1	614
6	0	610

Only the observations of *reading* for which the logical test specified inside the square brackets is true are selected for the computation of the mean. For example, among the first six observations in the dataset, only the values of *reading* that correspond to observations 1, 4, and 5 are included in this average. (See the table in the margin.) According to the output above, students who attended a small class earned about 633 points on the reading test, on average.

How about the students who attended a regular-size class? The code to compute this mean is identical to the one above, except that now the criterion of inclusion is that *small* must equal 0.

```
mean(star$reading[star$small==0])  # for control group
## [1] 625.492
```

Based on this output, students who attended a regular-size class earned about 625 points on the reading test, on average.

Now we can easily calculate the difference-in-means estimator as the difference between these two averages using the outputs above (633 − 625). Better yet, we can compute it all at once, by running the following piece of code:

```
## compute difference-in-means estimator for reading
mean(star$reading[star$small==1]) -
    mean(star$reading[star$small==0])
## [1] 7.210547
```

TIP: By convention, when we include in the R script a comment at the beginning of a line, as opposed to after some code, we use two # characters instead of one.

For the other two outcome variables, then, we can compute the corresponding difference-in-means estimators as follows:

```
## compute difference-in-means estimator for math
mean(star$math[star$small==1]) -
    mean(star$math[star$small==0])
## [1] 5.989905
```

```
## compute difference-in-means estimator for graduated
mean(star$graduated[star$small==1]) -
    mean(star$graduated[star$small==0])
## [1] 0.007031124
```

These two pieces of code are identical to the previous one, except that now we use *math* and *graduated*, respectively, instead of *reading* as the outcome variable of interest.

What can we conclude from these results? Assuming that the students who attended a small class were comparable before schooling to those who attended a regular-size class (a reasonable assumption given that the dataset comes from a randomized experiment), we estimate that attending a small class:

- increased student performance on the third-grade reading test by 7 points, on average
- increased student performance on the third-grade math test by 6 points, on average
- increased the proportion of students graduating from high school by about 1 percentage point, on average.

Notice that conclusion statements should mention the key elements of the analysis. (See TIP in the margin.) In addition, note that the unit of measurement of the difference-in-means estimator differs depending on the type of outcome variable. See the summary provided in outline 2.1. (Just as we did when discussing the interpretation of means in chapter 1, we exclude categorical variables from this discussion.)

TIP: Good conclusion statements are clear, are concise, and include the key elements of the analysis. For example, when estimating average causal effects with randomized experiments, be sure to convey:

- the assumption: the treatment and control groups are comparable based on pre-treatment characteristics; in this case, students who attended a small class were comparable before schooling to those who attended a regular-size class
- the justification for the assumption: dataset comes from a randomized experiment
- the treatment: attending a small class
- the outcome variable(s): third-grade reading test scores, third-grade math test scores, and proportion of students graduating from high school
- the direction, size, and unit of measurement of the causal effect(s): an increase of 7 points, an increase of 6 points, and an increase of a little less than 1 percentage point, respectively
- the fact that you are making a causal claim: use causal language (attending a small class *increased* student performance) rather than observational language (students attending a small class performed better than students attending a regular-size one)
- the fact that you are estimating *average* causal effects as opposed to individual causal effects.

OUTLINE 2.1. Unit of measurement of the difference-in-means estimator based on the type of outcome variable.

unit of measurement of the difference-in-means estimator	
if outcome variable is non-binary: in the same unit of measurement as the outcome variable	if outcome variable is binary: in percentage points (after multiplying the result by 100)

If the outcome variable is non-binary, the unit of measurement of the difference-in-means estimator will be the same as the unit of measurement of the outcome variable. For example, if the outcome variable is measured in points, as is the case with both *reading* and *math*, then the average outcomes for the treatment and control groups will also be in points (the average of points is measured in points) and so will be the estimator (points−points=points).

TIP: What is a percentage point? It is the unit of measurement for the arithmetic difference between two percentages. For example, if a student's proportion of correct answers on a test improved from 50% to 60%, we would state that the score increased by 10 percentage points:

$$\triangle score = score_{final} - score_{initial}$$
$$= 60\% - 50\% = 10 \text{ p.p.}$$

Why is this difference not referred to as 10%? Because percentage change is different from percentage-point change. If someone told us that the initial score was 50% and that it increased by 10%, the final score would be 55% (not 60%). Because an increase of 10% of 50% is an increase of 5 percentage points ($0.10 \times 50 = 5$ p.p.), the final score would be:

$$score_{final} = score_{initial} + \triangle score$$
$$= 50\% + 5 \text{ p.p.} = 55\%$$

If the outcome variable is binary, the unit of measurement of the difference-in-means estimator will be percentage points, sometimes abbreviated as p.p. (after multiplying the output by 100). Why?

- First, as explained in the previous chapter, the average of a binary variable should be interpreted as a percentage (after multiplying the output by 100), because it is equivalent to the proportion of the observations that have the characteristic identified by the variable. As a result, when the outcome variable is binary, as is the case with *graduated*, the average outcomes for the treatment and control groups will both be measured in percentages (after multiplying the output by 100).
- Second, the unit of measurement for the arithmetic difference between two percentages is percentage points (percentage−percentage=percentage points). (See TIP in the margin.) Therefore, if the outcome variable is binary, the difference-in-means estimator will be measured in percentage points (after multiplying the output by 100).

As an example, let's revisit the interpretation of the difference-in-means estimator for the binary variable *graduated*.

First, calculate the average of *graduated* for students attending a small class and for students attending a regular-size class, separately:

```
mean(star$graduated[star$small==1]) # for treatment group
## [1] 0.8735043
```

```
mean(star$graduated[star$small==0]) # for control group
## [1] 0.8664731
```

The top output above indicates that among students who attended a small class, the average high school graduation rate was 87.35% (0.8735×100=87.35%). The bottom output indicates that among students who attended a regular-size class, the average high school graduation rate was 86.65% (0.8665×100=86.65%).

Second, compute the difference-in-means estimator, which is the difference between the two averages above:

```
## difference-in-means for graduated
0.8735043 - 0.8664731
## [1] 0.0070312
```

As we already knew from our calculations above, the difference-in-means estimator for *graduated* equals 0.007. It should be interpreted as an increase in the probability of graduating from high school of 0.7 percentage points, on average (0.007×100=0.7 p.p. or 87.35%−86.65%=0.7 p.p.).

Now that we have clarified how to interpret the difference-in-means estimator, let's return to our estimates of the average treatment effects above. There are two caveats to these estimates:

- First, they indicate how much the average outcome across multiple individuals changes as a result of the treatment. They do not indicate how the treatment would affect any one individual's outcome. As we saw in the idealized scenario earlier in the chapter, individual-level treatment effects might differ significantly from average treatment effects. While we estimate that student performance on the reading test improved, on average, as a result of attending a small class, a particular student's performance might have suffered from it.
- Second, the validity of these estimates rests on the plausibility of the assumption that the treatment and control groups are comparable with respect to all the variables that might affect the outcome other than the treatment variable itself. In this case, we can confidently make this assumption because we are analyzing data from a randomized experiment.

There are still a few questions that we need to answer to complete this analysis. Two in particular are worth noting here:

- Can we generalize these results to a population of students other than those who participated in Project STAR?
- Do the estimated causal effects represent real systematic effects rather than noise in the data?

We learn how to answer the first type of question in chapter 5 and explore the second in chapter 7, once we have become acquainted with the relevant concepts.

TIP: Because an average causal effect estimates the *average change* in Y caused by a change in X, it should be interpreted as an average increase in Y if positive, as an average decrease in Y if negative, and as no average change in Y if zero.

2.6 SUMMARY

In this chapter, we learned about causal effects and some of the difficulties we face when attempting to estimate them.

If we could observe the outcomes of the same individual under both treatment and control conditions at the same time, we could compute the causal effect of the treatment on a particular individual's outcome as the difference between these two potential outcomes.

Unfortunately, observing both potential outcomes is not possible. In reality, we observe only the outcome under the condition each individual received (the factual outcome) and can never observe what would have happened had the individual received the opposite condition (the counterfactual outcome).

To estimate a causal effect, we have to rely on assumptions to approximate the counterfactual outcome. This leads us to estimate average treatment effects across multiple individuals rather than the treatment effect for each individual.

When the treatment and control groups are comparable, we can use the average observed outcome (the factual outcome) of one group as a good approximation for the average unobserved outcome (the counterfactual outcome) of the other. Under these circumstances, the difference-in-means estimator produces a valid estimate of the average treatment effect.

The best way of ensuring that treatment and control groups are comparable is to run a randomized experiment. By assigning individuals to the treatment or control group based on a random process such as a coin flip, we ensure that the two groups have identical pre-treatment characteristics, on average. Later in the book, we will learn how to estimate average causal effects when we cannot run a randomized experiment and, instead, must analyze observational data.

2.7 CHEATSHEETS

2.7.1 CONCEPTS AND NOTATION

concept/notation	description	example(s)
causal relationship	refers to the cause-and-effect connection between two variables in which a change in one variable systematically produces a change in the other; we represent a causal relationship with an arrow between the variables: $$X \rightarrow Y$$	in this chapter, we explore the causal relationship between attending a small class and student performance: $$small \rightarrow performance$$ the question we aim to answer is, does attending a small class increase, decrease, or have a zero effect on student performance, on average?
treatment variable (X)	variable whose change may produce a change in the outcome variable; variable where the change originates; in this book, the treatment variable is always binary: $$X_i = \begin{cases} 1 & \text{if individual } i \\ & \text{receives the treatment} \\ 0 & \text{if individual } i \text{ does not} \\ & \text{receive the treatment} \end{cases}$$ treatment variables are a type of independent variable	in Project STAR, the treatment variable is *small*, which we define as: $$small_i = \begin{cases} 1 & \text{if student } i \text{ attended} \\ & \text{a small class} \\ 0 & \text{if student } i \text{ attended} \\ & \text{a regular-size class} \end{cases}$$
outcome variable (Y)	variable that may change as a result of a change in the treatment variable; outcome variables are the same as dependent variables	in these causal relationships: $small \rightarrow reading$ $small \rightarrow math$ $small \rightarrow graduated$ *small* is the treatment variable, and *reading*, *math*, and *graduated* are the outcome variables
treatment condition	the condition when the treatment is present; condition when $X_i=1$	in Project STAR, students attending a small class were under the treatment condition
control condition	the condition when the treatment is absent; condition when $X_i=0$	in Project STAR, students attending a regular-size class were under the control condition
potential outcome under the treatment condition ($Y_i(X_i=1)$)	one of the two potential outcomes for individual i; potential outcome for individual i when the treatment is present; the value of Y_i if $X_i=1$	in Project STAR, the potential outcome under the treatment condition is student performance after attending a small class from kindergarten until third grade
potential outcome under the control condition ($Y_i(X_i=0)$)	one of the two potential outcomes for individual i; potential outcome for individual i when the treatment is absent; the value of Y_i if $X_i=0$	in Project STAR, the potential outcome under the control condition is student performance after attending a regular-size class from kindergarten until third grade
$\triangle$	Greek letter Delta; mathematical notation for change	$\triangle Y_i$ represents the change in Y for individual i

continues on next page...

2.7.1 CONCEPTS AND NOTATION (CONTINUED)

concept/notation	description	example(s)
individual causal effect of X on Y	change in the outcome variable Y caused by a change in the treatment variable X; if we could observe both potential outcomes for each individual, we could measure it as: $$individual\_effects_i = Y_i(X_i=1) \\ - Y_i(X_i=0)$$	suppose that the first student in the dataset ($i=1$) would have scored 720 points on the reading test after attending a small class, and 700 points after attending a regular-size class; therefore: - $reading_1(small_1=1) = 720$ - $reading_1(small_1=0) = 700$ in this hypothetical case, the individual causal effect of attending a small class on this student's performance on the reading test would have been: causal effect of *small* on *reading* = $$= Y_i(X_i=1) - Y_i(X_i=0)$$ $$= reading_1(small_1=1) - \\ reading_1(small_1=0)$$ $$= 720 - 700 = 20$$ attending a small class, as opposed to a regular-size one, would have increased this student's performance on the reading test by 20 points
factual outcome	potential outcome under whichever condition (treatment or control) was received in reality; we always observe the factual outcomes	if a student attended a small class, the factual outcome is this student's performance after attending a small class, which we observe
counterfactual outcome	potential outcome under whichever condition (treatment or control) was not received in reality; we never observe the counterfactual outcomes	if a student attended a small class, the counterfactual outcome is this student's performance after attending a regular-size class, which we do not observe
fundamental problem of causal inference	we never observe the counterfactual outcome; we cannot measure the individual causal effect of a treatment on an outcome because we never observe both potential outcomes; the individual causal effect is $Y_i(X_i=1) - Y_i(X_i=0)$, but we can observe only one of the two potential outcomes, $Y_i(X_i=1)$ or $Y_i(X_i=0)$, whichever occurs in reality	students attend either a small class or a regular-size class, but they cannot attend both types of classes at the same time; we can never observe each student's performance under both the treatment and control conditions, and therefore, we cannot measure the effect of attending a small class on a specific student's performance
average causal effect of X on Y or average treatment effect	effect that X has on Y at the aggregate level; average of the individual causal effects of X on Y across a group of observations: $$\overline{individual\_effects} = \frac{\sum_{i=1}^{n} individual\_effects_i}{n}$$ average change in the outcome variable Y caused by a change in the treatment variable X for a group of observations; if treatment and control groups were comparable before the treatment was administered, then we can estimate the average treatment effect using the difference-in-means estimator	(see difference-in-means estimator)

continues on next page...

2.7.1 CONCEPTS AND NOTATION (CONTINUED)

concept/notation	description	example(s)
randomized experiment	also known as a randomized controlled trial (RCT); type of study design in which treatment assignment (who receives and does not receive the treatment) is randomized; the randomization of the treatment assignment ensures that treatment and control groups are, on average, identical to each other in all observed and unobserved pre-treatment characteristics	Project STAR was a randomized experiment in which students were randomly assigned to attend either a small class or a regular-size class; as a result, the students who attended a small class should have similar pre-treatment characteristics as the students who attended a regular-size class; for example, the average age of the students in both groups should be comparable
treatment group	group of individuals who received the treatment; observations for which $X_i=1$	in Project STAR, students attending a small class were in the treatment group
control group	group of individuals who did not receive the treatment; observations for which $X_i=0$	in Project STAR, students attending a regular-size class were in the control group
pre-treatment characteristics	characteristics of the individuals in a study before the treatment is administered; by definition, these characteristics cannot be affected by the treatment	in Project STAR, before students were assigned to small or regular-size classes, researchers recorded students' demographic data, such as age, gender, and race/ethnicity
difference-in-means estimator	the difference-in-means estimator is defined as the average outcome for the treatment group minus the average outcome for the control group: $$\overline{Y}_{\text{treatment group}} - \overline{Y}_{\text{control group}}$$ when treatment and control groups are similar with respect to all the variables that might affect the outcome other than the treatment variable itself, it produces a valid estimate of the average causal effect of X on Y; in this case, it estimates the average change in Y caused by a change in X interpret as: - an average increase in Y if positive - an average decrease in Y if negative - no average change in Y if zero unit of measurement of this estimator: - if Y is non-binary: in the same unit of measurement as Y - if Y is binary: in percentage points (after multiplying the result by 100)	in the STAR dataset, the difference-in-means estimator for the reading test scores is 632.7 points – 625.49 points = 7.21 points because Project STAR was a randomized experiment, the difference-in-means is a valid estimator of the average causal effect of attending a small class on student performance; we conclude that attending a small class, as opposed to a regular-size one, increased students' reading test scores by 7.21 points, on average
percentage point	unit of measurement of the arithmetic difference between two percentages	in the STAR dataset, the difference-in-means estimator for *graduated* is 87.35% – 86.65% = 0.7 p.p.; attending a small class is estimated to increase the proportion of students graduating from high school by about 1 percentage point, on average

continues on next page...

2.7.1 CONCEPTS AND NOTATION (CONTINUED)

concept/notation	description	example(s)
average outcome for the treatment group ($\overline{Y}_{\text{treatment group}}$)	average observed outcome for the individuals who received the treatment (after the treatment)	in the STAR dataset, the average reading score of the students who attended a small class was about 632.7 points
average outcome for the control group ($\overline{Y}_{\text{control group}}$)	average observed outcome for the individuals who did not receive the treatment (after no treatment)	in the STAR dataset, the average reading score of the students who attended a regular-size class was about 625.49 points
experimental data	data from a randomized experiment	since Project STAR was a randomized experiment, the data we analyze in this chapter are experimental data
observational data	data collected about naturally occurring events, in which treatment was received or not received without the intervention of researchers	data on class sizes and student performance from districts where the size of the classes varies as a result of factors such as school budgets, student enrollment, or the physical limitations of the school buildings
observational study	type of study that analyzes observational data	(see previous entry)

2.7.2 R SYMBOLS AND OPERATORS

code	description	example(s)
==	relational operator used to test whether the observations of a variable are equal to a particular value; values should be in quotes if text but without quotes if numbers (see ")	data$variable==1 data$variable=="yes"
$	character used to identify an element inside an object, such as a variable inside a dataframe, either to access it or to create it; to its left, we specify the name of the object where the dataframe is stored (without quotes); to its right, we specify the name of the element or variable (without quotes)	data$variable # identifies the variable named variable inside the dataframe stored in the object named data
[]	operator used to extract a selection of observations from a variable; to its left, we specify the variable we want to subset; inside the square brackets, we specify the criteria of selection; for example, we can specify a logical test using the relational operator ==; only the observations for which the logical test is true will be extracted	data$var1[data$var2==1] # extracts the observations of the variable var1 for which the variable var2 equals 1

2.7.3 R FUNCTIONS

function	description	required argument(s)	example(s)
ifelse()	creates the contents of a new variable based on the values of an existing one	three, separated by commas, in the following order: (1) logical test (see ==) (2) return value if test is true (3) return value if test is false values should be in quotes if text but without quotes if numbers (see ")	ifelse(data$variable=="yes", 1, 0) # returns a 1 whenever the observation of variable equals "yes" and a 0 otherwise, creating the contents of a binary variable using the existing character variable variable

3. INFERRING POPULATION CHARACTERISTICS VIA SURVEY RESEARCH

Another common goal for data analysis in the social sciences is to estimate population characteristics using surveys. Surveys enable us to infer the characteristics of an entire population by measuring them in a representative sample. In this chapter, we explain how survey research works and discuss some methodological challenges that may arise in the process. We also learn how to visualize and summarize both the distribution of a single variable and the relationship between two variables. To illustrate these concepts, we analyze data from and about the 2016 British referendum on European Union (EU) membership.

R symbols, operators, and functions introduced in this chapter: table(), prop.table(), na.omit(), hist(), median(), sd(), var(), ^, plot(), abline(), and cor().

3.1 THE EU REFERENDUM IN THE UK

Faced with growing discontent among the British people with the relationship between the United Kingdom (UK) and the EU, in 2016 the UK government held a referendum. British voters were asked to weigh in on whether the UK should stay in or leave the EU. The second choice became known as Brexit, an abbreviation for "British exit."

This was a high-stakes referendum, with global political, legal, and socioeconomic ramifications. Leading up to the vote, a group of researchers from the British Election Study (BES) conducted a large survey to measure public opinion and predict the outcome. In the first few sections of this chapter, we analyze data from this survey to measure support for Brexit and determine the demographic makeup of Brexit supporters. Subsequently, we analyze the actual referendum results to determine whether patterns observed in the BES sample can also be observed in the population of interest as a whole.

Based on Sara B. Hobolt, "The Brexit Vote: A Divided Nation, a Divided Continent," *Journal of European Public Policy* 23, no. 9 (2016): 1259–77. The data come from Wave 7 of the British Election Study.

3.2 SURVEY RESEARCH

In the social sciences, we often want to know the characteristics of a population of interest. Yet collecting data from every individual in the target population may be prohibitively expensive or simply not feasible.

A **sample** is a subset of observations from a target population. A **representative sample** accurately reflects the characteristics of the population from which it is drawn.

In survey research, we collect data from a subset of observations in order to understand the target population as a whole. The subset of individuals chosen for study is called a **sample**. The number of observations in the sample is represented by n, and the number of observations in the target population is represented by N. For example, in the aforementioned BES survey, researchers collected data from just under 31,000 people to infer the attitudes of more than 46 million eligible UK voters (n=31,000; N=46 million). Even more remarkably, in the United States, researchers typically survey only about 1,000 people to infer the characteristics of more than 200 million adult citizens (n=1,000; N=200 million).

TIP: Recall, the notation n stands for the number of observations in a dataframe or in a variable. As we see here, it also stands for the number of observations in a sample.

In survey research, it is vital for the sample to be representative of the population of interest. A **representative sample** accurately reflects the characteristics of the population from which it is drawn. Characteristics appear in the sample at similar rates as in the population as a whole.

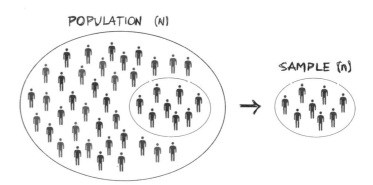

FIGURE 3.1. A sample is a subset of observations from a target population. In this case, the sample is clearly not representative of the population. The proportion of red individuals in the sample is substantially different than the proportion of red individuals in the population.

RECALL: The proportion of observations that meet a criterion is calculated as:

$$\frac{\text{number of observations that meet criterion}}{\text{total number of observations}}$$

To interpret this fraction as a percentage, we multiply the resulting decimal by 100.

If the sample is not representative, our inferences regarding the population characteristics based on the sample will be invalid. For example, in figure 3.1 above, the sample is clearly not representative of the population; the proportion of red individuals in the sample is 100% (8/8=1), while the proportion of red individuals in the population is only about 43% (19/44=0.43). As a result, the sample would lead us to infer the wrong population characteristics.

3.2.1 RANDOM SAMPLING

The best way to draw a representative sample is to select individuals at random from the population. This procedure is called **random sampling**. For example, to select individuals from a population randomly, we could number the individuals from 1 to N, write the numbers on slips of paper, put the slips of paper in a hat, shake the hat, and choose n slips of paper from the hat. (In practice, researchers do not use a hat but instead use a computer program like R to draw n random numbers from 1 to N.)

See figure 3.2 for an example of a randomly selected sample. In this case, the proportion of red individuals in the sample is 38% (3/8=0.38), which is not far from the proportion of red individuals in the population (43%). It is not exactly the same because n is relatively small. As we will see later in the book, as the sample size (n) increases, the characteristics of the sample will more closely approximate those of the population.

Random sampling consists of randomly selecting individuals from the population.

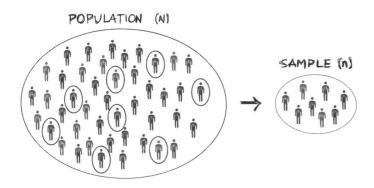

FIGURE 3.2. By randomly selecting individuals from the population, the proportion of red individuals in the sample more closely approximates the proportion of red individuals in the population than the sample shown in figure 3.1.

In the previous chapter, we saw how random assignment of individuals into treatment and control groups makes the two groups identical to each other, on average, before the treatment, in both observed and unobserved traits. Here, the random selection of individuals from the population makes the sample and the target population identical to each other, on average, in both observed and unobserved traits.

TIP: Do not confuse random treatment assignment with random sampling. Random treatment assignment means assigning treatment (deciding who receives it and who doesn't) at random; random sampling means selecting individuals from the population at random to be part of the sample.

> INFERRING POPULATION CHARACTERISTICS VIA RANDOM SAMPLING: By randomly selecting a sample of observations from the target population, we ensure that the target population and the sample are, on average, identical to each other in all observed and unobserved characteristics. In other words, we ensure that the sample is representative of the target population, which enables us to make valid inferences about the population.

The **sampling frame** is the complete list of individuals in a population. **Unit nonresponse** occurs when someone who has been selected to be part of the survey sample refuses to participate. **Item nonresponse** occurs when a survey respondent refuses to answer a certain question. **Misreporting** occurs when respondents provide inaccurate or false information.

3.2.2 POTENTIAL CHALLENGES

While random sampling is straightforward in theory, in practice it often faces complications that might invalidate the results.

First, to implement random sampling, we need the complete list of observations in the target population. This list is known as the **sampling frame**. In practice, the sampling frame of a population can be difficult to obtain. Lists of residential addresses, emails, or phone numbers often do not include the entire population of interest. More problematically, the individuals missing tend to be systematically different from those included. For example, a list of residential addresses may miss people who are either homeless or have recently moved, two segments of the population that are notably different from the rest. These omissions may render the lists not only incomplete but also unrepresentative of the population.

Second, even if we have access to a comprehensive list of the individuals in the population, some of those randomly selected might refuse to participate in the survey. This phenomenon is called **unit nonresponse**. If the individuals who refuse to participate differ systematically from those who agree, the resulting sample will be unrepresentative.

Third, participants might agree to answer some but not all of the questions in the survey. Respondents might feel uncomfortable sharing with strangers certain information about themselves. Whenever we have unanswered questions, we encounter what is called **item nonresponse**. If the missing answers differ systematically from the recorded answers, the data collected for the question at hand will not accurately reflect the characteristics of the population.

Fourth, participants might provide inaccurate or false information. This phenomenon, known as **misreporting**, is particularly likely when one answer is more socially acceptable or desirable than the others. For example, in the United States, official turnout rates in presidential elections have recently been around 60%, yet more than 70% of respondents in the American National Election Studies (ANES) report voting. Voting is often perceived to be a civic duty, so respondents might feel social pressure to lie about their voting behavior. As a rule, whenever we rely on self-reporting, we should be aware that misreporting might contaminate the data collected.

The statistical adjustments necessary to address these problems are beyond the scope of this book. For the purpose of our analysis, we assume that the sample from the BES survey is representative of the target population of interest, all eligible UK voters. Consequently, we use it to infer the population's support for Brexit.

3.3 MEASURING SUPPORT FOR BREXIT

Let's analyze the BES survey data to see how much support there was for Brexit a few weeks before the referendum occurred. (The survey was conducted between April 14 and May 4, 2016, and the referendum took place on June 23.)

The code for this chapter's analysis can be found in the "Population.R" file. Alternatively, you may choose to create a new blank R script and practice typing the code yourself. The file "BES.csv" contains the survey data, and table 3.1 provides the names and descriptions of the variables.

variable	description
vote	respondent's vote intention in the EU referendum: "leave", "stay", "don't know", or "won't vote"
leave	identifies leave voters: 1=intends to vote "leave" or 0=intends to vote "stay"; (NA=either "don't know" or "won't vote")
education	respondent's highest educational qualification: 1=no qualifications, 2=general certificate of secondary education (GCSE), 3=general certificate of education advanced level (GCE A level), 4=undergraduate degree, or 5=postgraduate degree; (NA=no answer)
age	respondent's age (in years)

TABLE 3.1. Description of the variables in the BES survey data, where the unit of observation is respondents.

Before starting our analysis of the BES survey dataset, we need to load and make sense of it, just as we did in chapter 1 with the STAR dataset. (See section 1.7 for details.)

First, we change the working directory so that R knows where to look for the data. Go ahead and run the code you used in chapter 1 to direct R to the DSS folder. Now we can read and store the dataset in an object named *bes* by running:

```
bes <- read.csv("BES.csv") # reads and stores data
```

RECALL: If the DSS folder is saved directly on your Desktop, to set the working directory, you must run setwd("~/Desktop/DSS") if you have a Mac and setwd("C:/*user*/Desktop/DSS") if you have a Windows computer (where *user* is your own username). If the DSS folder is saved elsewhere, please see subsection 1.7.1 for instructions on how to set the working directory.

To get a sense of the dataset, we can look at the first six observations using the function head():

```
head(bes)  # shows first observations
##          vote leave education age
## 1       leave     1         3  60
## 2       leave     1        NA  56
## 3        stay     0         5  73
## 4       leave     1         4  64
## 5 don't know    NA         2  68
## 6        stay     0         4  85
```

ADVANCED TIP: Recall that
ifelse() creates the contents of a
new variable based on the values
of an existing one. It requires
three arguments in the following
order, separated by commas: (1)
the logical test, (2) return value if
test is true, and (3) return value if
test is false. If the variable *leave*
had not been part of the dataframe,
we could have created it using one
ifelse() function nested in another:

```
bes$leave <-
  ifelse(bes$vote=="leave", 1,
    ifelse(bes$vote=="stay", 0, NA))
```

The observations of the variable
leave will be a 1 when *vote* equals
"leave", a 0 when *vote* equals "stay",
and an NA in all other cases. The
structure of this piece of code is as
follows: ifelse(test1, value if test1
is true, ifelse(test2, value if test1 is
false and test2 is true, value if both
test1 and test2 are false)).

Based on this output and table 3.1 (including the title of the table), we learn that each observation represents a survey respondent, and that the dataset contains four variables:

- *vote* captures how each respondent intended to vote in the referendum on Britain's EU membership at the time of the survey. It is a character variable that can take the following four values: "leave", "stay", "don't know", or "won't vote".

- *leave* is a binary variable that identifies leave voters, that is, Brexit supporters. It equals 1 if respondent intended to vote "leave" and 0 if respondent intended to vote "stay". For respondents who either didn't know how they would vote or did not intend to vote, we have NAs, which is how R represents missing values. (More on missing data soon.) Note that if this variable had not been part of the dataframe, we could have created it using the contents of *vote* by using multiple ifelse() functions. (See ADVANCED TIP in the margin.)

- *education* represents respondents' highest educational qualification. It is a non-binary numeric variable that can take five values: 1, 2, 3, 4, or 5. Each of these represents a different level of educational attainment, where 1 is the lowest level and 5 is the highest. Nonresponses are coded as NAs.

- *age* captures respondents' age in years, which means that it is a non-binary numeric variable that can take many values.

Putting it all together, for example, we interpret the first observation as representing a survey respondent who intended to vote "leave" in the EU referendum and was, therefore, a Brexit supporter, whose highest educational qualification was the general certificate of education advanced level (the British equivalent of a high school diploma), and who was 60 years old at the time of the survey.

Finally, to find out how many respondents were part of the survey, we run:

```
dim(bes) # provides dimensions of dataframe: rows, columns
## [1] 30895     4
```

Based on this output, we determine that the dataset contains information about 30,895 respondents. In other words, the sample size (*n*) is 30,895. (This is an impressively large survey!)

3.3.1 PREDICTING THE REFERENDUM OUTCOME

To predict the outcome of the referendum, we need to estimate the proportions of eligible UK voters who were (i) in favor of Brexit and (ii) opposed to Brexit, at the time the survey was conducted.

If the sample of respondents in the BES survey is representative of all eligible UK voters, then we can use the proportion of individuals' characteristics in the sample as good approximations of the proportion of individuals' characteristics in the entire target population.

To compute the proportions of individuals who were in favor of and opposed to Brexit in the BES sample, we create the table of proportions of the variable *vote*, but first we need to create a table of its frequencies.

3.3.2 FREQUENCY TABLES

The **frequency table** of a variable shows the values the variable takes and the number of times each value appears in the variable.

The **frequency table** of a variable shows the values the variable takes and the number of times each value appears in the variable.

For example, if $X=\{1, 0, 0, 1, 0\}$, the frequency table of X is:

values	0	1
frequencies	3	2

The table shows that X contains three observations that take the value of 0 and two observations that take the value of 1.

To create a frequency table in R, we use the function table(). The only required argument is the code identifying the variable to be summarized. In this case, to calculate the frequency table of *vote*, we run:

table() creates the frequency table of a variable. The only required argument is the code identifying the variable. Example: table(*data$variable*).

```
table(bes$vote) # creates frequency table
##     don't know      leave      stay    won't vote
##          2314       13692     14352          537
```

This frequency table shows that out of the 30,895 respondents in the BES survey, 2,314 were undecided, 13,692 intended to vote "leave", 14,352 intended to vote "stay", and 537 had no intention of voting. Note that the sum of all the frequencies equals the total number of observations in the sample, n (2314+13692+14352+537=30895).

RECALL: We use the $ character to access a variable inside a dataframe. To its left, we specify the name of the object where the dataframe is stored (without quotes). To its right, we specify the name of the variable (without quotes). Example: *data$variable*.

3.3.3 TABLES OF PROPORTIONS

The **table of proportions** of a variable shows the proportion of observations that take each value in the variable. By definition, the proportions in the table should add up to 1 (or 100%).

A **table of proportions** shows the proportion of observations that take each value in a variable.

For example, if $X=\{1, 0, 0, 1, 0\}$, the table of proportions of X is:

values	0	1
proportions	0.6	0.4

The table shows that 60% of the observations in X take the value of 0 and 40% take the value of 1. (Recall, to interpret a proportion as a percentage, we multiply the decimal value by 100.)

> prop.table() converts a frequency table into a table of proportions. The only required argument is the output of the function table() with the code identifying the variable inside the parentheses. Example: prop.table(table(*data$variable*)).

To create a table of proportions in R, we use the function prop.table(), which converts a frequency table into a table of proportions. This function takes as its main argument either (a) the name of the object containing the output of the function table() or (b) the function table() directly; in both cases, the variable of interest is specified inside the parentheses of table(). In our current example, then, to calculate the table of proportions of *vote*, we could run:

```
## option a: create frequency table  first
freq_table <- table(bes$vote)  # object with frequency table
prop.table(freq_table)  # creates table of proportions
##   don't know       leave        stay     won't vote
##      0.07490      0.44318     0.46454        0.01738
```

Alternatively, we could skip the step of creating an object with the frequency table and run instead:

```
## option b: do it  all  at once
prop.table(table(bes$vote))  # creates table of proportions
##   don't know       leave        stay     won't vote
##      0.07490      0.44318     0.46454        0.01738
```

Based on the proportions in the sample shown in the outputs above, we can estimate that when the survey was administered, 44% of eligible UK voters intended to vote "leave" and 46% to vote "stay"; more than 7% of the population was still undecided.

At this time, then, a slightly higher proportion of respondents intended to vote "stay" rather than "leave". The proportion of undecided, however, was larger than this difference (7% > 46%−44%), and thus, the survey results did not provide a clear prediction of the outcome of the referendum.

In reality, the referendum turned out to be quite close. The leave camp received 51.9% of the vote, and the stay camp received 48.1% of the vote. Thus, the leave camp won with a margin of only 3.8 percentage points (51.9%−48.1%=3.8 p.p.).

3.4 WHO SUPPORTED BREXIT?

We can also analyze the BES survey data to examine the characteristics of Brexit supporters and non-supporters. Specifically, we can determine how these two groups compare in terms of education level and age.

We begin this section by learning how different functions deal with missing data, and then we learn how to conduct our analysis on the observations that do not have missing information. Next, to compare the level of education of Brexit supporters to that of non-supporters, we explore the relationship between *leave* and *education* by creating a two-way table of frequencies and a two-way table of proportions. These tables are similar to the ones we created when exploring the contents of the variable *vote*, except that now we examine the contents of two variables at a time.

Then, to compare the age distribution of Brexit supporters to that of non-supporters, we explore the relationship between *leave* and *age*. In this case, we do not create a two-way table of frequencies or a two-way table of proportions. Because *age* (in years) can take a large number of distinct values, these tables would be too large to be informative. Instead, to visualize both age distributions and compare them to each other, we create histograms of *age* for supporters and non-supporters. Finally, to summarize and compare the characteristics of the two age distributions, we compute descriptive statistics such as the mean, median, standard deviation, and variance of *age* for each group.

3.4.1 HANDLING MISSING DATA

As we saw earlier, missing values are common in survey data. In the BES dataset, two variables contain NAs, which is how R represents missing values. The variable *leave* has NAs when respondents were undecided or didn't intend to vote. The variable *education* has NAs when respondents refused to provide an answer. (See the second and fifth observations of the dataframe shown in the output of head() at the beginning of section 3.3.)

Some functions in R automatically remove missing values before performing operations; others do not. For example, the function table() ignores missing values by default. If you want the function to include them, you need to specify the optional argument named exclude and set it to equal NULL. This asks R not to exclude any values from the table of frequencies. (See the RECALL in the margin for a brief overview of how optional arguments work.) In the current example, to create the table of frequencies of *education*, including missing values, we run:

RECALL: Inside the parentheses of a function, we can specify optional arguments by including the name of the optional argument (without quotes) and setting it to equal a particular value. TRUE, FALSE, NA, and NULL are special values in R and should not be written in quotes. Finally, optional arguments are specified after the required arguments, separated by commas.

```
table(bes$education, exclude=NULL) # table() including NAs
##     1     2     3     4     5   <NA>
##  2045  5781  6272 10676  2696   3425
```

Based on the output, a little more than 3,400 respondents refused to provide their level of education. The item nonresponse rate here, or the proportion of respondents who refused to provide an answer to this question, was about 11% (3425/30895=0.11).

The function mean() does not automatically exclude missing values. If a variable contains any NAs, R will not be able to compute

RECALL: In R, the function mean() calculates the mean of a variable. Example: mean(data$variable).

the average of the variable unless we change the default settings. For example, run the following:

```
mean(bes$leave) # mean() without removing NAs
## [1] NA
```

Here, R returns an NA, indicating the presence of missing values.

We can instruct R to remove the NAs before computing the average by specifying the optional argument named na.rm (which stands for "<u>NA</u> <u>re</u>move") and setting it to equal TRUE.

```
mean(bes$leave, na.rm=TRUE) # mean() removing NAs
## [1] 0.4882328
```

RECALL: The mean of a binary variable can be interpreted as the proportion of the observations that have the characteristic identified by the variable (that have a value of 1).

Now, R provides the result of the operation. We interpret the output as indicating that, in the BES survey, out of the respondents who had already made up their minds to vote for one camp or the other, about 49% were Brexit supporters ($0.49 \times 100 = 49\%$).

To see how other functions deal with missing values, we can use the help tab of RStudio (in the lower-right window). This tab provides descriptions of all the R functions, including the actions they perform, the arguments they require, and the settings they use by default as well as how to change them. To read about a particular function, all we need to do is manually select the help tab, type the name of the function next to the magnifying glass icon, and hit enter. (See figure 3.3 as an example.)

FIGURE 3.3. Example of the type of information displayed in RStudio's help tab.

Files   Plots   Packages   Help   Viewer

Arithmetic Mean   [Q mean ⊗]

Description
Generic function for the (trimmed) arithmetic mean

Usage
```
mean(x, trim = 0, na.rm = FALSE, ...)
```

Arguments

x	An R object...
trim	...
na.rm	a logical value indicating whether NA values should be stripped before the computation
...	

To remove from the dataframe all observations with missing values, we can use the function na.omit(). For our current purposes, to get rid of all observations with at least one NA from *bes*, we run:

```
bes1 <- na.omit(bes) # removes observations with NAs
```

The code `na.omit(bes)` returns the original dataframe without the observations that have any missing values. With the assignment operator `<-`, we store this new dataframe in an object named *bes1*. The environment (the storage room of the current R session shown in the upper-right window) should now contain two objects: *bes* (the original dataframe) and *bes1* (the new dataframe).

A word of caution: The function `na.omit()` instructs R to delete all observations with any missing data. To avoid removing observations needlessly, before applying this function to a dataframe, we should make sure that all the variables in the dataframe that contain any missing values are needed for the analysis. (Instructions for extracting the variables we want to use in the analysis from a dataframe are in the ADVANCED TIP in the margin.)

In the case of the BES survey, only two variables contain NAs: *leave* and *education*. We are not interested in the respondents for whom we have a missing value in *leave*. They either did not intend to vote or had not yet made up their minds about Brexit. And, since we will use *education* in our analysis, we will need to exclude respondents who refuse to provide their educational background. Consequently, applying `na.omit()` to *bes* does not result in unnecessarily removing any observations.

After using the function `na.omit()`, it is a good idea to (i) look at a few observations from both dataframes to ensure the function worked as expected, and (ii) compute how many observations were deleted.

To accomplish the first task, we can use the function `head()`:

```
head(bes) # shows first observations of original dataframe
##            vote leave education age
## 1         leave   1         3  60
## 2         leave   1        NA  56
## 3          stay   0         5  73
## 4         leave   1         4  64
## 5 don't know     NA         2  68
## 6          stay   0         4  85
```

```
head(bes1) # shows first observations of new dataframe
##            vote leave education age
## 1         leave   1         3  60
## 3          stay   0         5  73
## 4         leave   1         4  64
## 6          stay   0         4  85
## 7         leave   1         3  78
## 8         leave   1         2  51
```

`na.omit()` deletes all observations with missing data from a dataframe. The only required argument is the name of the object where the dataframe is stored.   Example: `na.omit(data)`.

ADVANCED TIP: Recall that `[]` is the operator used to extract a selection of observations from a variable.   It is also the operator used to extract a selection of observations from a dataframe.   In both cases, to its left, we specify what we want to subset (whether it is a variable or a dataframe), and inside the square brackets, we specify the criterion of selection.

To extract a subset of variables from a dataframe, we can use the `[]` operator in conjunction with the function `c()`, which combines values into a vector (as we will see in detail in chapter 6). Example:

```
reduced_data <-
    original_data[c("var1", "var2")]
```

This piece of code will create a new object, named *reduced_data*, containing a dataframe with the variables named *var1* and *var2* from the dataframe stored in *original_data*.

Comparing the two outputs above, we observe that, as expected, na.omit() deleted from the original dataframe the second and fifth observations because they both contain at least one NA. (Note that, by default, R keeps the original row numbers; as a result, *bes1* does not have any rows numbered 2 or 5.)

To accomplish the second task, we can use the function dim():

```
dim(bes)  # provides dimensions of original dataframe
## [1] 30895    4
```

```
dim(bes1)  # provides dimensions of new dataframe
## [1] 25097    4
```

By deleting observations with missing data, we reduced the dataset from 30,895 to 25,097 observations. A total of 5,798 observations, or close to 19% of the original observations, were removed because they contained at least one NA (30895−25097=5798 and 5798/30895=0.19).

Before continuing with the analysis, it is worth noting that removing observations with missing values from a dataset might make the remaining sample of observations unrepresentative of the target population, thereby rendering our inferences of population characteristics invalid. Here, for example, if respondents who refused to provide their level of education were all in favor of Brexit, our analysis of the new dataframe, *bes1*, would undermine the level of support for Brexit. The statistical methods used to address this problem are beyond the scope of this book. For our purposes, we assume that the sample from the BES survey is representative of all eligible UK voters, with or without the observations with missing values.

Going forward, we will analyze the data in the new dataframe, *bes1*, which does not contain any NAs. (The code identifying the variables will follow the structure *bes1$variable_name* instead of *bes$variable_name*.)

3.4.2 TWO-WAY FREQUENCY TABLES

A **two-way frequency table**, also known as a cross-tabulation, shows the number of observations that take each combination of values of two specified variables.

To see the level of education of Brexit supporters and non-supporters within the sample, we can create the two-way frequency table of *leave* and *education*. A **two-way frequency table**, also known as a cross-tabulation, shows the number of observations that take each combination of values of two specified variables.

For example, if X and Y are as defined in the first table below (the dataframe), the two-way frequency table of X and Y is the second table below:

i	X	Y
1	1	1
2	0	1
3	0	1
4	1	0
5	0	0

The two-way frequency table of X and Y is:

		values of Y	
		0	1
values	0	1	2
of X	1	1	1

The two-way frequency table shows that in the dataframe:

- there is one observation for which both X and Y equal 0 (the fifth observation)

- there are two observations for which X equals 0 and Y equals 1 (the second and third observations)

- there is one observation for which X equals 1 and Y equals 0 (the fourth observation)

- there is one observation for which both X and Y equal 1 (the first observation).

To produce a two-way frequency table, we use the function table(), just as we did to produce a one-way frequency table. For the two-way version, however, we need to specify two variables as required arguments (separated by a comma). In the study at hand, to create the two-way frequency table of *leave* and *education*, we run:

```
table(bes1$leave, bes1$education) # two-way frequency table
##        1    2    3    4    5
## 0    498 1763 3014 6081 1898
## 1   1356 3388 2685 3783  631
```

> table() creates a two-way frequency table when two variables are specified as required arguments (separated by a comma). In the output, the values of the first specified variable are shown in the rows; the values of the second specified variable are shown in the columns. Example: table(*data$variable1, data$variable2*).

In the output above, we can see that *leave* takes two values (0 or 1) and that *education* takes five (1, 2, 3, 4, or 5). (Note that the values of the variable specified as the first argument in the function are shown in the rows; the values of the second variable are shown in the columns.) The numbers in each cell indicate the frequency, or count, of each combination of values in the dataset. For example, we see from the first cell that in the BES sample, there were 498 respondents who were not Brexit supporters (*leave*=0) and had no educational qualification (*education*=1).

Two-way frequency tables can help us discover the relationship between two variables. For example, in the table above we observe that among respondents with no educational qualification (*education*=1), there were fewer Brexit non-supporters than supporters (498 non-supporters vs. 1,356 supporters). In contrast, among respondents with the highest educational qualification (*education*=5), there were more non-supporters than supporters (1,898 non-supporters vs. 631 supporters).

3.4.3 TWO-WAY TABLES OF PROPORTIONS

To infer the level of education of Brexit supporters and non-supporters among all eligible UK voters, we need to compute the proportion of individuals in the sample with each combination of relevant characteristics. Recall, if the sample is representative, characteristics should appear in similar proportions in the sample as in the population as a whole.

A **two-way table of proportions** shows the proportion of observations that take each combination of values of two specified variables.

To calculate the relevant proportions within the sample, we create a two-way table of proportions of *leave* and *education*. A **two-way table of proportions** shows the proportion of observations that take each combination of values of two specified variables.

Let's return to the simple example from the previous subsection. If X and Y are as defined in the first table below, the two-way table of proportions of X and Y is the second table below:

i	X	Y
1	1	1
2	0	1
3	0	1
4	1	0
5	0	0

The two-way table of proportions of X and Y is:

		values of Y	
		0	1
values	0	0.2	0.4
of X	1	0.2	0.2

The two-way table of proportions shows that in the dataframe:

- both X and Y equal 0 in 20% of the observations
- X equals 0 and Y equals 1 in 40% of the observations
- X equals 1 and Y equals 0 in 20% of the observations
- both X and Y equal 1 in 20% of the observations.

prop.table() converts a two-way frequency table into a two-way table of proportions. The only required argument is the output of the function table() with the code identifying the two variables inside the parentheses (separated by a comma). Example: prop.table(table(*data$variable1*, *data$variable2*)).

To create a two-way table of proportions in R, we use the same function as with the one-variable version: prop.table(). Here, though, we need to specify two variables inside the function table(), which is the required argument. By default, R produces the two-way table of proportions where the whole sample is the reference group (the denominator). Run:

```
## two-way table of proportions
prop.table(table(bes1$leave, bes1$education))
##           1         2         3         4         5
## 0   0.01984   0.07025   0.12009   0.24230   0.07563
## 1   0.05403   0.13500   0.10698   0.15074   0.02514
```

Because the whole sample is the reference group, the sum of all the proportions within the table equals 1. We interpret the first cell of the table as indicating that 2% of the respondents in the BES survey ($0.02 \times 100 = 2\%$) were against Brexit (*leave*=0) and had no educational qualification (*education*=1).

If we wanted to know proportions within subsets of the sample, we would need to change the reference group of the calculations. To do so, we specify the optional argument margin and set it to equal either 1 or 2. If it equals 1, R will use the first specified variable to set the reference groups. For example, to compute the proportion of different levels of education within Brexit supporters and within Brexit non-supporters, we run:

```
## two-way table of proportions with margin=1
prop.table(table(bes1$leave, bes1$education), margin=1)
##          1       2       3       4       5
## 0   0.03757 0.13302 0.22740 0.45880 0.14320
## 1   0.11450 0.28608 0.22672 0.31943 0.05328
```

Because we included the optional argument margin=1 and the first specified variable is *leave*, the proportions are calculated within two groups: Brexit non-supporters (*leave*=0) and Brexit supporters (*leave*=1). The proportions in each row now add up to 1. We interpret the first cell of the table as indicating that among all Brexit non-supporters in the sample, close to 4% had no educational qualification (*education*=1).

Alternatively, if we include the optional argument margin=2, R will use the second specified variable to define the reference groups. For example, to calculate the proportion of support for Brexit within each educational level, we run:

```
## two-way table of proportions with margin=2
prop.table(table(bes1$leave, bes1$education), margin=2)
##          1       2       3       4       5
## 0   0.26861 0.34226 0.52886 0.61648 0.75049
## 1   0.73139 0.65774 0.47114 0.38352 0.24951
```

The new proportions are calculated within five groups, one for each level of educational attainment. The proportions in each column now add up to 1. We interpret the first cell of the table as indicating that among respondents with no educational qualification (*education*=1), about 27% did not support Brexit (*leave*=0).

Two-way tables of proportions can also help us discover the relationship between two variables. For example, in the previous table, we find that among respondents with no educational qualification (*education*=1), the majority are Brexit supporters (27% non-supporters vs. 73% supporters). This phenomenon reverses with higher levels of education. Among respondents with the British equivalent of a high school diploma (*education*=3), Brexit supporters are in the minority by a slight margin (53% non-supporters vs. 47% supporters). Among respondents with the highest educational qualification (*education*=5), Brexit supporters are in the clear minority (75% non-supporters vs. 25% supporters).

If the BES sample is representative of all eligible UK voters, we can infer that voters with low levels of education were likely to support Brexit, and voters with high levels of education were likely to oppose Brexit.

3.4.4 HISTOGRAMS

The **histogram** of a variable is the visual representation of its distribution through bins of different heights. The position of the bins along the x-axis indicates the interval of values. The height of the bins indicates the frequency (or count) of the interval of values within the variable.

To compare Brexit supporters to non-supporters in terms of age, we can visualize the two age distributions by creating histograms. A **histogram** is a graphical representation of the variable's distribution, made up of bins (rectangles) of different heights. The position of the bins along the x-axis (the horizontal axis) indicates the interval of values. The height of the bins represents how often the variable takes the values in the corresponding interval.

For example, if $X=\{11, 11, 12, 13, 22, 26, 33, 43, 43, 48\}$, the histogram of X is the graph in the margin. It shows that the variable X contains:

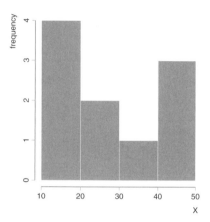

- four observations in the interval from 10 to 20
- two observations in the interval from 20 to 30
- one observation in the interval from 30 to 40
- three observations in the interval from 40 to 50.

The R function to create the histogram of a variable is hist(). In the case at hand, to produce the histogram of *age*, we run:

```
hist(bes1$age) # creates histogram
```

hist() creates the histogram of a variable. The only required argument is the code identifying the variable. Example: hist(*data$variable*).

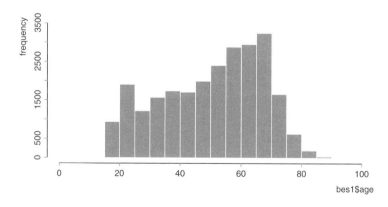

After running this piece of code, R will display the graph shown above in the plots tab of RStudio (the lower-right window). If R gives you the error message "Error in plot.new(): figure margins too large" instead, try making the lower-right window larger and then re-run the code that creates the plot. (Note that the graphs in the book might look a little different from those you see on your computer. To make the book easier to read, we often modify the default color schemes and styles of graphs. The overall patterns should be the same, however.)

Based on the histogram above, we see that the survey does not have any respondents below the age of 15. (The minimum value this variable takes is actually 18.) This makes sense since researchers purposely reached out only to eligible voters. We can see that the distribution roughly follows a bell curve, although it is skewed to the left. (See TIP in the margin for an explanation of what we mean by skewed.) The largest segment (the tallest bin) is made up of respondents between 65 and 70 years old.

The histogram above includes the age of both supporters and non-supporters. To compare the age distribution of Brexit supporters to that of non-supporters, we need to create two histograms, one for each group. For each of these histograms, we need to select only the observations of *age* that meet the criteria (the respondent must be a supporter or a non-supporter, respectively). For this purpose, we can use the [] operator in conjunction with the == operator, just as we did in chapter 2. (See subsection 2.5.3.) Then we can apply the hist() function to each subset. All together, the code to produce the two histograms is:

```
## create histograms
hist(bes1$age[bes1$leave == 0])  # for non-supporters
hist(bes1$age[bes1$leave == 1])  # for supporters
```

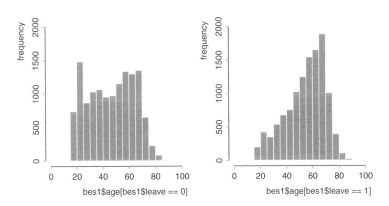

Looking at the histogram for non-supporters (the one on the left), we see that the age distribution is relatively uniform and that the largest segment is between 20 and 25 years old. In contrast, the histogram for supporters (the one on the right) shows that the age distribution approximates a bell curve, although clearly skewed to the left, and that the largest segment is between 65 and 70 years old. Based on the visual comparison of the age distributions of the two groups, we conclude that Brexit supporters tended to be older than non-supporters.

TIP: A bell curve is skewed to the left if the tail on the left side of the distribution is longer than the tail on the right side (as in the solid-line distribution below) and is skewed to the right if the opposite is true (as in the dashed-line distribution below).

skewed to the right   skewed to the left

RECALL: To extract a selection of observations from a variable, we use the [] operator. To its left, we specify the variable we want to subset. Inside the square brackets we specify the criterion of selection, using for example the relational operator ==. Only the observations for which the criterion is true are extracted. Example: *data$var1[data$var2==1]* extracts only the observations of the variable *var1* for which the variable *var2* equals 1.

TIP: In the uniform distribution, all values between the minimum and the maximum are equally likely.

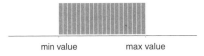

min value   max value

A **density histogram** uses densities instead of frequencies as the height of the bins, where densities are defined as the proportion of the observations in the bin divided by the width of the bin.

3.4.5 DENSITY HISTOGRAMS

Arguably a better option for visualizing the differences between the age distributions of the two groups is to use density histograms. Density histograms are especially useful for comparing groups with substantially different numbers of observations. In a **density histogram**, the height of each bin indicates the density of the bin, defined as the proportion of the observations in the bin divided by the width of the bin. This is true because the area of each bin (rectangle) is equivalent to the proportion of observations that fall in the bin, that is, that take any of the values within the interval identified by the position of the bin on the x-axis.

Here is the mathematical reasoning. The area of a rectangle or bin is computed as follows:

$$\text{area of the bin} = \text{height of the bin} \times \text{width of the bin}$$

To determine the height of each bin, we (i) rearrange the formula above and (ii) substitute the area of the rectangle with the proportion of observations because, as mentioned, in density histograms these two terms are equivalent:

$$\text{height of the bin} = \frac{\text{area of the bin}}{\text{width of the bin}}$$

$$= \frac{\text{proportion of observations in the bin}}{\text{width of the bin}}$$

$$= \text{density of the bin}$$

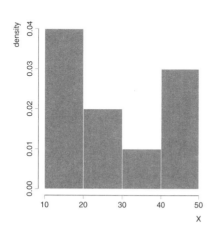

Let's return to the simple example from the previous subsection. If $X=\{11, 11, 12, 13, 22, 26, 33, 43, 43, 48\}$, the density histogram of X is the graph in the margin. As we can see, the height of the first bin is 0.04. Here is why:

- out of the 10 observations in the variable, 4 are in this bin; the proportion of observations in the bin is, therefore, 0.4 or 40% (4/10=0.4)
- the width of the bin is 10 because the bin is positioned from 10 to 20 on the x-axis (20−10=10)
- this results in a density of 0.04 (proportion/width=0.4/10=0.04).

Density histograms have two useful properties. First, if the width of the bins is constant, the relative height of the bins implies the relative proportion of observations that fall in the bins. In other words, if one bin is twice as high as another, it means that it contains twice as many observations.

For example, the density histogram above shows that in the variable X, there are:

- twice as many values in the interval from 10 to 20 as in the interval from 20 to 30
- twice as many values in the interval from 20 to 30 as in the interval from 30 to 40
- three times as many values in the interval from 40 to 50 as in the interval from 30 to 40.

Second, because the area of each bin equals the proportion of observations in the bin, the areas of all the bins in the density histogram add up to 1.

For example, the sum of the areas of all the bins in the density histogram above is:

$$\sum_{\text{all bins}} \text{height}_{\text{bin}} \times \text{width}_{\text{bin}} = (0.04 \times 10) + (0.02 \times 10) \\ + (0.01 \times 10) + (0.03 \times 10) = 1$$

Why are density histograms a better option than histograms for visualizing the differences between two distributions? Unlike frequencies, the unit of measurement of densities is comparable across distributions with different numbers of observations. Densities are related to proportions (percentages), which are not affected by changes in the total number of observations. In contrast, frequencies are related to counts, which are affected by changes in the total number of observations. As a result, whenever comparing two distributions with substantially different numbers of observations, it is better to use density histograms than histograms.

To illustrate this, let's compare the age distribution of respondents who have no educational qualifications with the age distribution of respondents who have an undergraduate degree but no postgraduate degree. Because the first group of respondents is much smaller than the second, this comparison highlights the advantages of using density histograms. As we saw earlier, in the BES survey only about 2,000 respondents have no educational qualification (*education*=1), but more than 10,000 have an undergraduate degree as their highest educational qualification (*education*=4).

To compare these two distributions, let's start by creating histograms where the height of the bins reflect frequencies:

```
## create histograms
hist(bes1$age[bes1$education==1]) # w/ no qualifications
hist(bes1$age[bes1$education==4]) # w/ undergraduate degree
```

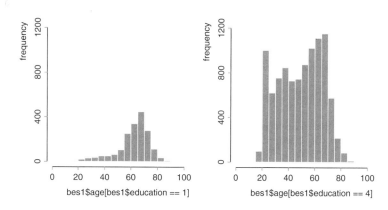

Is the proportion of respondents between 65 and 70 years old among those with no qualifications equivalent to the proportion of respondents in that age group among those with an undergraduate degree? Looking at the two histograms above, it is hard to say. The large difference in the size of the two groups makes comparisons difficult. To more easily compare these two distributions, we can create density histograms.

hist() creates the density histogram of a variable when the optional argument freq is set to equal FALSE. The only required argument is the code identifying the variable. Example: hist(*data*$*variable*, freq=FALSE).

To create a density histogram in R, we also use the hist() function, but we need to set the optional argument freq (which stands for "frequencies") to FALSE. In the current example, to produce the density histograms of *age* for respondents with no qualifications and for respondents with undergraduate degrees, we run:

```
## create density histograms
hist (bes1$age[bes1$education==1],
       freq=FALSE) # w/ no qualifications
hist (bes1$age[bes1$education==4],
       freq=FALSE) # w/ undergraduate degree
```

TIP: Here, to facilitate the comparison of the heights (or densities) of the bins across the two histograms, we purposely made both y-axes display the same range of values (from 0 to 0.05).

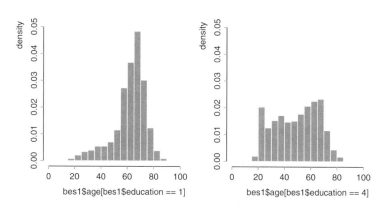

Looking at the density histograms, we can clearly see that the proportion of respondents between 65 and 70 years old among those with no qualifications (in the graph on the left) is about twice as large as the proportion of respondents in that age group among those with an undergraduate degree (in the graph on the right). We can draw this conclusion by just comparing the heights (or densities) of the bins across the two histograms because in both histograms the bins have all the same widths (5 years).

Now that we have learned the advantages of density histograms, let's return to exploring the distributions of *age* for Brexit supporters and non-supporters. To produce the two relevant density histograms, we run:

```
## create density histograms
hist (bes1$age[bes1$leave == 0]),
      freq=FALSE) # for non-supporters
hist (bes1$age[bes1$leave == 1]),
      freq=FALSE) # for supporters
```

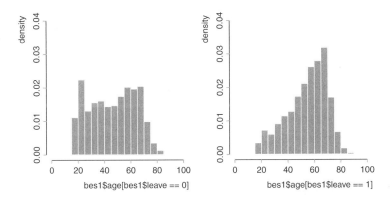

Here we can see, for example, that the proportion of respondents between 20 and 25 years old among Brexit non-supporters (in the graph on the left) is close to three times the proportion of respondents in the same age group among supporters (in the graph on the right). In addition, the proportion of respondents between 65 and 70 years old among Brexit supporters (in the graph on the right) is about one and a half times the proportion of respondents in that age group among non-supporters (in the graph on the left).

In practice, we rarely care about the exact value of each density. We usually just care about the shape of the histogram as demarcated by the height of the bins. We use this shape to describe or illustrate the different distributions. (See figure in the margin.)

3.4.6 DESCRIPTIVE STATISTICS

Another option for measuring the differences between Brexit supporters and non-supporters in terms of age distribution is to compute and compare **descriptive statistics**. Descriptive statistics numerically summarize the main traits of the distribution of a variable.

The **descriptive statistics** of a variable numerically summarize the main characteristics of its distribution.

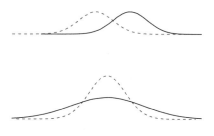

We can use two different types of descriptive statistics:

- Measures of centrality, such as the mean and the median, summarize the center of the distribution. (See the top figure in the margin, which shows two distributions that are identical except for their centrality.)

- Measures of spread, such as the standard deviation and the variance, summarize the amount of variation of the distribution relative to its center. (See the bottom figure in the margin, which shows two distributions that are identical except for their spread.)

RECALL: The average, or mean, of a variable equals the sum of the values across all observations divided by the number of observations. If the variable is non-binary, the mean should be interpreted as an average, in the same unit of measurement as the variable. If the variable is binary, the mean should be interpreted as a proportion, in percentages after multiplying the result by 100. In R, mean() calculates the mean of a variable. Example: mean(*data*$*variable*).

In chapter 1, we saw how to compute and interpret the **mean** of a variable. (See section 1.8.) In the running example, the code to compute the average age of each group is:

```
## compute mean
mean(bes1$age[bes1$leave == 0]) # for non-supporters
## [1] 46.89
```

```
mean(bes1$age[bes1$leave == 1]) # for supporters
## [1] 55.06823
```

TIP: If we were interested in calculating the average age among *all* respondents of the BES survey, we would run mean(bes1$age), without subsetting *age*.

Based on the results above, the average Brexit non-supporter was 47 years old, while the average supporter was 55 years old. This means that Brexit supporters were eight years older than non-supporters, on average (55−47=8).

The **median** of a variable is the value in the middle of the distribution that divides the data into two equal-size groups.

We can also describe the center of a distribution by using the **median**. The median is the value at the midpoint of the distribution that divides the data into two equal-size groups (or as close to it as possible). When the variable contains an odd number of observations, the median is the middle value of the distribution. When the variable contains an even number of observations, the median is the average of the two middle values.

For example, if $X=\{10, 4, 6, 8, 22\}$, the median of X is 8. To see this more clearly, we need to sort the values of X in ascending order (as they would be in the distribution). We end up with $\{4, 6, \underline{8}, 10, 22\}$. Now we clearly see that the value in the middle of the distribution is 8.

Unlike the mean, the median should always be interpreted in the same unit of measurement as the values in the variable, regardless of whether the variable is binary or non-binary.

median() calculates the median of a variable. The only required argument is the code identifying the variable. Example: median(*data*$*variable*).

The R function to calculate the median of a variable is median(). The only required argument is the code identifying the variable. In the running example, to calculate the medians of the two age distributions, we run:

```
## compute median
median(bes1$age[bes1$leave == 0]) # for non-supporters
## [1] 48

median(bes1$age[bes1$leave == 1]) # for supporters
## [1] 58
```

The median Brexit non-supporter was 48 years old, while the median supporter was 58 years old. In other words, about half of Brexit non-supporters were 48 years old or younger, and about half of supporters were 58 years old or younger.

In the case of the age distributions here, the mean values (47 and 55) are very similar to the median values (48 and 58), but this is not always true. One important distinction between the two statistics is that while the mean is sensitive to outliers (extreme values in the variable), the median is not. If, for example, we replaced the oldest Brexit supporter aged 97 with a Brexit supporter aged 107, the median value would remain the same because the value of the observation in the middle of the distribution would not have changed. In contrast, the new mean would be higher than the original, since the sum of all the observations (the numerator of the formula) would be 10 units larger.

To describe the amount of variation relative to the center of a distribution, we can use the **standard deviation**. Mathematically, it is the result of the following calculation:

$$sd(X) = \sqrt{\frac{\sum_{i=1}^{n}(X_i - \overline{X})^2}{n}}$$
$$= \sqrt{\frac{(X_1 - \overline{X})^2 + (X_2 - \overline{X})^2 + \cdots + (X_n - \overline{X})^2}{n}}$$

where:

- $sd(X)$ stands for the standard deviation of X
- X_i stands for a particular observation of X, where i denotes the position of the observation
- $\overline{X}$ stands for the mean of X
- n is the number of observations in the variable
- $\sum_{i=1}^{n}(X_i - \overline{X})^2$ means the sum of all $(X_i - \overline{X})^2$ from $i=1$ to $i=n$.

Roughly speaking, the standard deviation of a variable provides the average distance between the observations and the mean (in the same unit of measurement as the variable). To better understand this, let's look at a simple example step by step.

TIP: If we were interested in computing the median age among *all* respondents of the BES survey, we would run median(bes1$age).

The **mean** of a variable is more sensitive to outliers than the **median**.

The **standard deviation** of a variable measures the average distance of the observations to the mean. The larger the standard deviation, the flatter the distribution.

RECALL: The unit of measurement of the mean of a variable is the same as the unit of measurement of the variable, when the variable is non-binary.

If $X = \{2, 4, 6\}$ and the unit of measurement of X is miles:

- The average of X (including its unit of measurement) is:

$$\overline{X} = \frac{\sum_{i=1}^{n} X_i}{n} = \frac{2+4+6}{3} = \frac{12}{3} = 4 \text{ miles}$$

- For each i, we can calculate the term $X_i - \overline{X}$, which gives us a sense of the distance between each observation and the mean of X:
  - for $i=1$: $X_1 - \overline{X} = 2 - 4 = -2$ miles
  - for $i=2$: $X_2 - \overline{X} = 4 - 4 = 0$ miles
  - for $i=3$: $X_3 - \overline{X} = 6 - 4 = 2$ miles

- Note that the term $X_i - \overline{X}$ above can result in both negative and positive numbers. If we calculated the average of this term, positive distances would cancel out negative distances. We do not want such cancellation, since we are trying to measure the average deviation from the center of the distribution. To avoid the cancellation, we need to get rid of the signs. To do so, we square the term $X_i - \overline{X}$. The resulting term, $(X_i - \overline{X})^2$, provides the squared distance from the mean for each observation:
  - for $i=1$: $(X_1 - \overline{X})^2 = (2-4)^2 = (-2)^2 = 4$ miles^2
  - for $i=2$: $(X_2 - \overline{X})^2 = (4-4)^2 = (0)^2 = 0$ miles^2
  - for $i=3$: $(X_3 - \overline{X})^2 = (6-4)^2 = (2)^2 = 4$ miles^2

- To compute the average of the squared distances across all observations, we add them up and divide them by the number of observations:

$$\frac{\sum_{i=1}^{n}(X_i - \overline{X})^2}{n} = \frac{(X_1 - \overline{X})^2 + (X_2 - \overline{X})^2 + (X_3 - \overline{X})^2}{3}$$
$$= \frac{4+0+4}{3} = 2.67 \text{ miles}^2$$

- To return to the same unit of measurement as the original variable, we need to get rid of the square. To do so, we calculate the square root of the average of the squared distances across all observations:

$$sd(X) = \sqrt{\frac{\sum_{i=1}^{n}(X_i - \overline{X})^2}{n}} = \sqrt{2.67 \text{ miles}^2} = 1.63 \text{ miles}$$

- We can now interpret this number as the average distance between the observations and the mean in the same unit of measurement as the original variable (miles here).

In short, a smaller standard deviation indicates the observations are closer to the mean, on average. The distribution is concentrated around the mean, and consequently, the density is higher at the center. Analogously, a larger standard deviation indicates that the observations are farther from the mean, on average. The distribution is dispersed, and consequently, the density is lower at the center. For example, in the top figure in the margin, the standard deviation of the dashed distribution is smaller than the standard deviation of the solid distribution.

The R function to calculate the standard deviation of a variable is sd(). The only required argument is the code identifying the variable. Therefore, to compute the standard deviations of the age distributions of Brexit supporters and non-supporters, we run:

```
## compute standard deviation
sd(bes1$age[bes1$leave == 0])  # for non-supporters
## [1] 17.3464

sd(bes1$age[bes1$leave == 1])  # for supporters
## [1] 14.96106
```

> sd() calculates the standard deviation of a variable. The only required argument is the code identifying the variable. Example: sd(*data*$*variable*).

TIP: If we were interested in computing the standard deviation of the distribution of age among *all* respondents of the BES survey, we would run sd(bes1$age).

Among Brexit non-supporters, the average difference between respondents' age and the mean age is 17 years. Among supporters, the average difference is 15 years. If we look back at the two density histograms (at the end of subsection 3.4.5), we can see that the distribution of supporters is more concentrated around the mean than the distribution of non-supporters. It makes sense, then, that the standard deviation of the age distribution of supporters is smaller than that of non-supporters.

One final note about standard deviations: Knowing the standard deviation of a variable helps us understand the range of the data, especially when dealing with bell-shaped distributions known as normal distributions.

As we will see in detail later in the book, one of the distinct characteristics of normal distributions is that about 95% of the observations fall within two standard deviations from the mean (that is, are between the mean minus two standard deviations and the mean plus two standard deviations). For example, we know that the average *age* of Brexit supporters is 55, and the standard deviation of their age distribution is 15 years. If the age distribution of Brexit supporters were a perfect normal distribution, then 95% of Brexit supporters would be between 25 and 85 years old ($55-2\times15=25$ and $55+2\times15=85$). Looking at the histogram shown in the bottom figure in the margin, this seems about right, although the histogram is skewed to the left, and thus, the formula does not apply exactly.

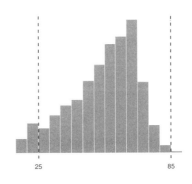

The **variance** of a variable is the square of the standard deviation.

We sometimes use another measure of the spread of a distribution called **variance**. The variance of a variable is simply the square of the standard deviation:

$$var(X) = sd(X)^2$$

where:

- $var(X)$ stands for the variance of X
- $sd(X)$ stands for the standard deviation of X.

var() calculates the variance of a variable. The only required argument is the code identifying the variable. Example: var(*data$variable*).

To calculate the variance of a variable in R, we can use the function var() or simply square the standard deviation of that variable using the ^ operator. For example, to calculate the variance of the age distribution of Brexit supporters, we can run either one of the following lines of code:

```
var(bes1$age[bes1$leave==1]) # calculates variance
## [1] 223.8334
sd(bes1$age[bes1$leave==1])^2 # calculates square of sd
## [1] 223.8334
```

^ is the operator that raises a number to a power. The number that follows it is the power, that is, the number of times we want to multiply the preceding number by itself. Example: 3^2 raises 3 to the 2nd power (3^2=9).

We are usually better off using standard deviations as our measure of spread. They are easier to interpret because, as we just saw, they are in the same unit of measurement as the variable. (The variance of a variable is in the unit of measurement of the variable squared.)

RECALL: sqrt() calculates the square root of the argument specified inside the parentheses. Example: sqrt(4).

If we know the variance of a variable, we take its square root to compute the standard deviation, using the sqrt() function:

```
sqrt(var(bes1$age[bes1$leave==1])) # square root of variance
## [1] 14.96106
```

Not surprisingly, running this code produces the same output as sd(bes1$age[bes1$leave==1]) on the previous page.

3.5 RELATIONSHIP BETWEEN EDUCATION AND THE LEAVE VOTE IN THE ENTIRE UK

Based on Sascha O. Becker, Thiemo Fetzer, and Dennis Novy, "Who Voted for Brexit? A Comprehensive District-Level Analysis," *Economic Policy* 32, no. 92 (2017): 601–50.

In the previous section, in our analysis of the data from the BES survey, we noted that respondents who had higher levels of education were less likely to support Brexit. In this section, we examine the actual referendum results to see whether a similar relationship can be identified in the whole population of UK voters. In particular, we use district-level data to explore how the proportion of residents with high levels of education (who earned at least an undergraduate degree or equivalent) relates to the vote share received by the leave camp. For this purpose, we learn how to create scatter plots to visualize the relationship between two variables and how to compute the correlation coefficient to summarize their linear relationship numerically.

For this analysis, we use a dataset that contains the referendum results on Brexit aggregated at the district level. The dataset is provided in the file "UK_districts.csv". Table 3.2 shows the names and descriptions of the variables included. (Note again that the dataset we use in this section is not from a sample of the population but rather from the entire population of interest.)

TIP: In an individual-level analysis, the unit of observation is individuals. By contrast, in an aggregate-level analysis, the unit of observation is collections of individuals. Here, our unit of observation is districts; each observation represents the residents of a particular district.

variable	description
name	name of the district
leave	vote share received by the leave camp in the district (in percentages)
high_education	proportion of district's residents with an undergraduate degree, professional qualification, or equivalent (in percentages)

TABLE 3.2. Description of the variables in the UK district-level data, where the unit of observation is districts.

In preparation for this section's analysis (assuming we have already set the working directory), we read and store the dataset by running:

```
dis <- read.csv("UK_districts.csv") # reads and stores data
```

RECALL: If the DSS folder is saved directly on your Desktop, to set the working directory, you must run setwd("~/Desktop/DSS") if you have a Mac and setwd("C:/*user*/Desktop/DSS") if you have a Windows computer (where *user* is your own username). If the DSS folder is saved elsewhere, please see subsection 1.7.1 for instructions on how to set the working directory.

To get a sense of the dataset, we look at the first few observations by using the function head():

```
head(dis)  # shows first observations
##              name   leave  high_education
## 1     Birmingham   50.42          22.98
## 2         Cardiff   39.98          32.33
## 3  Edinburgh City   25.56          21.92
## 4    Glasgow City   33.41          25.91
## 5        Liverpool  41.81          22.44
## 6         Swansea   51.51          25.85
```

Based on table 3.2 and the output above, we learn that each observation in the dataset represents a district in the UK, and that the dataset contains three variables:

- *name* is a character variable that identifies the district
- *leave* is a numeric non-binary variable that captures the vote share received by the leave camp in each district, measured in percentages
- *high_education* is a numeric non-binary variable that captures the proportion of residents in the district, measured in percentages, that had undergraduate degrees, professional qualifications, or the equivalent.

We interpret the first observation as representing the district called Birmingham, where leave received a little more than 50%

of the vote share, and about 23% of residents had a high level of education (at least an undergraduate degree or equivalent).

To determine the number of observations in the dataset, we use the function dim():

```
dim(dis) # provides dimensions of dataframe: rows, columns
## [1] 382    3
```

We find that the original dataframe contains information about 382 districts.

Although we did not see any NAs in the first six observations shown by head() above, there might be some missing values in the rest of the data. (Note that the description of variables does not always explicitly report on NAs.) In case there are any NAs in the dataset, we apply the function na.omit() to the dataframe. Because we will use all the variables in our analysis, this will not eliminate observations unnecessarily.

```
dis1 <- na.omit(dis) # removes observations with NAs
```

As is common practice, we use dim() to find out how many observations were deleted:

```
dim(dis1) # provides dimensions: rows, columns
## [1] 380    3
```

Deleting observations with missing values reduces the dataframe to 380 districts. This means that there were only two districts with at least one NA.

3.5.1 SCATTER PLOTS

A **scatter plot** is the graphical representation of the relationship between two variables, where one variable is plotted along the x-axis, and the other is plotted along the y-axis.

A **scatter plot** enables us to visualize the relationship between two variables by plotting one variable against the other in a two-dimensional space.

Imagine we have the dataframe shown below with two variables of interest, X and Y. The scatter plot of X and Y is the graph shown to its right:

i	X	Y
1	4	2
2	8	5
3	10	3

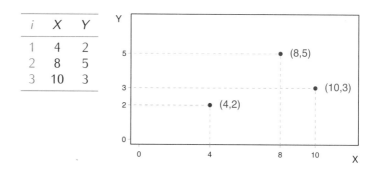

This dataframe contains only three observations. We can think of each observation *i* consisting of two coordinates in the two-dimensional space. The first coordinate indicates the position of the point on the x-axis (the horizontal axis), and the second coordinate indicates the position of the point on the y-axis (the vertical axis). Let's look at the first observation (the observation for which *i*=1). The value of X_1 is 4, which means that the dot for this observation should be lined up with the number 4 on the x-axis. The value of Y_1 is 2, which means that the dot for this observation should be lined up with the number 2 on the y-axis. Together, these two coordinates create the dot (4,2).

To create a scatter plot in R, we use the plot() function. It requires that we specify two arguments in a particular order: (1) the variable we want on the x-axis and (2) the variable we want on the y-axis. Alternatively, we can specify which variables we want to plot on the x- and y-axes by including the names of the arguments in the specification, which are x and y, respectively. Then, the order of the arguments no longer matters. To create the scatter plot of *high_education* and *leave* in the UK district-level dataset, we can run any of the following pieces of code:

```
plot(dis1$high_education, dis1$leave) # scatter plot X, Y

plot(x=dis1$high_education, y=dis1$leave) # scatter plot

plot(y=dis1$leave, x=dis1$high_education) # scatter plot
```

plot() creates the scatter plot of two variables. It requires two arguments, separated by a comma, in this order: (1) the variable to be plotted on the x-axis and (2) the variable to be plotted on the y-axis. Example: plot(*data$x_var, data$y_var*). As an alternative, we can specify which variables we want to plot on the x- and y-axes by including the names of the arguments in the specification, which are x and y, respectively. For example, both of these pieces of code will create the same scatter plot: plot(x=*data$x_var*, y=*data$y_var*) plot(y=*data$y_var*, x=*data$x_var*).

TIP: In R functions, the order of the arguments only matters when we do not specify the name of the arguments.

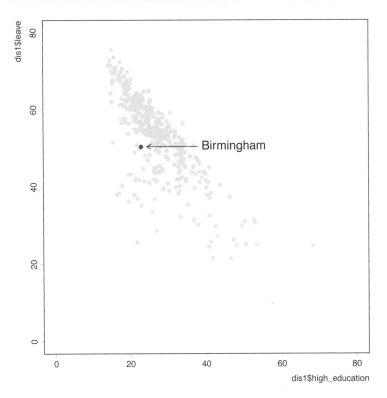

Just as in the simple example, every dot in the scatter plot above represents an observation, a district in this case. For example, the red dot is the observation that represents the district of Birmingham, where about 23% of residents had a high level of education, and close to 50% of the votes were cast in support of Brexit.

What can we learn from this scatter plot about the relationship between these two variables? Are districts with low proportions of highly educated residents likely to support Brexit? What about districts with high proportions of highly educated residents? An intuitive way to answer these questions is by finding the averages of both variables on the graph and using them to divide the graph into four parts (in our imagination or otherwise).

abline() adds a straight line to the most recently created graph. To add a vertical line, we set the argument v to equal the value on the x-axis where we want the line. To add a horizontal line, we set the argument h to equal the value on the y-axis where we want the line. To change the default solid line to a dashed line, we set the optional argument lty to equal "dashed". Examples: abline(v=2) and abline(h=3, lty="dashed").

To add straight lines to a graph in R, we can use the abline() function. To add a vertical line, we set the argument v to equal the value on the x-axis where we want the line drawn. To add a horizontal line, we set the argument h to equal the value on the y-axis where we want the line drawn. By default, R draws solid lines. To draw dashed lines, we set the lty argument (which stands for "line type") to equal "dashed". For example, go ahead and run:

```
## add straight dashed lines to the most recent graph
abline(v=mean(dis1$high_education), lty="dashed") # vertical
abline(h=mean(dis1$leave), lty="dashed") # horizontal
```

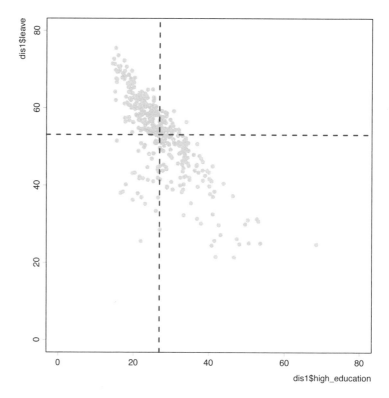

If you run the code in the sequence provided here, you should see the graph above. This is the scatter plot of *high_education* and *leave* we created earlier with the function plot(), with two added dashed lines: a vertical line marking the mean of *high_education* and a horizontal line marking the mean of *leave*. (Note that the function abline() will add lines to the most recently created graph, but R will give you an error message if you have yet to create a graph.)

As shown in the figure in the margin, the dashed lines divide the graph into four quadrants (from top right and counterclockwise):

- Quadrant I: values of the observations are above both means
- Quadrant II: observations have a value of *high_education* below the mean but a value of *leave* above the mean
- Quadrant III: values of the observations are below both means
- Quadrant IV: observations have a value of *high_education* above the mean but a value of *leave* below the mean

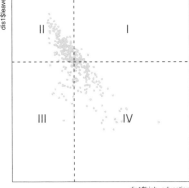

Now we can more easily answer our initial questions:

- Are districts with low proportions of highly educated residents likely to support Brexit? In other words, are districts with values of *high_education* below the mean likely to have values of *leave* above the mean?

  Looking at the bulk of the data in the scatter plot above, we determine that the answer is yes. Here is the logic: the districts with values of *high_education* below the mean are in quadrants II and III. Between these two quadrants, quadrant II contains a higher proportion of the data (more dots). This means that districts with values of *high_education* below the mean tend to have values of *leave* above the mean.

- Are districts with high proportions of highly educated residents likely to support Brexit? In other words, are districts with values of *high_education* above the mean likely to have values of *leave* also above the mean?

  Looking at the bulk of the data again, we see that the answer is no. The districts with values of *high_education* above the mean are in quadrants I and IV. Between these two quadrants, quadrant IV contains a higher proportion of the data. This means that districts with values of *high_education* above the mean tend to have values of *leave* below the mean.

We conclude that, at the district level, a higher proportion of highly educated residents is associated with a lower proportion of Brexit supporters. This is consistent with the individual-level relationship we observed using the BES survey data from a sample of the population.

The **correlation coefficient** summarizes the direction and strength of the linear association between two variables. It ranges from –1 to 1. The sign reflects the direction of the linear association: It is positive whenever the slope of the line of best fit is positive and negative whenever the slope of the line of best fit is negative. Its absolute value reflects the strength of the linear association, ranging from 0 (no linear association) to 1 (perfect linear association). The absolute value of the correlation coefficient increases as the observations move closer to the line of best fit and the linear association becomes stronger.

3.5.2 CORRELATION

While the scatter plot provides us with a visual representation of the relationship between two variables, sometimes it is helpful to summarize the relationship with a number. For that purpose, we use the **correlation coefficient**, or correlation for short. Before looking into how to compute this statistic, let's get a sense of how to interpret it.

The correlation coefficient ranges from –1 to 1, and it captures the following two characteristics of the relationship between two variables:

- the direction of their linear association, that is, the sign of the slope of the line of best fit (which is the line that best summarizes the data)
- the strength of their linear association, that is, the degree to which the two variables are linearly associated with each other.

While the direction of the linear association determines the sign of the correlation, the strength of the linear association determines the magnitude of the correlation. Let's look at this in detail.

Depending on the direction of the linear association, that is, whether the line that best fits the data slopes upward or downward, the correlation will be positive or negative:

- The correlation is positive whenever the two variables move in the same direction relative to their respective means, that is, when high values in one variable are likely to be associated with high values in the other, and low values in one variable are likely to be associated with low values in the other. In other words, the correlation is positive whenever the slope of the line of best fit is positive. For example, see the top scatter plot in the margin and the line of best fit that we added. Is the slope positive or negative? Positive. On average, higher values of X are associated with higher values of Y. This means that the correlation between X and Y is positive.

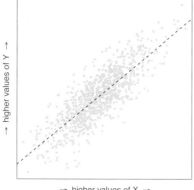

→ higher values of X →

- The correlation is negative whenever the two variables move in opposite directions relative to their respective means, that is, when high values in one variable are likely to be associated with low values in the other, and vice versa. For example, as we saw in the previous subsection, the variables *high_education* and *leave* in the UK district-level dataset move in opposite directions relative to their respective means. As shown in the bottom scatter plot in the margin, the slope of the line of best fit is negative. On average, higher values of *high_education* are associated with lower values of *leave*. This means that the correlation between *high_education* and *leave* is negative.

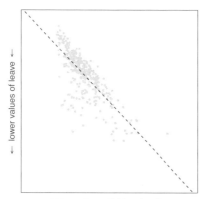

→ higher values of high_education →

 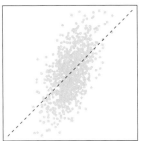 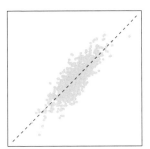 

Depending on the strength of the linear association, that is, how close the observations are to the line of best fit, the absolute value of the correlation coefficient will be closer to 0 or to 1:

- At one extreme, the absolute value of the correlation coefficient is approximately 0 when the linear relationship between the two variables is non-existent. This is the case in the first scatter plot of figure 3.4 above. Here, we would have a hard time fitting a line that would adequately summarize the data.

- At the opposite extreme, the absolute value of the correlation coefficient is exactly 1 if the association between the two variables is perfectly linear. This is the case in the last scatter plot of figure 3.4, where the points are all on a single line.

- All other linear relationships result in a correlation coefficient with an absolute value between 0 and 1. As the observations move closer to the line of best fit, the linear association between the two variables becomes stronger, and the absolute value of the correlation coefficient increases. See, for example, the progression from left to right in figure 3.4.

FIGURE 3.4. Scatter plots of variables with weaker to stronger linear associations. As the observations move closer to the line of best fit, the absolute value of the correlation coefficient increases. From left to right, the correlations are approximately 0, 0.5, 0.8, and 1.

Putting it all together, the correlation between two variables ranges from -1 to 1. The sign of the correlation indicates the direction of the linear association between the variables. And the absolute value of the correlation depicts the strength of the linear association between the variables. (See figure 3.5 above, which illustrates how the value of the correlation coefficient depends on the direction and strength of the linear association between the two variables.)

FIGURE 3.5. Scatter plots of variables with correlations ranging from -1 to 1. From left to right, the correlations are -1, -0.8, -0.5, approximately 0, 0.5, 0.8, and 1.

The **z-score** of an observation is the number of standard deviations the observation is above or below the mean.

How is the correlation coefficient computed? In order to understand the formula for the correlation coefficient, we first need to learn about z-scores. The z-score of an observation is the number of standard deviations the observation is above or below the mean. Specifically, the z-score of each observation of X is defined as:

$$Z_i^X = \frac{X_i - \overline{X}}{sd(X)}$$

where:

- Z_i^X stands for the z-score of observation X_i
- X_i stands for a particular observation of X, where i denotes the position of the observation
- $\overline{X}$ stands for the mean of X
- $sd(X)$ stands for the standard deviation of X.

Returning to the example we saw when learning about standard deviations, if $X=\{2, 4, 6\}$, then $\overline{X}=4$ and $sd(X)=1.63$ (as we computed earlier), and the z-score of each observation of X is:

- for $i=1$: $Z_1^X = \frac{X_1 - \overline{X}}{sd(X)} = \frac{2-4}{1.63} = -1.23$
- for $i=2$: $Z_2^X = \frac{X_2 - \overline{X}}{sd(X)} = \frac{4-4}{1.63} = 0$
- for $i=3$: $Z_3^X = \frac{X_3 - \overline{X}}{sd(X)} = \frac{6-4}{1.63} = 1.23$

The unit of measurement of z-scores is always in standard deviations, regardless of the unit of measurement of the original variable. In addition, the sign of the z-score indicates whether the observation is above or below the mean. For example, we interpret the three z-scores above as follows:

- for $i=1$: $Z_1^X=-1.23$ standard deviations; indicates that X_1 is a little more than one standard deviation below the mean of X
- for $i=2$: $Z_2^X=0$ standard deviations; indicates that X_2 is zero standard deviations away from the mean of X because X_2 and the mean coincide in value
- for $i=3$: $Z_3^X=1.23$ standard deviations; indicates that X_3 is a little more than one standard deviation above the mean of X.

To compute the correlation between two variables, X and Y, we first convert the observations of both variables to z-scores. Then, the correlation coefficient is calculated as the average of the products of the z-scores of X and Y. Mathematically, the correlation between X and Y is:

$$cor(X, Y) = \frac{\sum_{i=1}^{n} Z_i^X \times Z_i^Y}{n}$$

$$= \frac{Z_1^X \times Z_1^Y + Z_2^X \times Z_2^Y + \cdots + Z_n^X \times Z_n^Y}{n}$$

where:

- $cor(X, Y)$ stands for correlation between X and Y
- Z_i^X and Z_i^Y denote the z-scores of observation i for X and Y, respectively
- $\sum_{i=1}^{n} Z_i^X \times Z_i^Y$ stands for the sum of the product of the z-scores of X and Y from $i=1$ to $i=n$, meaning from the first observation to the last one
- n is the number of observations.

For example, if X and Y are as defined in the first two columns of the table below, the z-scores of X and Y are as shown in the adjacent two columns:

i	X	Y	Z^X	Z^Y
1	2	6	-1.23	1.23
2	4	4	0	0
3	6	2	1.23	-1.23

And the correlation coefficient between X and Y is:

$$cor(X, Y) = \frac{\sum_{i=1}^{n} Z_i^X \times Z_i^Y}{n}$$

$$= \frac{-1.23 \times 1.23 + 0 \times 0 + 1.23 \times -1.23}{3} = -1$$

The product of the two z-scores for each observation is:

- positive when both z-scores are positive (the observation is above the mean in both variables)
- positive when both z-scores are negative (the observation is below the mean in both variables)

- negative when one z-score is negative, but the other is positive (the observation is below the mean in one variable but above the mean in the other).

As a result, the sign of the correlation coefficient will be:

- positive when the two variables tend to move in the same direction relative to their respective means, that is, when above-average values in one variable are usually associated with above-average values in the other (both z-scores are positive), and when below-average values in one variable are usually associated with below-average values in the other (both z-scores are negative)
- negative when the two variables tend to move in the opposite direction relative to their respective means, that is, when above-average values in one variable are usually associated with below-average values in the other (the two z-scores are of opposite signs).

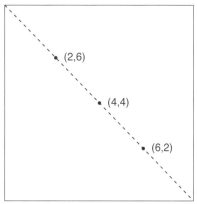

In the formula in detail above, we manually computed that, if $X=\{2, 4, 6\}$ and $Y=\{6, 4, 2\}$, the correlation between X and Y is -1. What does this tell us?

- The negative sign indicates that the two variables tend to move in opposite directions relative to their respective means. (As we can see in the scatter plot of these two variables shown in the margin, the slope of the line of best fit is indeed negative.)
- The absolute value of 1 indicates that the two variables have a perfect linear association with each other. (As we can see in the same scatter plot, all the points are on the line of best fit.)

Note that this is an extreme example. Most correlations are between -1 and 1, not including the endpoints. If we change the second observation in the example above to $(4,0)$ instead of the original $(4,4)$, then the new correlation between X and Y is about -0.65. As we can see in the new scatter plot shown in the margin, while the slope of the line of best fit continues to be negative, now the points are no longer on the line of best fit. This means that the negative linear association is no longer perfect, which explains why the correlation is no longer exactly -1.

To calculate the correlation coefficient between two variables in R, we use the function cor(). Inside the parentheses, we must identify the two variables (separated by a comma and in no particular order). For example, to calculate the correlation between *high_education* and *leave*, we run:

```
cor(dis1$high_education, dis1$leave) # computes correlation
## [1] -0.7633185
```

The correlation between *high_education* and *leave* is -0.76, a strong negative correlation. It is negative because the slope of the line of best fit is negative. Its absolute value is closer to 1 than to 0 because the observations are scattered tightly around the line of best fit. (See the scatter plot of *high_education* and *leave* on the left side of the figure in the margin.)

A few final remarks about the correlation coefficient. First, the correlation between Y and X is the same as the correlation between X and Y. Mathematically: $cor(Y, X) = cor(X, Y)$. For example, by running the following code we see that the correlation between *leave* and *high_education* is the same as the correlation between *high_education* and *leave* (computed above):

```
cor(dis1$leave, dis1$high_education) # computes correlation
## [1] -0.7633185
```

By switching the order of the variables, we are flipping the axes of the scatter plot—the variable that was on the x-axis is now on the y-axis, and vice versa—but the relationship between the variables does not change. Both the direction and strength of their linear association remain the same. Compare the scatter plot of *leave* and *high_education* on the right side of the figure in the margin to the scatter plot of *high_education* and *leave* on the left side. The slope of both lines of best fit are negative, and the points are equally clustered around both lines.

Second, a steeper line of best fit does not necessarily mean a higher correlation in absolute terms, or vice versa. What determines the absolute value of the correlation coefficient is how close the observations are to the line of best fit. For example, in figure 3.6, the absolute value of the correlation is lower in the second scatter plot than in the first (despite the steeper line) because the observations are farther away from the line of best fit.

cor() calculates the correlation coefficient between two variables. It requires the code identifying the two variables (separated by a comma and in no particular order). Example: cor(*data$variable1*, *data$variable2*).

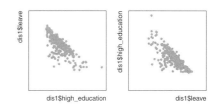

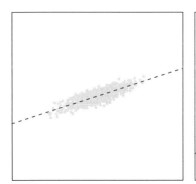
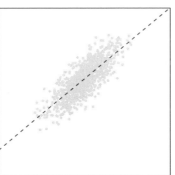

FIGURE 3.6. A steeper line of best fit does not necessarily mean a higher correlation in absolute terms.

Third, if two variables have a correlation coefficient of zero, it does not necessarily mean that there is no relationship between them. It just means that there is no *linear* relationship between them. For example, the two variables depicted in the figure in the margin have a strong parabolic relationship. Their correlation is approximately zero, however, because there is no line that would summarize the relationship well.

Finally, correlation does not necessarily imply causation. Just because two variables have a strong linear association does not mean that changes in one variable cause changes in the other. As we will see in detail in chapter 5, correlation does not necessarily imply causation when the treatment and control groups are not comparable with respect to all the variables that affect the outcome (not including the treatment itself).

> CORRELATION DOES NOT NECESSARILY IMPLY CAUSATION: Just because two variables are highly correlated with each other does not necessarily mean that changes in one variable cause changes in the other.

Despite the strong negative correlation between *high_education* and *leave*, without further evidence we cannot conclude that if UK voters became more highly educated, they would also become less likely to support Brexit. In other words, we do not know whether voters' level of education and support for Brexit are causally related in any way. Perhaps the observed relationship is spurious, that is, the product of some third variable that affects both the education level of voters and their support for Brexit, such as the local economy. (We will discuss spurious relationships in more detail in chapter 5.)

3.6 SUMMARY

This chapter introduced us to survey research. We saw how random sampling can help us obtain a representative sample from a population, enabling us to infer population characteristics from a subset of observations.

In addition, we learned some tools that we can use to visualize and summarize the distribution of one variable or the relationship between two. Most data analyses in the social sciences, whether for the purpose of measurement, prediction, or explanation, involve exploring one variable at a time and/or trying to understand the relationship between two variables. In this chapter, we have seen various methods we can use for these purposes in different contexts. Below is a quick review.

To explore one numeric variable at a time, we can:

- create a frequency table
- create a table of proportions
- create a histogram with frequencies or densities to visualize the distribution of the variable
- numerically summarize the center of the distribution by computing the mean and/or the median
- numerically summarize the spread of the distribution by computing the standard deviation and/or the variance.

When exploring the relationship between two numeric variables, we can:

- create a two-way frequency table
- create a two-way table of proportions
- create a scatter plot to visualize their relationship
- numerically summarize the direction and strength of their linear association by computing the correlation coefficient.

These are major building blocks of data analysis, and we will use them in many of the analyses in the remainder of the book.

3.7 CHEATSHEETS

3.7.1 CONCEPTS AND NOTATION

concept/notation	description	example(s)
sample	subset of observations from a target population	the subset of students in a particular class constitutes a sample from the population of students who attend the school
representative sample	sample that accurately reflects the characteristics of the population from which it is drawn; characteristics appear in the sample at similar rates as in the population as a whole	if we randomly select students from those who attend a particular school, we will end up with a representative sample of the population of students from that school; the characteristics of the sample should resemble those of the population; they should have the same proportion of political science majors, females, foreign-born students, and so on
random sampling	procedure that consists of randomly selecting a sample of individuals from the target population	to draw observations from a population randomly, we could number the individuals in the population from 1 to N (where N stands for the number of observations in the population), write the numbers on slips of paper, put the slips in a hat, shake the hat, and choose n slips of paper from the hat (where n stands for the number of observations in the sample)
sampling frame	complete list of individuals in a population	the directory of students attending a particular school is the sampling frame of the population of students in that school
unit nonresponse	phenomenon that occurs when someone who has been selected to be part of a survey sample refuses to participate	when you refuse to participate in a survey via phone or in person, your lack of participation is referred to as a unit nonresponse
item nonresponse	phenomenon that occurs when a survey respondent refuses to answer a certain question	survey respondents might feel uncomfortable answering questions about income and leave those questions blank
misreporting	phenomenon that occurs when respondents provide inaccurate or false information	respondents might claim to have voted in the last election, even if they did not, to conform with social norms
frequency table of a variable	table that shows the values the variable takes and the number of times each value appears in the variable	if $X=\{1, 0, 0, 1, 0\}$, the frequency table of X is: values 0 1 frequencies 3 2 the table shows that X contains three observations that take the value of 0 and two observations that take the value of 1

continues on next page...

3.7.1 CONCEPTS AND NOTATION (CONTINUED)

concept/notation	description	example(s)
table of proportions of a variable	table that shows the proportion of observations that take each value in a variable; by definition, the proportions in the table should add up to 1 (or 100%)	if $X=\{1, 0, 0, 1, 0\}$, then the table of proportions of X is:

values	0	1
proportions	0.6	0.4

the table shows that 60% of the observations in X take the value of 0 and 40% take the value of 1

two-way frequency table of two variables	also known as a cross-tabulation, shows the number of observations that take each combination of values of two specified variables	if X and Y are as defined in the dataframe below:

i	X	Y
1	1	1
2	0	1
3	0	1
4	1	0
5	0	0

then the two-way frequency table of X and Y is:

		values of Y	
		0	1
values of X	0	1	2
	1	1	1

the two-way frequency table shows that in the dataframe:
- there is one observation for which both X and Y equal 0 (the fifth observation)
- there are two observations for which X equals 0 and Y equals 1 (the second and third observations)
- there is one observation for which X equals 1 and Y equals 0 (the fourth observation)
- there is one observation for which both X and Y equal 1 (the first observation)

continues on next page. . .

3.7.1 CONCEPTS AND NOTATION (CONTINUED)

concept/notation	description	example(s)
two-way table of proportions of two variables	shows the proportion of observations that take each combination of values of two specified variables; by definition, the proportions in the table should add up to 1 (or 100%)	if X and Y are as defined in the dataframe below:

i	X	Y
1	1	1
2	0	1
3	0	1
4	1	0
5	0	0

then the two-way table of proportions of X and Y is:

		values of Y	
		0	1
values	0	0.2	0.4
of X	1	0.2	0.2

the two-way table of proportions shows that in the dataframe:
- both X and Y equal 0 in 20% of the observations
- X equals 0 and Y equals 1 in 40% of the observations
- X equals 1 and Y equals 0 in 20% of the observations
- both X and Y equal 1 in 20% of the observations

concept/notation	description	example(s)
histogram of a variable	visual representation of a variable's distribution through bins of different heights; the position of the bins along the x-axis indicates the interval of values; the height of the bins indicates the frequency (or count) of the interval of values within the variable	if $X=\{11, 11, 12, 13, 22, 26, 33, 43, 43, 48\}$, the histogram of X is:

the histogram shows that the variable X contains:

- four observations in the interval from 10 to 20
- two observations in the interval from 20 to 30
- one observation in the interval from 30 to 40
- three observations in the interval from 40 to 50

continues on next page. . .

3.7.1 CONCEPTS AND NOTATION (CONTINUED)

concept/notation	description	example(s)
density histogram of a variable	histogram that uses densities instead of frequencies as the height of the bins, where densities are defined as the proportion of the observations in the bin divided by the width of the bin; because the width of the bins is constant, the relative height of the bins in a density histogram implies the relative proportion of the observations in the bins; the sum of the areas of all the bins in a density histogram always equals 1	if $X=\{11, 11, 12, 13, 22, 26, 33, 43, 43, 48\}$, the density histogram of X is: the density histogram shows that in the variable X, there are: - twice as many values in the interval from 10 to 20 as in the interval from 20 to 30 - twice as many values in the interval from 20 to 30 as in the interval from 30 to 40 - three times as many values in the interval from 40 to 50 as in the interval from 30 to 40
descriptive statistics of a variable	numerically summarize the main characteristics of a variable's distribution: (i) measures of centrality such as mean and median, and (ii) measures of spread such as standard deviation and variance	see mean (in chapter 2), median, standard deviation, and variance
median of a variable; $median(X)$	characterizes the central tendency of the variable; value in the middle of the distribution that divides the data into two equal-size groups; it equals the middle value of the distribution when the variable contains an odd number of observations; it equals the average of the two middle values when the variable contains an even number of observations	if $X=\{10, 4, 6, 8, 22\}$, the median of X is 8 because the middle value of the distribution of X is 8: $\{4, 6, \underline{8}, 10, 22\}$ (recall that the values in the distribution are always sorted in ascending order) if $X=\{10, 4, 6, 8, 22, 5\}$, the median of X is 7 because the average of the two middle values of the distribution (6 and 8) is 7: $\{4, 5, \underline{6}, \underline{8}, 10, 22\}$
standard deviation of a variable; $sd(X)$	characterizes the spread of the variable's distribution; it measures the average distance of the observations to the mean; the larger the standard deviation, the flatter the distribution $$sd(X) = \sqrt{\frac{\sum_{i=1}^{n}(X_i-\overline{X})^2}{n}}$$ it is the square root of the variable's variance $$sd(X) = \sqrt{var(X)}$$	the standard deviation of the dashed distribution is smaller than that of the solid one: if $var(X) = 4$, then $sd(X) = \sqrt{4} = 2$

continues on next page...

3.7.1 CONCEPTS AND NOTATION (CONTINUED)

concept/notation	description	example(s)
variance of a variable; $var(X)$	characterizes the spread of the variable's distribution; it is the square of the variable's standard deviation $$var(X) = sd(X)^2$$	if $sd(X) = 2$, then $var(X) = 2^2 = 4$
scatter plot of X and Y	graphical representation of the relationship between two variables, X and Y; the X variable is plotted along the horizontal axis, and the Y variable is plotted along the vertical axis	if X and Y are as defined in the dataframe below: 	i	X	Y	 |---|---|---| | 1	4	2	 | 2	8	5	 | 3	10	3	 then the scatter plot of X and Y is:
z-score of an observation of X; Z_i^X	number of standard deviations the observation is above or below the mean of the variable; to transform the observations of a variable into z-scores, we subtract the mean, and then divide the result by the standard deviation: $$Z_i^X = \frac{X_i - \overline{X}}{sd(X)}$$	if $X = \{2, 4, 6\}$, then $\overline{X} = 4$, $sd(X) = 1.63$, and the z-score of each observation of X is: - for $i=1$: $Z_1^X = \frac{X_1 - \overline{X}}{sd(X)} = \frac{2-4}{1.63} = -1.23$ - for $i=2$: $Z_2^X = \frac{X_2 - \overline{X}}{sd(X)} = \frac{4-4}{1.63} = 0$ - for $i=3$: $Z_3^X = \frac{X_3 - \overline{X}}{sd(X)} = \frac{6-4}{1.63} = 1.23$

continues on next page...

3.7.1 CONCEPTS AND NOTATION (CONTINUED)

concept/notation	description	example(s)
correlation or correlation coefficient between two variables; $cor(X, Y)$	statistic that summarizes the direction and strength of the linear association between two variables it ranges from –1 to 1	$cor(X, Y) = -1$ perfect negative correlation
	the sign reflects the direction of the linear association: it is positive whenever the slope of the line of best fit is positive, and negative whenever the slope of the line of best fit is negative	$cor(X, Y) = -0.8$
	its absolute value reflects the strength of the linear association, ranging from 0 (no linear association) to 1 (perfect linear association); the absolute value of the correlation coefficient increases as the observations move closer to the line of best fit and the linear association becomes stronger	$cor(X,Y) = -0.5$
	a strong correlation between X and Y does not imply that either X causes Y or that Y causes X; correlation does not necessarily imply causation; more on this in chapter 5	$cor(X, Y) = 0$ no linear relationship
	to compute the correlation between two variables, X and Y, we first convert the observations of both variables to z-scores; then, the correlation coefficient is calculated as the average of the products of the z-scores of X and Y: $$cor(X, Y) = \frac{\sum_{i=1}^{n} Z_i^X \times Z_i^Y}{n}$$	$cor(X, Y) = 0.5$
		$cor(X, Y) = 0.8$
		$cor(X, Y) = 1$ perfect positive correlation

3.7.2 R SYMBOLS AND OPERATORS

code	description	example(s)
^	operator that raises a number to a power; the number that follows this symbol is the power, that is, the number of times we want to multiply the preceding number by itself	3^2 # raises 3 to the 2nd power $(3^2=9)$

3.7.3 R FUNCTIONS

function	description	required argument(s)	example(s)
table()	creates the frequency table of one variable or the two-way frequency table of two variables	code identifying the variable(s) (separated by a comma, if two) optional argument exclude: if set to equal NULL, the table includes NAs	table(*data*$*variable*) # frequency table table(*data*$*variable1*, *data*$*variable2*) # two-way frequency table table(*data*$*variable*, exclude=NULL) # includes NAs
prop.table()	converts a frequency table into a table of proportions and a two-way frequency table into a two-way table of proportions	either (a) the name of the object containing the output of the function table() or (b) the function table() directly; in both cases the code identifying the variable(s) should be specified inside the parentheses of table() optional argument margin for two-way table of proportions: if set to equal 1, the first specified variable defines the groups of reference; if set to equal 2, the second specified variable defines the groups of reference; if unspecified, the whole sample is the reference group	freqtable <- table(*data*$*variable*) prop.table(freqtable) # or prop.table(table(*data*$*variable*)) # table of proportions prop.table(table(*data*$*variable1*, *data*$*variable2*)) # two-way table of proportions; the whole sample is the reference group prop.table(table(*data*$*variable1*, *data*$*variable2*, margin=1)) # two-way table of proportions; variable1 defines the reference groups
na.omit()	deletes all observations with missing data from a dataframe	name of object where the dataframe is stored	na.omit(*data*)
hist()	creates the histogram of a variable; by default, it creates the histogram where the heights of the bins indicate frequencies	code identifying the variable optional argument freq: if set to equal FALSE, the function creates the density histogram	hist(*data*$*variable*) # frequency histogram hist(*data*$*variable*, freq=FALSE) # density histogram
mean()	calculates the mean of a variable; by default, it does not exclude missing values	code identifying the variable optional argument na.rm: if set to equal TRUE, R ignores the NAs when computing the average of the variable	mean(*data*$*variable*) # without removing NAs mean(*data*$*variable*, na.rm=TRUE) # removing NAs

continues on next page...

3.7.3 R FUNCTIONS (CONTINUED)

function	description	required argument(s)	example(s)
median()	calculates the median of a variable	code identifying the variable	median(*data$variable*)
sd()	calculates the standard deviation of a variable	code identifying the variable	sd(*data$variable*)
var()	calculates the variance of a variable	code identifying the variable	var(*data$variable*)
plot()	creates the scatter plot of two variables	two, separated by a comma and in this order: (1) variable on the x-axis (2) variable on the y-axis alternatively, we can specify the arguments x and y to indicate which variables we want to plot on the x and y axes, respectively	## all of these pieces of code produce the same scatter plot: plot(*data$x_var, data$y_var*) plot(x=*data$x_var*, y=*data$y_var*) plot(y=*data$y_var*, x=*data$x_var*)
abline()	adds a straight line to the most recently created graph; by default, it draws a solid line	to add a vertical line, we set the argument v to equal the value on the x-axis where we want the line; to add a horizontal line, we set the argument h to equal the value on the y-axis where we want the line optional argument lty: if set to equal "dashed", R draws a dashed line instead of a solid one	abline(v=2) # draws solid vertical line at 2 abline(h=3) # draws solid horizontal line at 3 abline(v=3, lty="dashed") # draws dashed vertical line at 3
cor()	calculates the correlation coefficient between two variables	code identifying the two variables, separated by a comma and in no particular order	cor(*data$variable1, data$variable2*)

4. PREDICTING OUTCOMES USING LINEAR REGRESSION

R symbols, operators, and functions introduced in this chapter: lm() and log().

We have already seen how we can analyze data to estimate causal effects and to infer population characteristics. Another goal of data analysis in the social sciences is to make predictions. In this chapter, we learn how to summarize with a line the relationship between the outcome variable of interest and another variable called a predictor (a process known as fitting a linear regression model). We then use this summary line to estimate the most likely value of the outcome, given a specific value of the predictor. As an illustration, we analyze data from 170 countries to predict GDP growth based on changes in night-time light emissions.

4.1 GDP AND NIGHT-TIME LIGHT EMISSIONS

Based on J. Vernon Henderson, Adam Storeygard, and David N. Weil, "Measuring Economic Growth from Outer Space," *American Economic Review* 102, no. 2 (2012): 994–1028.

To assess a country's economic activity, we often want to measure its gross domestic product (GDP). The GDP of a country is the monetary value of goods produced and services provided in that country during a specific period of time. The data required to construct GDP measures, however, may be either unreliable or hard to collect consistently, especially in developing countries. Consequently, we need good ways of predicting GDP using other observed variables.

In recent years, a group of social scientists noticed that changes in night-time light emissions, as measured from satellites circling the earth, were highly correlated with economic activity. As economic activity increases, so does use of electricity at night. As a result, change in a country's night-time light emissions as measured from space might be a good predictor of that country's GDP growth. In this chapter, we explore this connection and predict GDP growth using night-time light emission changes over time. We begin, though, with a simpler example. To practice fitting linear models and interpreting the results, we start by predicting a country's GDP at one point in time using a prior value of GDP.

4.2 PREDICTORS, OBSERVED VS. PREDICTED OUTCOMES, AND PREDICTION ERRORS

In the social sciences, we are often unable to observe the value of a particular variable of interest, Y, either because it hasn't occurred yet or because it is difficult to measure. In these situations, we typically observe the values of other variables that, if correlated with Y, can be used to predict Y. On the basis of these other variables, we can make an educated guess about what the value of Y is currently or will likely be at a different point in time, on average.

When analyzing data for the purpose of making predictions, we refer to the variable or variables that we use to make predictions as the **predictor(s)** and to the variable of interest that we want to predict as the **outcome variable**.

When making predictions, we distinguish between two types of variables:
- the **predictor(s)** (X): variable(s) that we use as the basis for our predictions
- the **outcome variable** (Y): variable that we are trying to predict based on the values of the predictor(s).

TIP: Predictors are also known as independent variables, and outcome variables as dependent variables.

For example, if we are interested in predicting GDP using prior GDP, then GDP is the outcome variable, and prior GDP is the predictor. If we are interested in predicting GDP growth using the change in night-time light emissions, then GDP growth is the outcome variable, and the change in night-time light emissions is the predictor.

In mathematical notation, we represent the predictor as X and the outcome variable as Y. Although we use the same mathematical notation as when estimating causal effects, the relationship between the X and Y variables here is not necessarily causal.

As we will see in detail later, to make good predictions, we choose predictors that are highly correlated with the outcome variable of interest. In other words, we choose predictors that have a strong linear association with the outcome variable. (Note that, when we speak of a "high degree of correlation," we mean that the correlation coefficient is high in absolute terms, regardless of its sign.) As discussed in chapter 3, correlation does not necessarily imply causation. Just because two variables are highly correlated with each other does not necessarily mean that changes in one variable cause changes in the other. When analyzing data for predictive purposes, then, we do not assume that there is a causal relationship between X and Y; we simply rely on a high degree of correlation between them and use one variable to estimate the value of the other.

RECALL: The correlation coefficient ranges from –1 to 1 and summarizes the direction and strength of the linear association between two variables. The closer the correlation coefficient is in absolute value to 1, the stronger the linear association between the two variables (that is, the closer the observations are to the line of best fit).

Making predictions is a two-step process. Once we have identified our X and Y variables, we need to understand how these two variables relate to each other. Our first step, then, is to analyze a dataset that contains both variables and summarize the relationship between X and Y with a mathematical model. We call this process "model fitting" because it consists of fitting to the data a model that characterizes how X is related to Y, on average.

The **predicted outcomes**, $\widehat{Y}$, are the values of Y we predict based on (i) the fitted model that summarizes the relationship between X and Y in a dataset where we observe both X and Y for each observation and (ii) the observed values of X.

Later, once we are in a situation where we cannot observe Y but we observe X, we use the fitted model to predict specific average values of the outcome variable for each observed value of the predictor. We refer to our predictions of Y as the **predicted outcomes**, and we denote them as $\widehat{Y}$ (pronounced Y-hat).

---

1. FIT A MODEL

- we observe both X and Y

- we summarize the relationship between the average Y and X with a model

2. MAKE PREDICTIONS

- we observe X but not Y

- we compute $\widehat{Y}$ by plugging the observed value of X into the fitted model

---

The prediction **error**, $\widehat{\epsilon}$, also known as a residual, measures how far our prediction is from the observed value; it is the difference between the observed outcome and the predicted outcome.

When making predictions, we aim to be as accurate as possible. In other words, we aim to minimize the prediction **errors** (also known as residuals). These are defined as the difference between the observed outcomes and the predicted outcomes and are denoted by $\widehat{\epsilon}$ (the Greek letter epsilon with a "hat" on top).

Note that to differentiate between observed and predicted variables, we often refer to Y as the *observed* outcome—and not just the outcome—to distinguish it more clearly from the *predicted* outcome $\widehat{Y}$.

4.3 SUMMARIZING THE RELATIONSHIP BETWEEN TWO VARIABLES WITH A LINE

When fitting a model for predictive purposes, we could use many different mathematical functions. In this book, we always summarize the relationship between X and Y with a line and, in particular, the line of best fit.

Let's get a sense of how this works using a hypothetical example. Suppose that the scatter plot of the X and Y variables (in the dataset where we can observe both) is as shown in the margin. As in all scatter plots, every dot represents a particular observation of X and Y. In this case, each dot is located based on the value of the predictor and the value of the observed outcome for a given observation. In the figure in the margin, we highlight, as an example, the dot representing the first observation of this imaginary dataset: (X_1, Y_1).

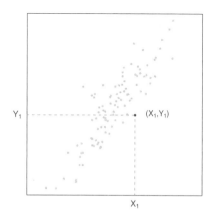

By looking at the scatter plot of X and Y, we get a general sense of how Y relates to X. In this case, given the observed upward slope of the data cloud, we conclude that high values of Y are likely to be associated with high values of X, and low values of Y are likely to be associated with low values of X. While this is helpful information for predicting Y using X, it would be even better if we could summarize the relationship with a mathematical formula so that for each value of X, we could compute a predicted value of Y.

For example, we can summarize the relationship between X and Y with a line. In the top figure in the margin, in addition to the scatter plot of X and Y, we have plotted such a line, which we call the fitted line. Now, for every value of X, we can find a predicted Y ($\widehat{Y}$), by finding the value of X we are interested in on the x-axis, going up to the fitted line, and finding the height of the corresponding point on the line. For example, if we were interested in the value of X in the first observation in the dataset (X_1), based on the fitted line drawn on the plot, we would predict a Y equal to $\widehat{Y_1}$.

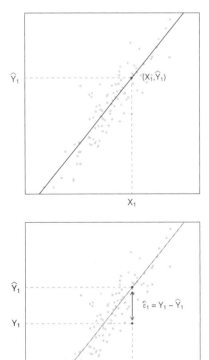

By looking at the scatter plot with the line, we get a sense of the prediction errors this fitted model would produce. If we use the line to compute the predicted outcomes for every observation, then we can measure the prediction errors ($\widehat{\epsilon}$) as the difference between the observed outcomes (Y) and the predicted outcomes ($\widehat{Y}$). ($\widehat{\epsilon_i} = Y_i - \widehat{Y_i}$.) Note that for each observation, this difference is equivalent to the vertical distance between the dot and the fitted line. See, for example, the bottom figure in the margin, where we show the prediction error of the first observation. In general, the closer the dots are to the fitted line, the smaller the prediction errors, and the farther the dots are from the line, the larger the prediction errors. To make the best possible predictions, then, we always summarize the relationship between X and Y with the line of best fit, which is the line closest to the data. (In subsection 4.3.4, we will explain the precise method used to choose this line.)

4.3.1 THE LINEAR REGRESSION MODEL

Now let's introduce some mathematical notation. The linear model, also known as the linear regression model, is defined as:

$$Y_i = \alpha + \beta X_i + \epsilon_i$$

where:

- Y_i is the outcome for observation i
- α (the Greek letter alpha) is the intercept coefficient
- β (the Greek letter beta) is the slope coefficient
- X_i is the value of the predictor for observation i
- ϵ_i (pronounced epsilon sub i) is the error for observation i.

This is the theoretical model that we assume reflects the true relationship between X and Y. If we knew the values of the

TIP: In statistics, we use Greek letters to represent quantities we do not know, such as α, β, and ϵ_i. The two coefficients, α and β, are not subscripted by i because they do not vary by observation. They are constants and not variables.

coefficients (α and β), as well as the values of the errors for each observation (ϵ_i), we could use this formula to compute the outcomes for each observation (Y_i) based on the observed values of the predictors (X_i). (By plugging the values of α, β, X_i, and ϵ_i into the formula above, we would compute Y_i.)

Unfortunately, we do not know the values of α, β, and ϵ_i. We have to estimate them based on data. We start by estimating the intercept (α) and the slope (β), the two coefficients that define the line. This is equivalent to fitting a line to the data, that is, finding the line that best summarizes the relationship between X and Y.

The formula of the line we fit to the data is:

$$\widehat{Y}_i = \widehat{\alpha} + \widehat{\beta} X_i$$

where:

- $\widehat{Y}_i$ (pronounced Y-hat sub i) is the predicted outcome for observation i
- $\widehat{\alpha}$ (pronounced alpha-hat) is the estimated intercept coefficient
- $\widehat{\beta}$ (pronounced beta-hat) is the estimated slope coefficient
- X_i is the value of the predictor for observation i.

Note that in this formula, Y, α, and β have a "hat" on top. This indicates that they are estimates or approximations. In addition, this formula no longer includes the errors (ϵ_i), which means that the resulting outcomes do not necessarily equal the true values of Y (Y_i); they equal the predicted values of Y ($\widehat{Y}_i$). In other words, for every value of X, this formula provides the corresponding value of Y *on the fitted line* (instead of on the observed data point). Note that the value of $\widehat{Y}$ produced by a fitted model is an *average* predicted value; it is the average predicted value of Y associated with a particular value of X. Indeed, predicted outcomes ($\widehat{Y}$) are equivalent to average outcomes ($\overline{Y}$).

The difference between the observed values of Y and the predicted values of Y are the estimated errors or residuals:

$$\widehat{\epsilon}_i = Y_i - \widehat{Y}_i$$

where:

- $\widehat{\epsilon}_i$ is the estimated error, or residual, for observation i
- Y_i is the observed outcome for observation i
- $\widehat{Y}_i$ is the predicted outcome for observation i.

These are the prediction errors that we try to minimize by using the line that best fits the data.

TIP: You might have seen the equation of a line written as $Y = mX + b$ where m is the slope and b the intercept. If so, it may be helpful for you to think that $\widehat{\alpha}$ is the b and $\widehat{\beta}$ is the m of the familiar model.

To recap, to make predictions using the linear regression model, we start by analyzing a dataset that contains both X and Y for each observation. We summarize the relationship between them with the line of best fit, which is the line with the smallest prediction errors possible. Fitting this line involves estimating the two coefficients that define any line: the intercept ($\widehat{\alpha}$) and the slope ($\widehat{\beta}$). Once we have fitted the line, we can use it to obtain the most likely average value of Y based on the observed value of X.

1. FIT A LINEAR REGRESSION MODEL	2. MAKE PREDICTIONS
- we observe both X and Y - we find the line that best summarizes the relationship between them; we estimate the intercept ($\widehat{\alpha}$) and slope ($\widehat{\beta}$) of the line with the smallest prediction errors possible	- we observe X but not Y - we compute $\widehat{Y}$ by plugging the observed value of X into the fitted linear regression model: $$\widehat{Y} = \widehat{\alpha} + \widehat{\beta}X$$

Let's take a moment now to understand what the two coefficients of a line measure and how to interpret them.

4.3.2 THE INTERCEPT COEFFICIENT

Generally speaking, the **intercept** of a line specifies the vertical location of the line. See, for example, the lines in the margin, which have different intercepts but the same slope. Increasing and decreasing the intercept moves the line up and down.

Specifically, the intercept ($\widehat{\alpha}$) is the value of $\widehat{Y}$ when $X=0$.

Indeed, as we can see below, if in the fitted linear model, we plug in $X=0$, then $\widehat{Y}$ equals $\widehat{\alpha}$. So, $\widehat{\alpha}$ is the $\widehat{Y}$ when $X=0$.

$$\widehat{Y} = \widehat{\alpha} + \widehat{\beta} \times 0 = \widehat{\alpha} \quad \text{(if } X=0\text{)}$$

This definition of the intercept is helpful. We can use it to figure out the value of $\widehat{\alpha}$ of any line on a graph. We just need to find $X=0$ on the x-axis, go up to the fitted line, and then find the height of the corresponding point. The value of $\widehat{Y}$ at the point on the fitted line where $X=0$ is the value of the intercept of the line. (See figure in the margin.) Note that the y-axis is not always drawn at $X=0$, and therefore, the intercept is *not* necessarily the value of $\widehat{Y}$ at the point where the line crosses the y-axis.

The **intercept** ($\widehat{\alpha}$) is the $\widehat{Y}$ when $X=0$.

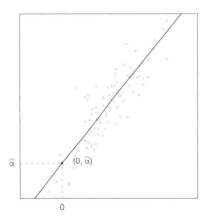

We can also use the definition above to help us substantively interpret the value of $\widehat{\alpha}$. In predictive models, we interpret the intercept as the predicted outcome, $\widehat{Y}$, when the predictor X equals zero. (We will see concrete examples soon.)

4.3.3 THE SLOPE COEFFICIENT

Generally speaking, the **slope** of a line specifies the angle, or steepness of the line. See, for example, the lines in the margin, which have different slopes but the same intercept. The top line has a positive slope, the middle line has a slope of zero, and the bottom line has a negative slope.

The **slope** $(\widehat{\beta})$ is $\triangle\widehat{Y}$ divided by $\triangle X$ between two points on the line.

Specifically, the slope $(\widehat{\beta})$ is the change in $\widehat{Y}$ divided by the change in X between two points on the line, commonly known as "rise over run":

$$\widehat{\beta} = \frac{\text{rise}}{\text{run}} = \frac{\triangle\widehat{Y}}{\triangle X} = \frac{\widehat{Y}_{\text{final}} - \widehat{Y}_{\text{initial}}}{X_{\text{final}} - X_{\text{initial}}}$$

TIP: The change in a variable between two points (initial and final) is equivalent to the difference between the value of the variable at the final point and the value of the variable at the initial point. Examples:

$$\triangle\widehat{Y} = \widehat{Y}_{\text{final}} - \widehat{Y}_{\text{initial}}$$
$$\triangle X = X_{\text{final}} - X_{\text{initial}}$$

where $\triangle$ (the Greek letter Delta) represents change, and thus, $\triangle\widehat{Y}$ is the change in $\widehat{Y}$ and $\triangle X$ is the change in X.

For example, see figure 4.1, which shows the change in $\widehat{Y}$ ($\triangle\widehat{Y}$) and the change in X ($\triangle X$) associated with two points on the line.

FIGURE 4.1. The slope $(\widehat{\beta})$ can be computed as "rise over run," where rise is the change in $\widehat{Y}$ and run is the change in X between two points on the line.

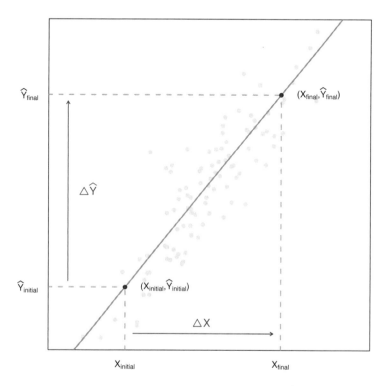

Substantively speaking, we can interpret the value of the slope as the change in $\widehat{Y}$ associated with a one-unit increase in X. In mathematical notation, when $\triangle X=1$, $\widehat{\beta}=\triangle\widehat{Y}$:

$$\widehat{\beta} = \frac{\triangle\widehat{Y}}{1} = \triangle\widehat{Y} \quad \text{(if } \triangle X=1)$$

The **slope** ($\widehat{\beta}$) represents the $\triangle\widehat{Y}$ associated with a one-unit increase in X.

In predictive models, then, we interpret the slope as the predicted change in the outcome, $\triangle\widehat{Y}$, associated with a one-unit increase in the predictor X. Since $\widehat{\beta}$ measures a *change* in $\widehat{Y}$, we interpret it as an increase when positive, a decrease when negative, and as no change when zero.

THE FITTED LINE IS:

$$\widehat{Y} = \widehat{\alpha} + \widehat{\beta}X$$

where:

- $\widehat{\alpha}$ is the estimated intercept coefficient, which can be interpreted as the $\widehat{Y}$ when $X=0$
- $\widehat{\beta}$ is the estimated slope coefficient, which can be interpreted as the $\triangle\widehat{Y}$ associated with $\triangle X=1$.

Before moving on to learning how to find the line of best fit, let's practice figuring out the specific formula of a line by looking at its depiction in a graph. (See figure in the margin.)

We start by finding the values of two points on the line:

- the point that corresponds to $X=0$
- the point that corresponds to a higher value of X than 0.

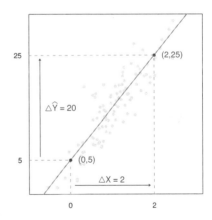

In the figure in the margin, these two points are (0,5) and (2,25). Given the values of these two points, we can conclude that:

- the intercept coefficient ($\widehat{\alpha}$) equals 5 because that is the value of $\widehat{Y}$ when $X=0$ (see the point (0,5) on the line)
- the slope coefficient ($\widehat{\beta}$) equals 10 because that is the value of $\triangle\widehat{Y}/\triangle X$ between the two points on the line:

$$\widehat{\beta} = \frac{\triangle\widehat{Y}}{\triangle X} = \frac{25-5}{2-0} = \frac{20}{2} = 10$$

This particular fitted line is then: $\widehat{Y}=5+10X$.

We can check that the two points shown in the figure on the previous page—(0,5) and (2,25)—belong to the line $\widehat{Y} = 5 + 10X$. For each point, we plug the value of X into the formula of the line and find the corresponding $\widehat{Y}$:

$$\widehat{Y} = 5 + 10 \times 0 = 5 \qquad \text{(if } X{=}0\text{)}$$
$$\widehat{Y} = 5 + 10 \times 2 = 25 \qquad \text{(if } X{=}2\text{)}$$

The math above confirms that these two points are indeed on the line $\widehat{Y} = 5 + 10X$.

4.3.4 THE LEAST SQUARES METHOD

We could draw an infinite number of lines on a scatter plot, but some lines do a better job than others at summarizing the relationship between X and Y. For example, of the three lines shown in figure 4.2, we can agree that the last one does the best job of depicting how Y relates to X. (Intuitively, we know that the line of best fit should be as close to the dots as possible.)

FIGURE 4.2. Three lines that we could draw on the scatter plot of X and Y out of the infinite number of possible lines.

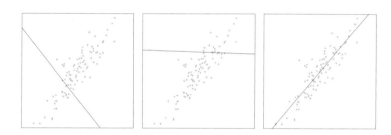

FIGURE 4.3. The fit of the line improves from left to right. The last line best summarizes the relationship between X and Y; it is closest to the observations, which means that it produces the smallest prediction errors (shown as red dashed lines).

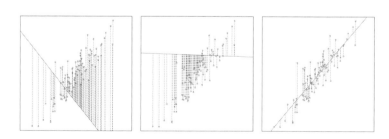

How do we choose the line that best summarizes the relationship between X and Y? Given that we want our predictions to be as accurate as possible, generally speaking, we choose the line that reduces the prediction errors ($\widehat{\epsilon}$), that is, the vertical distance between each dot and the fitted line. As we can observe in figure 4.3, the line on the right produces the smallest prediction errors (shown as red dashed lines). Therefore, we would choose this line over the other two to summarize the relationship between X and Y.

Formally, to choose the line of best fit, we use the "least squares" method, which identifies the line that minimizes the "sum of the squared residuals," known as SSR. (Recall that residuals is a different name for prediction errors; this method minimizes the sum of the squared prediction errors.)

$$\text{SSR} = \sum_{i=1}^{n} \widehat{\epsilon}_i^2$$

Why do we want to minimize the sum of the *squared* residuals rather than the sum of the residuals? Because in the minimization process we want to avoid having positive prediction errors cancel out negative prediction errors. By squaring the residuals, we convert them all to positive numbers. (This procedure for choosing the line of best fit is called the "least squares" method because it *minimizes* the sum of the *squared* residuals.)

In practice, we do not undertake this minimization process ourselves. Instead, we rely on R to make the necessary computations. In the next section, we will go over a simple example and learn how to ask R to estimate the two coefficients of the line that minimizes the sum of the squared residuals. In other words, we will learn how to use R and the least squares method to find the line of best fit.

4.4 PREDICTING GDP USING PRIOR GDP

The code for this chapter's analysis can be found in the "Prediction.R" file. The dataset we analyze is provided in the file "countries.csv", and table 4.1 shows the names and descriptions of the variables included.

variable	description
country	name of the country
gdp	country's GDP from 2005 to 2006 (in trillions of local currency units)
prior_gdp	country's GDP from 1992 to 1993 (in trillions of local currency units)
light	country's average level of night-time light emissions from 2005 to 2006 (in units on a scale from 0 to 63, where 0 is complete darkness and 63 is extremely bright light)
prior_light	country's average level of night-time light emissions from 1992 to 1993 (in units on a scale from 0 to 63, where 0 is complete darkness and 63 is extremely bright light)

TABLE 4.1. Description of the variables in the countries dataset, where the unit of observation is countries.

RECALL: If the DSS folder is saved directly on your Desktop, to set the working directory, you must run setwd("~/Desktop/DSS") if you have a Mac and setwd("C:/*user*/Desktop/DSS") if you have a Windows computer (where *user* is your own username). If the DSS folder is saved elsewhere, please see subsection 1.7.1 for instructions on how to set the working directory.

As always, we begin by reading and storing the data (assuming we have already set the working directory):

```
co <- read.csv("countries.csv") # reads and stores data
```

To get a sense of the dataset, we look at the first few observations:

```
head(co)  # shows first observations
##    country     gdp prior_gdp    light prior_light
## 1      USA  11.107     7.373    4.227       4.482
## 2    Japan 543.017   464.168   11.926      11.808
## 3  Germany   2.152     1.793   10.573       9.699
## 4    China  16.558     4.901    1.451       0.735
## 5       UK   1.098     0.754   11.856      13.392
## 6   France   1.582     1.208    8.513       6.909
```

Based on table 4.1 and the output above, we learn that each observation in the dataset represents a country, and that the dataset contains five variables:

- *country* is a character variable that identifies the country.
- *gdp* and *prior_gdp* are each country's GDP at two different points in time, 13 years apart, from 2005 to 2006 and from 1992 to 1993. They are measured in trillions of local currency units (that is, in trillions of dollars in the case of the United States, trillions of yen in the case of Japan, trillions of euros in the case of Germany, and so on).
- *light* and *prior_light* are each country's average night-time light emissions at two different points in time, 13 years apart, from 2005 to 2006 and from 1992 to 1993. They are measured on a scale from 0 to 63, where 0 represents no light and 63 is extremely bright light.

We interpret the first observation as representing the United States, where GDP was $11 trillion from 2005 to 2006 and $7 trillion from 1992 to 1993, and average night-time light emissions were 4.2 units from 2005 to 2006 and 4.5 units from 1992 to 1993 (as measured on a scale from 0 to 63).

To find the total number of observations in the dataset, we run:

```
dim(co) # provides dimensions of dataframe: rows, columns
## [1] 170    5
```

The dataset contains information about 170 countries.

4.4.1 RELATIONSHIP BETWEEN GDP AND PRIOR GDP

To get a sense of the relationship between a country's GDP at two points in time, we analyze how the two measures of GDP that we have in the dataset, *gdp* and *prior_gdp*, relate to each other. Since these two variables were measured 13 years apart, our conclusions refer to the relationship between a country's GDP at one point in time and its GDP about 13 years prior.

We start the analysis by creating a scatter plot using the function plot() to visualize the relationship between the two variables of interest. Note that we always plot the predictor on the x-axis and the outcome variable on the y-axis. In this case, to visualize the relationship between *gdp* and *prior_gdp*, we run:

RECALL: plot() creates the scatter plot of two variables. Examples: plot(*data$x_var, data$y_var*), plot(x=*data$x_var*, y=*data$y_var*), or plot(y=*data$y_var*, x=*data$x_var*). Also, if R gives you the error message "Error in plot.new(): figure margins too large", try making the lower-right window larger and then re-run the code that creates the plot.

```
plot(x=co$prior_gdp, y=co$gdp) # creates scatter plot
```

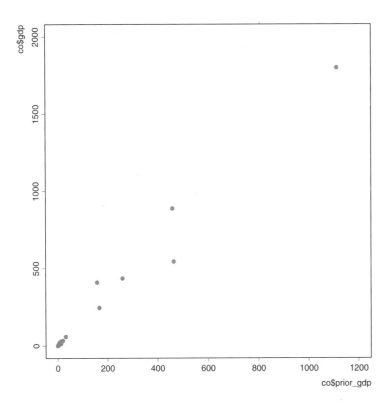

Looking at the scatter plot, we observe a positive association between the two variables. Higher values of prior GDP tend to be associated with higher values of GDP. In addition, we notice that the relationship between the two variables appears to be strongly linear. To further investigate the direction and strength of the linear association, we can compute the correlation coefficient using the function cor():

RECALL: The correlation coefficient ranges from –1 to 1 and summarizes the direction and strength of the linear association between two variables. In R, the function cor() calculates the correlation coefficient between two variables. Example: cor(*data$variable1, data$variable2*).

TIP: When writing the model for the first time, it is helpful to (i) emphasize that the variables may take different values for each observation by adding the subscript i, and (ii) specify what each observation, i, represents. In this case, the unit of observation, i, is countries.

lm() fits a linear model. It requires a formula of the type $Y \sim X$, where Y identifies the Y variable and X identifies the X variable. To specify the object where the dataframe is stored, we can either use the $ character in the code identifying each variable or set the optional argument data. Examples: lm(data$y_var $\sim$ data$x_var) or lm(y_var $\sim$ x_var, data=data).

```
cor(co$gdp, co$prior_gdp) # computes correlation
## [1] 0.9903451
```

The correlation coefficient between the two variables turns out to be 0.99, which confirms what we noticed in the scatter plot above.

Now that we have a general sense of how the two variables relate to each other, we can fit a linear model to summarize their relationship. This is the model we will use later to make predictions. Since our outcome of interest is *gdp* and our predictor is *prior_gdp*, the line we want to fit is:

$$\widehat{gdp_i} = \widehat{\alpha} + \widehat{\beta} \ prior\_gdp_i \quad (i = \text{countries})$$

where:

- $\widehat{gdp_i}$ is the average predicted GDP from 2005 to 2006 among countries in which the value of *prior_gdp* equals *prior_gdp_i*
- *prior_gdp_i* is the GDP of country i from 1992 to 1993.

Once we estimate $\widehat{\alpha}$ and $\widehat{\beta}$, we will be able to plug into the formula above any value of *prior_gdp* and get a $\widehat{gdp}$ in return.

To estimate the coefficients of the linear model using the least squares method in R, we use the function lm(), which stands for "<u>l</u>inear <u>m</u>odel." This function requires that we specify as the main argument a formula of the type $Y \sim X$, where Y identifies the outcome variable and X identifies the predictor. To fit a line to summarize the relationship between GDP and prior GDP, we run:

```
lm(co$gdp ~ co$prior_gdp) # fits linear model
##
## Call:
## lm(formula = co$gdp ~ co$prior_gdp)
##
## Coefficients:
## (Intercept)   co$prior_gdp
##      0.7161        1.6131
```

Note that since the variables in the model should always come from the same dataframe, there is an alternative way of specifying the lm() function. Instead of using the $ character for each variable, we can use the optional argument data and set it to equal the name of the object where the dataframe containing all the variables is stored. For example, lm(gdp $\sim$ prior_gdp, data=co) produces the same output as the code above.

As we can see in the output of the function lm() above, the estimated intercept ($\widehat{\alpha}$) is 0.72, and the estimated slope ($\widehat{\beta}$), the coefficient for the variable *prior_gdp*, is 1.61.

The fitted linear model is then:

$$\widehat{gdp} = 0.72 + 1.61 \ prior\_gdp$$

How should we interpret $\widehat{\alpha}$=0.72? The value of $\widehat{\alpha}$ equals the $\widehat{Y}$ when X=0. Here, since Y is GDP and X is prior GDP (both measured in trillions of local currency units), we interpret the estimated intercept coefficient as indicating that when prior GDP is 0 trillion local currency units, we predict that GDP is 0.72 trillion local currency units, on average. (Note that the interpretation of the intercept does not always make substantive sense, especially when the range of observed values of the predictor does not include zero. This is a good example. It does not make sense for a country to have a prior GDP of 0 trillion local currency units. When we make predictions beyond the observed range of data, we make the strong assumption that the relationship between X and Y continues to hold. This is called "extrapolation," and it may lead to nonsensical predictions.)

How should we interpret $\widehat{\beta}$=1.61? The value of $\widehat{\beta}$ equals the $\triangle\widehat{Y}$ associated with $\triangle X$=1. Here, since the Y is GDP and the X is prior GDP (both measured in trillions of local currency units), we interpret the estimated slope coefficient as indicating that an increase in prior GDP of 1 trillion local currency units is associated with a predicted increase in GDP of 1.61 trillion local currency units, on average.

To make it easier to work with the fitted model, we may want to store it as an object using the assignment operator <-. (Here, we chose the name *fit*, but we could have chosen another name.)

```
fit <- lm(gdp ~ prior_gdp, data=co) # stores fitted model
```

For example, now we can easily add the fitted line to the scatter plot by using the function abline(). As we saw in the previous chapter, this function adds a straight line to the most recently created graph. There, we saw how to draw horizontal and vertical lines. Here, we learn that this function will draw the fitted line when we specify as the main argument the object that contains the output of the fitted model. Go ahead and run:

```
abline( fit ) # adds line to scatter plot
```

Remember, that R will give you an error message if you run this piece of code without having first created a graph. If you run all the code provided in this section, in sequence, you should see the figure shown in the margin.

Now that we have fitted a line to summarize the relationship between our two variables of interest (also known as fitting a linear regression model), we can use the fitted model to make predictions.

TIP: In what units of measurement are the two estimated coefficients, $\widehat{\alpha}$ and $\widehat{\beta}$?
- If Y is non-binary, both $\widehat{\alpha}$ and $\widehat{\beta}$ are in the same unit of measurement as Y.
- If Y is binary, $\widehat{\alpha}$ is in percentages, and $\widehat{\beta}$ is in percentage points (after multiplying both outputs by 100).

Here, since *gdp* is non-binary and measured in trillions of local currency units, both $\widehat{\alpha}$ and $\widehat{\beta}$ are measured in trillions of local currency units.

abline() adds the fitted line to the most recently created graph when we specify as the main argument the object that contains the output of the lm() function. Example: fit <- lm(Y ~ X) and then abline(fit).

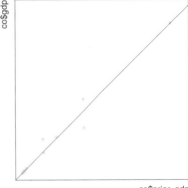

TIP: In what units of measurement are our predictions, $\widehat{Y}$ and $\triangle\widehat{Y}$?
- If Y is non-binary, both $\widehat{Y}$ and $\triangle\widehat{Y}$ are in the same unit of measurement as Y.
- If Y is binary, $\widehat{Y}$ is in percentages and $\triangle\widehat{Y}$ is in percentage points (after multiplying both outputs by 100).

Here, since *gdp* is non-binary and measured in trillions of local currency units, both $\widehat{Y}$ and $\triangle\widehat{Y}$ are measured in trillions of local currency units.

Generally speaking, there are two types of predictions we may be interested in making. First, we may want to predict the average value of the outcome variable given a value of the predictor. When this is the case, we use the formula of the fitted line directly.

> TO COMPUTE $\widehat{Y}$ BASED ON X: We plug the value of X into the fitted linear model and calculate $\widehat{Y}$.
> $$\widehat{Y} = \widehat{\alpha} + \widehat{\beta}X$$

For example, suppose that we want to know the current GDP of a country, and for some reason we cannot measure it. But we do know that 13 years ago, the country's GDP was 400 trillion local currency units. What would our best guess be for current GDP, given the relationship between GDP and prior GDP that we estimated above? To predict the value of a country's current GDP based on the value of that country's GDP 13 years prior, we plug the value of prior GDP into the fitted linear model:

$$\widehat{gdp} = 0.72 + 1.61 \ prior\_gdp$$
$$= 0.72 + 1.61 \times 400 = 644.72$$

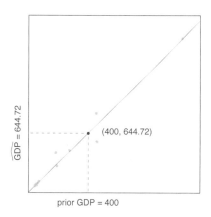

Based on the fitted line, we predict that the country has a current GDP of about 644.72 trillion local currency units. (See figure in the margin to visualize how we would arrive at the same conclusion using the fitted line drawn in the scatter plot.)

Second, we may want to predict the average change in the outcome variable associated with a change in the value of the predictor. When this is the case, we use the formula that computes the change in the predicted outcome, shown below.

TIP: We arrive at this formula by using the definition of either (a) the slope coefficient or (b) the change in the predicted outcome between two points (initial and final).

(a) Since $\widehat{\beta} = \triangle\widehat{Y}/\triangle X$, then $\triangle\widehat{Y} = \widehat{\beta}\triangle X$

(b) $\triangle\widehat{Y} = \widehat{Y}_{final} - \widehat{Y}_{initial}$
$= (\widehat{\alpha} + \widehat{\beta}\,X_{final}) - (\widehat{\alpha} + \widehat{\beta}\,X_{initial})$
$= \widehat{\beta}\,(X_{final} - X_{initial}) = \widehat{\beta}\triangle X$

> TO COMPUTE $\triangle\widehat{Y}$ ASSOCIATED WITH $\triangle X$: We plug the value of $\triangle X$ into the formula below and calculate $\triangle\widehat{Y}$.
> $$\triangle\widehat{Y} = \widehat{\beta}\triangle X$$

For example, imagine that we want to predict the change in GDP associated with an increase in prior GDP of 400 trillion local currency units. To make the calculations here, we start with the formula of change in the predicted GDP and plug in the value of change in prior GDP:

$$\triangle \widehat{gdp} = 1.61 \, \triangle prior\_gdp$$
$$= 1.61 \times 400 = 644$$

We predict that an increase in GDP 13 years ago of 400 trillion in local currency would likely be associated with an increase in current GDP of about 644 trillion local currency units. (Again, see figure in the margin to visualize how we would arrive at the same conclusion using the fitted line drawn in the scatter plot.)

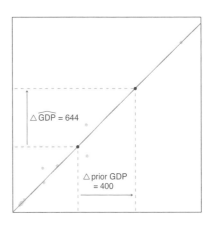

4.4.2 WITH NATURAL LOGARITHM TRANSFORMATIONS

In the previous subsection, we saw how to fit a line using our two variables of interest, *gdp* and *prior_gdp*, without any transformations. To improve the fit of the line, there are times when we might want to transform one or both of our variables of interest. As we will soon see, these transformations affect how we interpret the coefficients.

When a variable contains a handful of either extremely large or extremely small values, the distribution of the variable will be skewed. (Recall that a distribution is considered skewed when it is not symmetric because one of its tails is longer than the other.) Under these circumstances, it is often a good idea to transform the variable by taking its natural logarithm. This transformation will make the variable of interest more normally distributed and, in turn, improve the fit of the line to the data. In the example at hand, we will transform both variables of interest by taking the natural logarithm, and then we will re-fit the line.

TIP: The natural logarithm is the inverse of the exponential function. The base of the natural logarithm is the constant *e*, known as Euler's number, which is approximately 2.7183. The natural logarithm of X, $\log(X)$, is the power to which *e* would have to be raised to equal X (if $X = e^Y$, then $\log(X) = Y$).

In R, the function to compute a natural logarithm is `log()`. To calculate the natural logarithm of each of the values inside a variable, we specify the code identifying the variable as the main argument. Then, to save the results as a new variable, we can use the assignment operator `<-`. To store this new variable inside the existing dataframe, we use the `$` character. Returning to the running example, to create the log-transformed GDP variables, *log_gdp* and *log_prior_gdp*, we run:

`log()` computes the natural logarithm of the argument specified inside the parentheses. Example: `log(10)`.

```
## create log-transformed GDP variables
co$log_gdp <- log(co$gdp) # gdp
co$log_prior_gdp <- log(co$prior_gdp)  # prior gdp
```

To check that the new variables were created correctly, we could look at the first few observations of the dataframe *co*. If you run `head(co)` again, you should see that the value of the first observation of *log_gdp* is 2.4 (since $gdp_1 = 11.1$ and $\log(11.1) = 2.4$), and the value of the first observation of *log_prior_gdp* is approximately 2 (since $prior\_gdp_1 = 7.4$ and $\log(7.4) = 2$).

RECALL: hist() creates the histogram of a variable. Example: hist(*data$variable*).

To visualize how the transformation affected the distribution of our two variables of interest, we can create the histograms of the original and log-transformed variables by running:

```
## create histograms
hist(co$gdp) # gdp
hist(co$log_gdp) # log-transformed gdp
hist(co$prior_gdp) # prior gdp
hist(co$log_prior_gdp) # log-transformed prior gdp
```

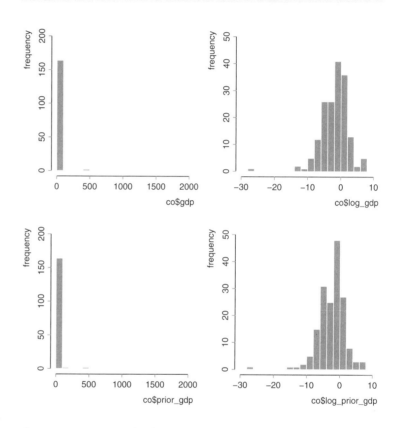

As we can see in the histograms on the left, the two original measures of GDP contained a handful of extremely large values, which skewed their distributions. (In both cases, the tail on the right is longer than the tail on the left). While most observations had values below 200 trillion local currency units, there were a few outliers. For example, Indonesia had a GDP of more than 1,100 trillion rupiahs in 1993 and of almost 1,800 trillion rupiahs in 2006. As we can see in the histograms on the right, the distributions become more symmetrical and bell-shaped once we log-transform the variables.

Now, we can visualize how the transformation of the variables affected the fit of the line by creating the scatter plots between the original variables and between the log-transformed variables:

```
## create scatter plots
plot(x=co$prior_gdp, y=co$gdp) # original
plot(x=co$log_prior_gdp, y=co$log_gdp) # log-transformed
```

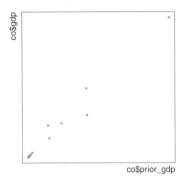
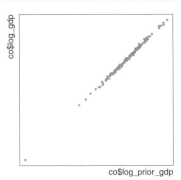

Comparing the two scatter plots, we clearly see that the natural logarithm transformation makes the relationship between the two variables of interest more linear. To confirm this, we can compute the correlation coefficient between the log-transformed variables:

```
cor(co$log_gdp, co$log_prior_gdp) # computes correlation
## [1] 0.9982696
```

Indeed, the new correlation coefficient is even closer to 1 than it was before the logarithmic transformation (0.998 vs. 0.990).

Now that we have a sense of how the two log-transformed variables relate to each other, we can fit the following linear model to summarize their relationship:

$$\widehat{log\_gdp}_i = \widehat{\alpha} + \widehat{\beta} \; log\_prior\_gdp_i \quad (i=\text{countries})$$

where:

- $\widehat{log\_gdp}_i$ is the average predicted natural logarithm of GDP from 2005 to 2006 among countries in which the value of log_prior_gdp equals $log\_prior\_gdp_i$
- $log\_prior\_gdp_i$ is the natural logarithm of the GDP of country i from 1992 to 1993.

To estimate the coefficients of this new line of best fit, we use the lm() function again and run:

```
lm(log_gdp ~ log_prior_gdp, data=co) # fits linear model
##
## Call:
## lm(formula = log_gdp ~ log_prior_gdp, data=co)
##
## Coefficients:
## (Intercept)   log_prior_gdp
##      0.4859          1.0105
```

RECALL: lm() fits a linear model. It requires a formula of the type Y ~ X. To specify the object where the dataframe is stored, we can use the optional argument data or the $ character. Examples: lm(y_var ~ x_var, data=data) or lm(data$y_var ~ data$x_var).

Using the estimated coefficients provided above, we can write the new fitted linear model as follows:

$$\widehat{log\_gdp} = 0.49 + 1.01 \; log\_prior\_gdp$$

The fitted **log-log linear model** is a fitted linear model in which both Y and X have been log-transformed:

$$\widehat{\log(Y)} = \widehat{\alpha} + \widehat{\beta}\log(X)$$

In this model, we interpret $\widehat{\beta}$ as the predicted percentage change in the outcome associated with an increase in the predictor of 1 percent.

This type of model, in which both the outcome and the predictor have been log-transformed, is called the **log-log linear model**. While we could interpret the coefficients the same way as in the normal linear model, in practice, we use an approximation to avoid dealing with the logarithms, especially when interpreting $\widehat{\beta}$.

As shown in the appendix near the end of this chapter, we interpret $\widehat{\beta}$ as the predicted *percentage* change in the outcome associated with an increase in the predictor of 1 *percent*. Since here $\widehat{\beta}=1.01$, an increase of prior GDP of 1% is associated with a predicted increase in GDP of 1.01%, on average. Note that in this interpretation of $\widehat{\beta}$, both the change in X and the change in $\widehat{Y}$ are measured in *percentages*, instead of in units, as is the case in the standard linear model. In other words, in the log-log model, we estimate change in relative rather than absolute terms.

4.5 PREDICTING GDP GROWTH USING NIGHT-TIME LIGHT EMISSIONS

Let's figure out how to fit a model to predict changes in GDP using changes in night-time light emissions. As mentioned earlier, being able to predict GDP growth using night-time light emissions would be quite useful. In remote areas of the world, where measuring GDP is difficult, measures of night-time light emissions are readily available through satellite imagery.

We start the analysis by creating the two variables whose relationship we want to understand. In this model, our outcome of interest is the percentage change in GDP between two points in time, which is defined as:

$$gdp\_change = \frac{gdp - prior\_gdp}{prior\_gdp} \times 100$$

As we saw in chapter 1, R understands arithmetic operators such as $+$, $-$, $*$, and $/$. Thus, to create this variable, we can run:

```
## create GDP percentage change variable
co$gdp_change <-
   ((co$gdp - co$prior_gdp) / co$prior_gdp) * 100
```

Our predictor is the percentage change in night-time light emissions over the same period of time, which is defined as:

$$light\_change = \frac{light - prior\_light}{prior\_light} \times 100$$

To create this variable, we run:

```
## create light percentage change variable
co$light_change <-
   ((co$light - co$prior_light) / co$prior_light) * 100
```

We could check that the new variables were created correctly by looking at the first few observations of the dataframe *co*. If you run head(co) again, you should see that the value of the first observation of *gdp_change* is approximately 51, and the value of the first observation of *light_change* is about -6. Since both new variables measure change as a percentage, we interpret the first number as indicating that the GDP of that country grew by 51% in the 13-year period under study; we interpret the second number as indicating that the night-time light emissions in that same country declined by 6% during the same time period.

To get a better sense of the contents of *gdp_change* and *light_change*, we can create their histograms by running:

```
## create histograms
hist(co$gdp_change) # of percentage change in gdp
hist(co$light_change) # of percentage change in light
```

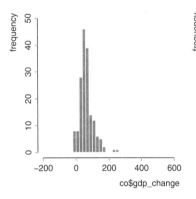 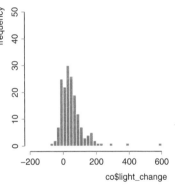

TIP: Do not confuse percentage change with percentage-point change. The percentage change is defined as the change relative to the baseline:

$$\frac{Y_{final} - Y_{initial}}{Y_{initial}} \times 100$$

In contrast, the percentage-point change is defined as the difference between the final and initial values when these values are measured in percentages:

$$Y_{final} - Y_{initial} \quad \text{(both measured in \%)}$$

For example, if the voter turnout rate increased from 50% to 60%, the percentage change would be:

$$\frac{60\% - 50\%}{50\%} \times 100 = 20\%$$

And, the percentage-point change:

$$60\% - 50\% = 10 \text{ p.p.}$$

We could describe this change as an increase of either (a) 20 percent or (b) 10 percentage points.

Here we observe that both variables are more or less normally distributed and that while almost all countries saw their GDP grow by between 0 and 200% over the 13-year period, a fair number of countries saw their night-time light emissions either grow by more than 200% or actually decline.

RECALL: We always plot the predictor on the x-axis and the outcome variable on the y-axis.

Now that we have constructed and learned how to interpret our two variables of interest, we can create their scatter plot to get a sense of how they relate to each other:

```
## create scatter plot
plot(x=co$light_change, y=co$gdp_change)
```

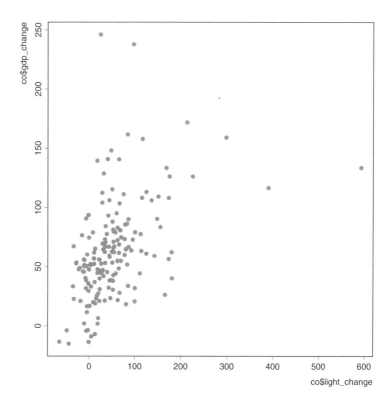

As expected, looking at the scatter plot, we can see that higher values of night-time light change tend to be associated with higher values of GDP change. In other words, increases in a country's night-time light emissions are usually accompanied by increases in that country's GDP. The relationship appears to be only moderately linear, however. To confirm this, we compute the correlation coefficient:

```
cor(co$gdp_change, co$light_change) # computes correlation
## [1] 0.4577672
```

The correlation between the two variables is 0.46, which is consistent with what we saw in the scatter plot above.

To predict GDP growth using the change in night-time light emissions, we are interested in the following linear model:

$$\widehat{gdp\_change}_i = \widehat{\alpha} + \widehat{\beta} \ light\_change_i \quad (i=\text{countries})$$

where:

- $\widehat{gdp\_change}_i$ is the average predicted percentage change in GDP from 1992–1993 to 2005–2006 among countries in which the value of *light_change* equals *light_change*$_i$
- *light_change*$_i$ is the percentage change in night-time light emissions experienced by country i from 1992–1993 to 2005–2006.

To estimate the coefficients of the linear model, we can use the function lm() and run:

```
lm(gdp_change ~ light_change, data=co) # fits linear model
##
## Call:
## lm(formula = gdp_change ~ light_change, data = co)
##
## Coefficients:
## (Intercept)   light_change
##      49.8202        0.2546
```

Based on the estimated coefficients above, we write the fitted model as:

$$\widehat{gdp\_change} = 49.82 + 0.25 \ light\_change$$

Now we can use the fitted model to make predictions. Imagine, for example, that we want to know a country's GDP growth over a period of 13 years but do not have the data necessary to measure it. Suppose also that we observe that night-time light emissions increased by 20% in that country over the same period of time. What would be our best guess for its GDP growth? To compute this prediction, we plug into the fitted linear model a *light_change* equal to 20:

$$\begin{aligned}\widehat{gdp\_change} &= 49.82 + 0.25 \ light\_change \\ &= 49.82 + 0.25 \times 20 = 54.82\end{aligned}$$

Based on the fitted model, we predict that the country's GDP grew by an average of about 55% during the 13-year period.

4.6 MEASURING HOW WELL THE MODEL FITS THE DATA WITH THE COEFFICIENT OF DETERMINATION, R^2

R^2, also known as the **coefficient of determination**, ranges from 0 to 1 and measures the proportion of the variation of the outcome variable explained by the model. The higher the R^2, the better the model fits the data.

Whenever we use a model to make predictions, we want to know how well the model fits the data because a poor fit can lead to inaccurate predictions. For this purpose, we use a statistic called **coefficient of determination**, or R^2 (pronounced r-squared). The value of R^2 ranges from 0 to 1 and represents the proportion of the variation of Y explained by the model. For example, we interpret an R^2 of 0.8 as indicating that the model explains 80% of the variation of Y ($0.8 \times 100 = 80\%$). Therefore, the higher the R^2, the better the model fits the data.

FORMULA IN DETAIL

In mathematical terms, R^2 is defined as:

$$R^2 = 1 - \frac{SSR}{TSS} = 1 - \frac{\sum_{i=1}^{n}(Y_i - \hat{Y}_i)^2}{\sum_{i=1}^{n}(Y_i - \overline{Y})^2}$$

where:

- SSR stands for the "<u>s</u>um of the <u>s</u>quared <u>r</u>esiduals" and measures the variation of Y *not* explained by the model. This is what we minimize by using the least squares method when choosing the line of best fit. More precisely:

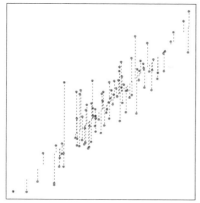

$$SSR = \sum_{i=1}^{n}\hat{\epsilon}_i^2 = \sum_{i=1}^{n}(Y_i - \hat{Y}_i)^2$$

In other words, SSR sums the squared distances between the dots and the line of best fit (shown as dashed red lines in the top figure in the margin).

- TSS stands for "<u>t</u>otal <u>s</u>um of <u>s</u>quares" and measures the total variation of Y, explained and unexplained. This is the numerator of the variance of Y, which, as we saw in chapter 3, is a measure of the spread of the variable. More precisely:

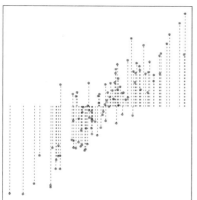

$$TSS = \sum_{i=1}^{n}(Y_i - \overline{Y})^2$$

In other words, TSS sums the squared distances between the dots and the mean of Y (shown as dashed red lines in the bottom figure in the margin).

Given the definitions above, we can interpret SSR/TSS as the proportion of the variation of Y *not* explained by the model. Therefore, $1-(SSR/TSS)$ is the proportion of the variation of Y that is explained by the model.

At one extreme, when the model perfectly fits the data, the model will produce no residuals, SSR will equal 0, and R^2 will equal 1. At the other extreme, when the model does not explain any of the variation of the outcome variable, SSR will equal TSS, and R^2 will equal 0. Most situations fall somewhere in between.

When we use a simple linear model, that is, a linear model with only one X variable, as is the case in this chapter, R^2 is also equivalent to the correlation between X and Y squared:

$$R^2 = cor(X, Y)^2$$

Given this definition of R^2, it becomes clear that the higher the correlation between X and Y (in absolute terms), the better the model fits the data.   As the linear association between X and Y becomes stronger (for example, moving from the first scatter plot in figure 4.4 to the second one), the prediction errors in the model (the vertical distance between the dots and the line) become smaller, and the proportion of the variation of Y explained by the model (the value of R^2) increases.

TIP: Linear models with only one X variable are known as simple linear regression models (or just simple linear models) to differentiate them from multiple linear regression models, which use more than one X variable. Linear models with only one X variable are also known as bivariate linear models because they estimate the relationship between two variables, X and Y ("bi" means two, and "variate" means variable).

 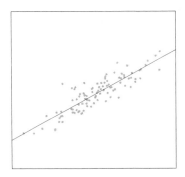

FIGURE 4.4.   The higher the absolute value of the correlation between X and Y, the higher the R^2 and the better the model fits the data. For example, the correlation between the variables in the first plot is 0.48, and the R^2 of the model is 0.23 ($0.48^2=0.23$). By comparison, the correlation between the variables in the second plot is 0.88, and the R^2 of the model is 0.77 ($0.88^2=0.77$).

At one extreme, when the relationship between X and Y is perfectly linear (the correlation between X and Y equals either 1 or -1), the model explains 100% of the variation of Y ($R^2=1^2=1$ and $R^2=(-1)^2=1$). At the other extreme, when there is no linear relationship between X and Y (the correlation between X and Y equals 0), the model explains 0% of the variation of Y ($R^2=0^2=0$).

When building predictive models, then, we look for variables that are highly correlated with Y so that we can use them as predictors. The higher the correlation between X and Y (in absolute terms), the better the fitted linear model will usually be at predicting Y using X.

PREDICTING OUTCOMES USING LINEAR REGRESSION: We look for X variables that are highly correlated with Y because the higher the correlation between X and Y (in absolute terms), the higher the R^2 and the better the fitted linear model will usually be at predicting Y using X.

4.6.1 HOW WELL DO THE THREE PREDICTIVE MODELS IN THIS CHAPTER FIT THE DATA?

Let's evaluate the three predictive models we fitted in this chapter. Figure 4.5 shows the three scatter plots with their fitted lines.

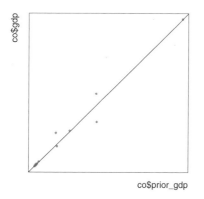 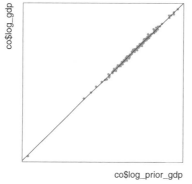 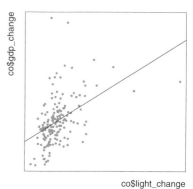

FIGURE 4.5. The first model predicts GDP using prior GDP. The second predicts the natural logarithm of GDP using the natural logarithm of prior GDP. The third predicts GDP growth using changes in night-time light emissions.

They were all simple linear models, so to compute R^2, we can square the correlation between the two variables of interest:

```
## compute R-squared for each predictive model
cor(co$gdp, co$prior_gdp)^2 # model 1
## [1] 0.9807834
```

```
cor(co$log_gdp, co$log_prior_gdp)^2 # model 2
## [1] 0.9965443
```

```
cor(co$gdp_change, co$light_change)^2 # model 3
## [1] 0.2095928
```

We can interpret the R^2 of the first model as indicating that the linear model that uses prior GDP as a predictor explains about 98% of the variation of GDP. If we compare the R^2 of the first model to that of the second (0.98 vs. approximately 1), we can see that the fit of the model improves ever so slightly by log-transforming both measures of GDP. In either case, the predictive models appear to fit the data remarkably well.

Finally, we can interpret the R^2 of the third model as indicating that the linear model that uses night–time light emission changes as a predictor explains about 21% of the variation in GDP growth. While this might appear to be a low R^2 at first, given how difficult it is to predict GDP growth, this model is quite good in relative terms. (Note that we should only compare R^2s between models that have the same outcome variable because some outcomes are intrinsically harder to predict than others.)

4.7 SUMMARY

This chapter introduced us to the linear regression model for making predictions. We learned how to fit a line to summarize the relationship between a predictor and an outcome variable. Then, we learned how to use the fitted line to (i) predict the average value of the outcome variable given a value of the predictor, and (ii) predict the average change in the outcome variable associated with a change in the value of the predictor. Along the way, we learned about prediction errors, the difference between observed and predicted outcomes, and how to interpret the two coefficients of a line: the intercept and the slope. We ended the chapter by learning how to compute and interpret R^2 to measure how well a model fits the data. In the next chapter, we will see how to use the linear regression model for the purpose of estimating causal effects.

4.8 APPENDIX: INTERPRETATION OF THE SLOPE IN THE LOG-LOG LINEAR MODEL

In the log-log linear model, both the outcome and the predictors have been log-transformed:

$$\widehat{\log(Y)} = \widehat{\alpha} + \widehat{\beta}\log(X)$$

RECALL: The slope refers to the change in the predicted outcome between two specific points on the line. In addition, the change in a variable between two points (initial and final) is equivalent to the difference between the value of the variable at the final point and the value of the variable at the initial point. For example:

$$\triangle\widehat{Y} = \widehat{Y}_{\text{final}} - \widehat{Y}_{\text{initial}}$$

Since we are interested in the interpretation of $\widehat{\beta}$, let's start with the formula for the change in the predicted outcome between two points on the line:

$$\widehat{\log(Y_{\text{final}})} - \widehat{\log(Y_{\text{initial}})} = \left[\widehat{\alpha} + \widehat{\beta}\log(X_{\text{final}})\right] - \left[\widehat{\alpha} + \widehat{\beta}\log(X_{\text{initial}})\right]$$
$$= \widehat{\alpha} - \widehat{\alpha} + \widehat{\beta}\log(X_{\text{final}}) - \widehat{\beta}\log(X_{\text{initial}})$$
$$= \widehat{\beta}\left[\log(X_{\text{final}}) - \log(X_{\text{initial}})\right]$$

If we multiply both sides by 100, we arrive at:

$$\left[\widehat{\log(Y_{\text{final}})} - \widehat{\log(Y_{\text{initial}})}\right] \times 100 = \widehat{\beta}\left[\log(X_{\text{final}}) - \log(X_{\text{initial}})\right] \times 100$$

TIP: Based on the formula in detail below, we can make the following approximations:

$$\left[\widehat{\log(Y_{\text{final}})} - \widehat{\log(Y_{\text{initial}})}\right] \times 100 \approx$$
$$\approx \frac{\triangle\widehat{Y}}{\widehat{Y}_{\text{initial}}} \times 100$$

$$\left[\log(X_{\text{final}}) - \log(X_{\text{initial}})\right] \times 100 \approx$$
$$\approx \frac{\triangle X}{X_{\text{initial}}} \times 100$$

Now, if we use the approximations shown in the TIP in the margin, the formula becomes:

$$\frac{\triangle\widehat{Y}}{\widehat{Y}_{\text{initial}}} \times 100 \approx \widehat{\beta}\frac{\triangle X}{X_{\text{initial}}} \times 100$$

where:

- $\triangle\widehat{Y}/\widehat{Y}_{\text{initial}} \times 100$ is the predicted percentage change in the outcome variable
- $\widehat{\beta}$ is the estimated slope coefficient
- $\triangle X/X_{\text{initial}} \times 100$ is the percentage change in the predictor.

Given the formula above, if the predictor increases by 1 percent (that is, $\triangle X/X_{\text{initial}} \times 100 = 1$), then the outcome is predicted to increase by $\widehat{\beta}$ percent:

$$\frac{\triangle\widehat{Y}}{\widehat{Y}_{\text{initial}}} \times 100 \approx \widehat{\beta} \times 1 \approx \widehat{\beta}$$

Putting it all together, in the log-log model, the estimated slope coefficient $\widehat{\beta}$ is the predicted *percentage* change in the outcome associated with an increase in the predictor of 1 *percent*.

The difference between the natural logarithms of two values in a variable is approximately equal to the percentage change between those two values in that variable, when the distance between the two values is relatively small. Here is the math:

$$\left[\log(X_{\text{final}}) - \log(X_{\text{initial}})\right] \times 100 =$$

$$= \left[\log(X_{\text{initial}} + \triangle X) - \log(X_{\text{initial}})\right] \times 100 \qquad \text{because } X_{\text{final}} = X_{\text{initial}} + \triangle X$$

$$= \left[\log\left(X_{\text{initial}} + X_{\text{initial}}\frac{\triangle X}{X_{\text{initial}}}\right) - \log(X_{\text{initial}})\right] \times 100 \qquad \text{because } \frac{X_{\text{initial}}}{X_{\text{initial}}} = 1$$

$$= \left[\log\left(X_{\text{initial}}\left(1 + \frac{\triangle X}{X_{\text{initial}}}\right)\right) - \log(X_{\text{initial}})\right] \times 100$$

$$= \left[\log(X_{\text{initial}}) + \log\left(1 + \frac{\triangle X}{X_{\text{initial}}}\right) - \log(X_{\text{initial}})\right] \times 100 \qquad \text{because } \log(A \times B) = \log(A) + \log(B)$$

$$= \log\left(1 + \frac{\triangle X}{X_{\text{initial}}}\right) \times 100$$

$$\approx \frac{\triangle X}{X_{\text{initial}}} \times 100 \qquad \text{because } \log(1 + A) \approx A \text{ when } A \text{ is small}$$

4.9 CHEATSHEETS

4.9.1 CONCEPTS AND NOTATION

concept/notation	description	example(s)
predictor (X)	variable that we use as the basis for our predictions; predictors are also known as independent variables	when trying to predict a country's current GDP based on prior GDP, the predictor is prior GDP
outcome variable (Y)	variable that we are trying to predict based on the values of the predictor(s); outcome variables are also known as dependent variables	when trying to predict a country's current GDP based on prior GDP, the outcome variable is current GDP
predicted outcomes ($\widehat{Y}$)	pronounced Y-hat; values of Y we predict based on (i) the fitted model that summarizes the relationship between X and Y, and (ii) the observed values of X	(see computing $\widehat{Y}$ based on X below)
observed outcomes (Y)	observed values of Y, in contrast with predicted values of Y, which are estimated, not observed	(see prediction errors below)
prediction errors ($\widehat{\epsilon}$)	pronounced epsilon-hat; also known as residuals; difference between the observed outcomes and the predicted outcomes: $$\widehat{\epsilon}_i = Y_i - \widehat{Y}_i$$ for each observation, this difference is equivalent to the vertical distance between the dot and the fitted line	if the observed outcome equals 5 and the predicted outcome equals 3, the prediction error equals 2 $$\widehat{\epsilon}_i = 5 - 3 = 2$$
linear model	also known as simple linear regression model, simple linear model, and bivariate linear model; theoretical model that we assume reflects the true relationship between X and Y $$Y_i = \alpha + \beta X_i + \epsilon_i$$ where: - Y_i is the outcome for observation i - α is the intercept coefficient - β is the slope coefficient - X_i is the value of the predictor for observation i - ϵ_i is the error for observation i	$Y_i = 2 - 3X_i + \epsilon_i$
fitted linear model	also known as fitted simple linear regression model and fitted simple linear model; line fitted to the data to summarize the relationship between X and Y $$\widehat{Y}_i = \widehat{\alpha} + \widehat{\beta} X_i$$ where: - $\widehat{Y}_i$ is the predicted outcome for observation i - $\widehat{\alpha}$ is the estimated intercept coefficient - $\widehat{\beta}$ is the estimated slope coefficient - X_i is the value of the predictor for observation i	$\widehat{Y}_i = 2 - 3X_i$

continues on next page...

4.9.1 CONCEPTS AND NOTATION (CONTINUED)

concept/notation	description	example(s)
estimated intercept $(\widehat{\alpha})$	pronounced alpha-hat; estimated coefficient of the fitted line that specifies the vertical location of the line it is the $\widehat{Y}$ when $X=0$ unit of measurement of $\widehat{\alpha}$: - if Y is non-binary: in the same unit of measurement as Y - if Y is binary: in percentages (after multiplying the result by 100)	if $\widehat{Y}=2-3X$: the estimated intercept, $\widehat{\alpha}$, is 2 when X equals 0, we predict that Y will equal 2 units, on average
estimated slope $(\widehat{\beta})$	pronounced beta-hat; estimated coefficient of the fitted line that specifies the angle, or steepness of the line; it equals the change in the predicted outcome divided by the change in the predictor between two points on the line ("rise over run") it is the $\triangle\widehat{Y}$ associated with $\triangle X=1$ interpret as: - an average increase in Y if positive - an average decrease in Y if negative - no average change in Y if zero unit of measurement of $\widehat{\beta}$: - if Y is non-binary: in the same unit of measurement as Y - if Y is binary: in percentage points (after multiplying the result by 100)	if $\widehat{Y}=2-3X$: the estimated slope, $\widehat{\beta}$, is -3 when X increases by 1, we predict an associated decrease in Y of 3 units, on average
computing $\widehat{Y}$ based on X	plug the value of X into the fitted linear model: $$\widehat{Y}=\widehat{\alpha}+\widehat{\beta}X$$ unit of measurement of $\widehat{Y}$: - if Y is non-binary: in the same unit of measurement as Y - if Y is binary: in percentages (after multiplying the result by 100)	if $\widehat{Y}=2-3X$ and $X=2$: $$\widehat{Y}=2-3\times2=\text{-}4$$ when X equals 2, we predict that Y will equal -4 units, on average
computing $\triangle\widehat{Y}$ associated with $\triangle X$	plug the value of $\triangle X$ into the formula below: $$\triangle\widehat{Y}=\widehat{\beta}\,\triangle X$$ interpret as: - an average increase in Y if positive - an average decrease in Y if negative - no average change in Y if zero unit of measurement of $\triangle\widehat{Y}$: - if Y is non-binary: in the same unit of measurement as Y - if Y is binary: in percentage points (after multiplying the result by 100)	if $\widehat{Y}=2-3X$ and $\triangle X=2$: $$\triangle\widehat{Y}=-3\times2=\text{-}6$$ when X increases by 2, we predict an associated decrease in Y of 6 units, on average

continues on next page...

4.9.1 CONCEPTS AND NOTATION (CONTINUED)

concept/notation	description	example(s)
fitted log-log linear model	fitted linear model in which both Y and X have been log-transformed; in this model, we interpret the slope coefficient as the predicted percentage change in the outcome associated with an increase in the predictor of 1 percent $$\widehat{\log(Y)} = \widehat{\alpha} + \widehat{\beta}\log(X)$$	if $\widehat{\log(Y)} = 2 + 3\log(X)$: the estimated slope, $\widehat{\beta}$, is 3 when X increases by 1%, we predict an associated increase in Y of 3%, on average
R^2 or coefficient of determination	pronounced r-squared; statistic that measures the proportion of the variation of the outcome variable explained by the model it ranges from 0 to 1 the higher the R^2, the better the model fits the data in the simple linear model: $$R^2 = cor(X, Y)^2$$ when building predictive models, we look for X variables that are highly correlated with Y because the higher the correlation between X and Y (in absolute terms), the higher the R^2 and the better the fitted linear model will usually be at predicting Y using X	if the R^2 of a model equals 0.80, it means that 80% of the variation of the outcome variable is explained by the model

4.9.2 R FUNCTIONS

function	description	required argument(s)	example(s)
lm()	fits a linear model	formula of the type $Y \sim X$, where Y identifies the outcome variable and X identifies the X variable optional argument data: specifies the object where the dataframe is stored; alternative to using $ for each variable	## both of these pieces of code fit the same linear model: lm(data$y_var ~ data$x_var) lm(y_var ~ x_var, data=data)

abline()	adds a straight line to the most recently created graph	to add the fitted line, we specify as the main argument the object that contains the output of the lm() function; (for other uses, see page 97)	fit <- lm(y_var ~ x_var, data=data)
			 # stores fitted line into an object named fit
			 abline(fit)
			 # adds the fitted line to the most recently created graph

log()	computes the natural logarithm	what we want to compute the natural logarithm of	log(10)

5. ESTIMATING CAUSAL EFFECTS WITH OBSERVATIONAL DATA

In chapter 2, we learned how to estimate average causal effects using data from randomized experiments. Here, we learn how to estimate them when we cannot randomly assign the treatment and instead have to rely on observational data. As an illustration, we estimate the causal effects of Russian TV reception on the 2014 Ukrainian parliamentary election.

5.1 RUSSIAN STATE-CONTROLLED TV COVERAGE OF 2014 UKRAINIAN AFFAIRS

Ukraine became independent from the Soviet Union in 1991. Since then, attitudes toward Russia have often been a point of contention. For a long time, the Ukrainian population and political parties were divided into pro-Russian and anti-Russian.

Leading up to the 2014 Ukrainian elections, Russia and Ukraine (which, at the time, was governed by a party with an "anti-Russian" agenda) were in fierce political and military conflict. Russian state-controlled TV coverage of the conflict, and of the issues at stake in the Ukrainian elections, was intense and one-sided. For instance, the coverage deemed the Ukrainian government illegitimate and claimed that the revolution that brought it to power had been organized by foreign countries. Such coverage was aired not only in Russian territory but also in parts of Ukraine. Some Ukrainians living close to the border received the signal, and thus, could be exposed to pro-Russia propaganda.

In this chapter, we estimate the effect of Russian TV reception on Ukraine's 2014 parliamentary election. We do so at two levels. First, we analyze individual-level survey data to estimate the impact on an individual's propensity to vote for a pro-Russian party. Second, we analyze aggregate-level data to estimate the effect on the vote share of pro-Russian parties at the precinct level. In both cases, we focus on areas close to the Russian border.

Based on Leonid Peisakhin and Arturas Rozenas, "Electoral Effects of Biased Media: Russian Television in Ukraine," *American Journal of Political Science* 62, no. 3 (2018): 535–50. To simplify the analyses, we consider that a signal strength of 50 dBuV or above provides reception, and we limit the number of potential confounders.

5.2 CHALLENGES OF ESTIMATING CAUSAL EFFECTS WITH OBSERVATIONAL DATA

As we discussed in chapter 2, to estimate causal effects, we must find or create a situation in which the treatment and control groups are comparable with respect to all the variables that might affect the outcome other than the treatment variable itself. Only when this assumption is satisfied can we use the average factual or observed outcome of one group as a good estimate of the average counterfactual outcome of the other group.

RECALL: The fundamental problem of causal inference is that we can never observe the counterfactual outcome. Yet to infer causal effects, we need to compare the factual outcome with the counterfactual outcome.

As we have already seen, in randomized experiments, we can rely on the random assignment of the treatment to make treatment and control groups, on average, identical to each other in terms of all observed and unobserved pre-treatment characteristics. But what happens when we cannot conduct a randomized experiment and have to analyze observational data instead? We can no longer assume that treatment and control groups are comparable. To estimate causal effects using observational data, we have to first identify any relevant differences between treatment and control groups—known as confounding variables or confounders—and then statistically control for them so that we can make the two groups as comparable to each other as possible.

RECALL: Observational data are data collected about naturally occurring events, where researchers do not assign treatment.

We begin this section by defining confounding variables. Then, we explore why their presence poses a problem when estimating causal effects and discuss how the randomization of treatment assignment eliminates all potential confounders in randomized experiments.

5.2.1 CONFOUNDING VARIABLES

A **confounding variable**, also known as a **confounder**, is a variable that affects both (i) the likelihood of receiving the treatment X and (ii) the outcome Y.

A **confounding variable**, or **confounder**, denoted as Z, is a variable that affects both (i) the likelihood of receiving the treatment X and (ii) the outcome Y.

In mathematical notation, just as we represent the treatment variable as X and the outcome variable as Y, we represent a potential confounding variable as Z. The diagram in figure 5.1 shows the causal relationships between these variables. Note that the arrows between Z and X and between Z and Y both originate from Z, indicating that changes in Z affect the values of X and Y but not the other way around.

FIGURE 5.1. Representation of the causal relationships between the confounding variable, Z, the treatment variable, X, and the outcome variable, Y. (Recall, we represent a causal relationship with an arrow; the direction of the arrow indicates which one of the variables affects the other.)

Let's look at a simple hypothetical example to get a better sense of how this works. Suppose we are interested in the average causal effect of attending a private school, as opposed to a public one, on student performance. Given the goal of our research:

- the treatment variable, X, is a binary variable indicating whether the student attended a private school (call it *private school*)
- the outcome variable, Y, is student performance on a standardized test such as the SAT (call it *test scores*).

If we are collecting data from the real world, where children attend the school their parents choose, can we think of any variable that affects both (i) the likelihood of attending a private school and (ii) student performance on a test? In other words, can we think of a confounding variable, Z?

One potential confounding variable is *family wealth*. Given that private schools require that students pay tuition, private school students are likely to come from wealthier families than public school students. Thus, family wealth affects the likelihood that a student attends a private school.

$$family\ wealth \rightarrow private\ school$$

Family wealth also affects the likelihood that a student receives after-school help such as one-on-one tutoring, which, in turn, will improve performance on standardized tests.

$$family\ wealth \rightarrow tutoring \rightarrow test\ scores$$

Thus, since *family wealth* affects both *private school* and *test scores*, it is a confounding variable.

5.2.2 WHY ARE CONFOUNDERS A PROBLEM?

Why does the presence of a confounder pose a problem when estimating causal effects? Because confounders obscure the causal relationship between X and Y.

Returning to the example above, if we observed that, on average, private school students perform better on tests than public school students, we would not know whether it is because they attended a private school or because they came from wealthier families that could afford to provide them with after-school help. In other words, if we were to calculate the difference in average test scores between the two groups (the difference-in-means estimator), we would not know what portion of this difference, if any, could be attributed to the treatment (attending a private school) and what portion was the result of the confounding variable (coming from a wealthier family).

In the presence of confounders, correlation does not necessarily imply causation. Just because we observe that two variables are highly correlated with each other does not automatically mean that one causes the other. There could be a third variable—a confounder—that affects both variables.

In the extreme, by affecting both X and Y at the same time, confounding variables might create a completely spurious relationship between X and Y, misleading us into thinking that X and Y are causally related to each other when, in fact, there is no direct causal link between the two.

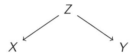

For example, ice cream sales and the number of drownings are positively correlated with each other. When we observe a larger number of ice cream sales, we usually also observe a larger number of drownings. That does not mean that eating ice cream causes one to drown. There is an obvious confounder: heat.

When it is hot, people are more likely to eat ice cream, and they are also more likely to go swimming, which might sadly lead to some drownings. The presence of the confounder, heat, then, makes ice cream sales and number of drownings positively correlated with each other. As far as we know, however, there is no direct causal link between them. Eating ice cream does not make one more likely to drown. (Note the lack of a causal link/arrow between *ice cream* and *drownings* in the diagram in the margin.)

Not all cases are this extreme. Typically, there is a causal link between the treatment and the outcome, but the presence of a confounder makes it difficult for us to estimate the causal effect of X on Y accurately (as we saw in the example of the effect of attending a private school on student test scores).

In short, when there is a confounding variable Z affecting X and Y, we should not trust correlation as a measure of causation, and thus, we cannot use the difference-in-means estimator to estimate average causal effects.

IN THE PRESENCE OF CONFOUNDING VARIABLES:
Treatment and control groups are not comparable, correlation does not necessarily imply causation, and the
difference-in-means estimator does *not* provide a valid
estimate of the average treatment effect.

Note that in order for a variable to be considered a confounder,
it has to affect both (i) the likelihood of being treated and (ii) the
outcome. If it affects only one, it is not a confounding variable,
and therefore, its presence does not complicate the estimation of
causal effects. (See scenarios I and II in figure 5.2.)

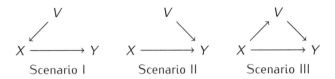

Scenario I   Scenario II   Scenario III

FIGURE 5.2. Representation of scenarios where the variable V, despite its being
causally linked to X, or Y, or both, is not
a confounding variable.

For example, perhaps students who are raised Catholic are more
likely to attend a private school. As long as being raised Catholic
does not also affect test performance, it does not constitute a
confounder (Scenario I).

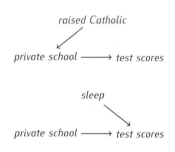

Similarly, perhaps students who get more sleep perform better
academically, but if sleeping more doesn't affect the likelihood of
attending a private school, then it is not a confounding variable
(Scenario II).

Also, mechanisms by which the treatment affects the outcome are
not confounders (Scenario III). For example, private schools might
have smaller classes than public schools, and smaller classes may
improve student performance. The use of smaller classes in private
schools is not a confounder but may be one of the mechanisms
by which private schools improve student performance. One easy
way of seeing this distinction is by thinking about the direction
of the causal relationships. A confounder causally affects the
treatment and outcome rather than the other way around.

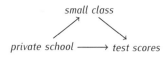

5.2.3 CONFOUNDERS IN RANDOMIZED EXPERIMENTS

Why don't we have to worry about confounders in randomized
experiments? Randomization of treatment assignment eliminates
all potential confounders. It ensures that treatment and control
groups are comparable by breaking the link between any potential
confounder and the treatment.

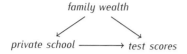

Let's return to the example above, where we were interested in the causal effect of attending a private school on student performance. As discussed, if parents choose the school their children attend, a potential confounding variable is *family wealth*.

If we are designing our study and want to ensure that there are no confounders, how should we decide who attends and does not attend a private school? We can flip a coin (or use any other method of random assignment) to determine which students attend a private school and which attend a public school. If, for example, there were more applicants than open seats in a private school voucher program, we could ensure that there would be no confounders by allocating the vouchers through a method of random assignment such as a lottery.

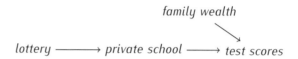

Now, students from non-wealthy families would be as likely as students from wealthy families to receive the voucher, and thus, attend a private school. In other words, by assigning students to attend a private school with the flip of a coin, we break the link between *family wealth* and *private school*. As a result, *family wealth* is no longer a confounder, since it no longer affects the probability of receiving the treatment (although it continues to affect the outcome).

In general, by assigning the treatment at random, we ensure that nothing related to the outcome is also related to the likelihood of receiving the treatment, including factors that we cannot observe such as student aptitude or motivation. Random assignment of treatment, then, eliminates any potential confounders. This is why in chapter 2 we stated that by randomly assigning treatment, we ensure that treatment and control groups have identical pre-treatment characteristics, on average.

> WHY ARE THERE NO CONFOUNDING VARIABLES IN RANDOMIZED EXPERIMENTS? By randomly assigning treatment, we break the link between any potential confounders and the treatment variable, thereby eliminating all potential confounding variables.

This is the reason randomized experiments are regarded as the gold standard for establishing causal relationships in many scientific disciplines. Randomization of treatment assignment makes the estimation of valid causal effects relatively straightforward. All we need to do is compute the difference-in-means estimator.

5.3 THE EFFECT OF RUSSIAN TV ON UKRAINIANS' VOTING BEHAVIOR

In this section, we learn how to estimate average treatment effects using observational, as opposed to experimental, data. As our running example, we study the effects of receiving Russian TV on the voting behavior of Ukrainians in the 2014 parliamentary election. In particular, we analyze data from a survey conducted a few months after the election on a random sample of Ukrainians living in precincts within 50 kilometers (about 31 miles) of the Russian border. (See figure 5.3.)

FIGURE 5.3. The precincts studied are within 50 kilometers of the border with Russia (shown in black).

The dataset is provided in the file "UA_survey.csv". Table 5.1 shows the names and descriptions of the variables included.

variable	description
russian_tv	identifies whether the respondent's precinct receives Russian TV: 1=there is reception or 0=there is no reception
pro_russian_vote	identifies respondents who reported having voted for a pro-Russian party in the 2014 parliamentary election: 1=voted for a pro-Russian party or 0=did not
within_25km	identifies whether the respondent's precinct is within 25 kilometers of the Ukraine-Russia border: 1=it is within 25 kilometers of the border or 0=it is not

TABLE 5.1. Description of the variables in the UA_survey dataset, where the unit of observation is respondents.

The code for this chapter's analysis can be found in the "Observational.R" file. As always, we begin by reading and storing the data (assuming we have already set the working directory):

```
uas <- read.csv("UA_survey.csv") # reads and stores data
```

To get a sense of the dataset, we look at the first few observations:

```
head(uas) # shows first observations
##   russian_tv pro_russian_vote within_25km
## 1          1                0           1
## 2          1                1           1
## 3          0                0           0
## 4          0                0           1
## 5          0                0           1
## 6          1                0           0
```

Based on table 5.1 and the output above, we learn that each observation in the dataset represents a respondent, and that the dataset contains three variables:

- *russian_tv* is a binary variable that identifies whether the respondent's precinct received Russian TV
- *pro_russian_vote* is a binary variable that identifies whether the respondent reported having voted for a pro-Russian party in the 2014 Ukrainian parliamentary election
- *within_25km* is a binary variable that identifies whether the respondent's precinct is very close to the border with Russia (defined as within 25 kilometers).

We interpret the first observation as representing a respondent who lived in a precinct that received Russian TV, did not vote for a pro-Russian party, and lived in a precinct within 25 kilometers (km) of the border.

To find the total number of observations in the dataset, we run:

```
dim(uas) # provides dimensions of dataframe: rows, columns
## [1] 358   3
```

The dataset contains information for 358 survey respondents.

5.3.1 USING THE SIMPLE LINEAR MODEL TO COMPUTE THE DIFFERENCE-IN-MEANS ESTIMATOR

RECALL: Simple linear models use only one X variable to predict Y.

In this subsection, we learn to fit a simple linear model that produces an estimated coefficient that is equivalent to the difference-in-means estimator. This procedure is a stepping stone toward fitting a more complex model in which we estimate an average causal effect while statistically controlling for confounders.

While we use the same statistical method as in the previous chapter, we do so with a different goal in mind. In chapter 4, we fitted a linear model to *predict* a quantity of interest, that is, to predict the outcome Y given a value of the predictor X. In this chapter, we fit a linear model to *explain* a quantity of interest, that is, to estimate the causal relationship between the treatment X and the outcome Y. (Recall, X denotes the predictor when we are making predictions, but it denotes the treatment variable when we are estimating causal effects.) As we will soon see, the goal of the analysis does not affect the mathematical underpinnings of the model (the method used to fit the line and the mathematical definitions of the coefficients remain the same), but it does affect the substantive interpretations of the coefficients.

Let's analyze the UA_survey dataset as an example. Here, we are interested in estimating the average causal effect that receiving Russian TV had on a respondent's probability of voting for a pro-Russian party in the 2014 Ukrainian parliamentary election. In other words, we are interested in the causal link between *russian_tv* and *pro_russian_vote*, where *russian_tv* is the treatment variable and *pro_russian_vote* is the outcome variable.

$$Russian\ TV\ reception\ \rightarrow\ pro\text{-}Russian\ vote$$

Can we use the difference-in-means estimator to estimate this average treatment effect? The information contained in this dataset does not come from a randomized experiment, but rather from naturally occurring events. The reception of Russian TV was not randomly assigned to different precincts. Instead, Russian TV reception was determined by factors such as the terrain and distance between the precinct where the respondent lived and the Russian TV transmitters. The data we are analyzing are therefore observational, not experimental.

Having said that, while the factors that determined Russian TV reception were outside the researchers' control, one could argue that they produced an "as-if-random" variation of treatment that had nothing to do with the determinants of individual voting behavior. For example, small differences in terrain affected Russian TV reception but probably did not affect voting behavior directly. For now, then, we assume that the respondents who received Russian TV were similar in all relevant characteristics to those who did not and use the difference-in-means estimator to estimate the average treatment effect. (Later, we will see what happens when we relax this assumption.)

In the running example, to compute the difference-in-means estimator (just as we did in subsection 2.5.3), we run:

```
## calculate the difference-in-means estimator
mean(uas$pro_russian_vote[uas$russian_tv==1])-
  mean(uas$pro_russian_vote[uas$russian_tv==0])
## [1] 0.1191139
```

RECALL: The difference-in-means estimator is defined as the average outcome for the treatment group minus the average outcome for the control group:

$$\overline{Y}_{\text{treatment group}} - \overline{Y}_{\text{control group}}$$

It produces a valid estimate of the average treatment effect when treatment and control groups are comparable, that is, when there are no confounders present.

RECALL: In R, mean() calculates the mean of a variable and [] is the operator used to extract a selection of observations from a variable. Example: mean(*data*$*var1*[*data*$*var2*==1]) calculates the mean of the observations of the variable *var1* for which the variable *var2* equals 1.

RECALL: The difference-in-means estimator is measured in:
- the same unit of measurement as Y, if
  Y is non-binary
- percentage points (after multiplying the
  output by 100), if Y is binary.

Here, since *pro_russian_vote* is binary, the
estimator is measured in percentage points
(after multiplying the output by 100).

Based on this output, we would write the following conclusion
statement: Assuming that respondents who received Russian TV
were comparable to those who did not, we estimate that receiving
Russian TV increased a respondent's probability of voting for a
pro-Russian party by 12 percentage points, on average.

As we will see next, we can arrive at the same estimate by fitting
a line where X is our treatment variable and Y is our outcome
variable of interest. Then, the estimated slope coefficient ($\widehat{\beta}$) is
numerically equivalent to the difference-in-means estimator.

> TO COMPUTE THE DIFFERENCE-IN-MEANS ESTIMA-
> TOR: We can either
>
> (a) calculate it directly, or
>
> (b) fit a simple linear model where Y is our outcome vari-
>   able of interest and X is the treatment variable. In this
>   case, the estimated slope coefficient ($\widehat{\beta}$) is equivalent to
>   the difference-in-means estimator.

Recall that the formula of the fitted line is:

$$\widehat{Y} = \widehat{\alpha} + \widehat{\beta}X$$

where the estimated slope coefficient ($\widehat{\beta}$) equals the change in the
predicted outcome associated with a one-unit increase in X.

RECALL: In this book, we define a treatment variable, X, as binary and identifying
receipt of treatment:

$$X_i = \begin{cases} 1 \text{ if individual } i \text{ received} \\ \quad \text{the treatment} \\ 0 \text{ if individual } i \text{ did not receive} \\ \quad \text{the treatment} \end{cases}$$

When X is the treatment variable, a one-unit increase in X occurs
when X changes from 0 to 1, since those are the only two values that the treatment variable can take. This increase in X is
equivalent to changing from not receiving the treatment ($X=0$) to
receiving the treatment ($X=1$). The value of $\widehat{\beta}$ is, therefore, the
estimated average change in the outcome variable ($\triangle\widehat{Y}$) associated with the change from the control condition to the treatment
condition, also known as the difference-in-means estimator. (See
the formula in detail below for a step-by-step explanation.)

FORMULA IN DETAIL

As we learned in chapter 4, the estimated slope coefficient
equals the change in $\widehat{Y}$ associated with a one-unit increase
in X:

$$\widehat{\beta} = \triangle\widehat{Y} \quad (\text{if } \triangle X=1)$$

The change in $\widehat{Y}$ can be calculated as $\widehat{Y}_{\text{final}} - \widehat{Y}_{\text{initial}}$:

$$\widehat{\beta} = \widehat{Y}_{\text{final}} - \widehat{Y}_{\text{initial}} \quad (\text{if } \triangle X = 1)$$

When the X is the treatment variable, a one-unit increase in X is equivalent to changing from the control group ($X=0$) to the treatment group ($X=1$). This makes the control group the initial state, and the treatment group the final state:

$$\widehat{\beta} = \widehat{Y}_{\text{treatment group}} - \widehat{Y}_{\text{control group}}$$

Finally, recall that $\widehat{Y}$ is an *average* predicted value. In this case, it turns out that the $\widehat{Y}$s are exactly equal to the $\overline{Y}$s for their respective groups. The estimated slope coefficient is, then:

$$\widehat{\beta} = \overline{Y}_{\text{treatment group}} - \overline{Y}_{\text{control group}}$$

When in a fitted linear model the X variable is the treatment variable, then the estimated slope coefficient $\widehat{\beta}$ is numerically equivalent to the difference-in-means estimator.

Now, let's take a moment to figure out the substantive interpretation of $\widehat{\beta}$ in this model. As we just saw, $\widehat{\beta}$ is equivalent to the difference-in-means estimator, which, under certain conditions, produces a valid estimate of the average treatment effect, defined as the average change in the outcome variable *caused by* a change in the treatment variable. As a result, when interpreting $\widehat{\beta}$ in a linear model where X is the treatment variable, we use causal as opposed to predictive language. We interpret the value of $\widehat{\beta}$ as the estimated change in the outcome variable *caused by*, not just *associated with*, the treatment. The validity of this causal interpretation depends on the extent to which the treatment and control groups are comparable, that is, on the absence of confounding variables.

INTERPRETATION OF THE ESTIMATED SLOPE COEF-FICIENT IN THE SIMPLE LINEAR MODEL:

- By default, we interpret $\widehat{\beta}$ using predictive language: It is the $\triangle \widehat{Y}$ *associated with* $\triangle X = 1$.
- When X is the treatment variable, then $\widehat{\beta}$ is equivalent to the difference-in-means estimator, and thus, we interpret $\widehat{\beta}$ using causal language: It is the $\triangle \widehat{Y}$ *caused by* $\triangle X = 1$ (the presence of the treatment). This causal interpretation is valid if there are no confounding variables present, and thus, the treatment and control groups are comparable.

RECALL: This model uses the true values of α, β, and ϵ_i (that is, without the hats) because it is the theoretical model that we assume reflects the true relationship between X and Y. Since we do not know these values, we have to estimate them by fitting the model to the data.

Turning back to the running example, given that our treatment variable is *russian_tv* and our outcome variable is *pro_russian_vote*, the linear model we are interested in is:

$$pro\_russian\_vote_i = \alpha + \beta\ russian\_tv_i + \epsilon_i \quad (i=\text{respondents})$$

where:

- *pro_russian_vote$_i$* is the binary variable that identifies whether respondent *i* voted for a pro-Russian party in the 2014 Ukrainian parliamentary election
- *russian_tv$_i$* is the treatment variable, which indicates whether the precinct where respondent *i* lives received Russian TV
- ϵ_i is the error term for respondent *i*.

RECALL: lm() fits a linear model. It requires a formula of the type $Y \sim X$. To specify the object where the dataframe is stored, we can use the optional argument data or the $ character. Examples: lm(y_var ~ x_var, data=data) or lm(data$y_var ~ data$x_var).

To fit the linear model to the data, we use the lm() function:

```
lm(pro_russian_vote ~ russian_tv,
    data=uas) # fits linear model
##
## Call:
## lm(formula = pro_russian_vote ~ russian_tv, data = uas)
##
## Coefficients:
## (Intercept)    russian_tv
##      0.1709        0.1191
```

RECALL: The fitted model uses the estimated coefficients, $\widehat{\alpha}$ and $\widehat{\beta}$, but it does not include ϵ_i (the residuals or error terms). For every value of X, the fitted model provides an average value of Y, that is, the value of $\widehat{Y}$ on the line.

Based on the output, the fitted linear model is:

$$\widehat{pro\_russian\_vote} = 0.17 + 0.12\ russian\_tv$$

In this type of analysis, we typically go straight to the interpretation of $\widehat{\beta}$, since that is the coefficient that helps us estimate the average treatment effect.

RECALL: The estimated slope coefficient, $\widehat{\beta}$, is measured in:
- the same unit of measurement as Y, if Y is non-binary
- percentage points (after multiplying the output by 100), if Y is binary.

Here, since *pro_russian_vote* is binary, $\widehat{\beta}$ is measured in percentage points (after multiplying the output by 100).

How should we interpret $\widehat{\beta}=0.12$? The value of $\widehat{\beta}$ equals the $\triangle\widehat{Y}$ associated with $\triangle X=1$, and because here *russian_tv* (the X variable in the model) is the treatment variable, $\widehat{\beta}$ is also equivalent to the difference-in-means estimator. (Note that the value of $\widehat{\beta}$ is indeed the same value we arrived at above, when we calculated the difference-in-means estimator directly.) As a result, we interpret the value of $\widehat{\beta}$ as estimating that receiving Russian TV (as compared to not receiving it) increased a respondent's probability of voting for a pro-Russian party by 12 percentage points, on average. This causal interpretation would be valid if respondents who received Russian TV were comparable to those who did not. (In the formula in detail below, we show how the fitted line on the scatter plot relates to the substantive interpretation of the two coefficients in this model.)

FORMULA IN DETAIL

As shown in the scatter plot, if X is the treatment variable:

- $\widehat{\alpha} + \widehat{\beta}$, which is the height of the point on the line that corresponds to $X=1$, can be interpreted as the average outcome for the treatment group ($\overline{Y}_{\text{treatment group}}$)

- $\widehat{\alpha}$, which is the height of the point on the line that corresponds to $X=0$, can be interpreted as the average outcome for the control group ($\overline{Y}_{\text{control group}}$)

- $\widehat{\beta}$, which is the difference between these two heights, is then equivalent to the difference-in-means estimator ($\overline{Y}_{\text{treatment group}} - \overline{Y}_{\text{control group}}$).

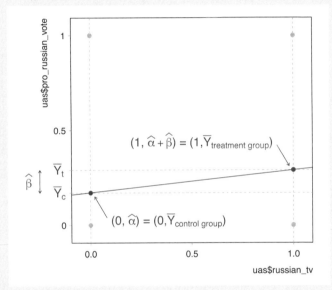

TIP: When X and Y are both binary, the scatter plot will show at most four dots representing all observations in the dataset. These correspond to the only four possible combinations of 0s and 1s: (0,1), (1,1), (1,0), and (0,0). In this case, we will not be able to discern how many observations in the dataset have the same combination of values because the dots that represent them will be displayed on top of each other.

In the running example:

- $\widehat{\alpha} + \widehat{\beta} = 0.29$; indicates that 29 percent of the respondents who lived in a precinct with Russian TV reception (*russian_tv*=1) voted for a pro-Russian party

- $\widehat{\alpha} = 0.17$; indicates that 17 percent of the respondents who lived in a precinct without Russian TV reception (*russian_tv*=0) voted for a pro-Russian party

- $\widehat{\beta} = 0.12$; estimates that receiving Russian TV increased the probability of voting for a pro-Russian party by 12 percentage points, on average (29%−17%=12 p.p.).

RECALL: The predicted outcome, $\widehat{Y}$, and the estimated intercept coefficient, $\widehat{\alpha}$, are measured in:
- the same unit of measurement as Y, if Y is non-binary
- percentages (after multiplying the output by 100), if Y is binary.

Here, since *pro_russian_vote* is binary, both $\widehat{Y}$ and $\widehat{\alpha}$ are measured in percentages (after multiplying the output by 100).

Had the UA_survey dataset come from a randomized experiment, we could interpret the difference-in-means estimator as a valid estimate of the average treatment effect. Here, we are working with observational data, however, and so we need to worry about potential confounders.

5.3.2 CONTROLLING FOR CONFOUNDERS USING A MULTIPLE LINEAR REGRESSION MODEL

When dealing with observational data, our first step should be to identify every potential confounding variable in the relationship between X and Y. In the case at hand, we might worry about whether living *very* close to the Russian border affected both (i) the likelihood of receiving Russian TV and (ii) respondents' attitudes toward pro-Russian parties.

TIP: A confounder can affect the likelihood of receiving the treatment and the outcome in opposite directions. In our example, living very close to the border might increase the chances of receiving Russian TV but decrease the probability of voting for a pro-Russian party.

On the one hand, residents living very close to the border should be more likely to receive Russian TV, given their geographical proximity to Russian TV transmitters ($Z \rightarrow X$). On the other hand, given the military fortifications along the border during this time period, residents living very close to the border were probably less likely to vote for a pro-Russian party ($Z \rightarrow Y$).

In the months leading up to the 2014 election, Ukraine prepared to defend itself from a possible Russian invasion by deploying its army to the border. The Ukrainian army built military fortifications (trenches and defensive walls) at a distance of up to 10 km from the border, depending on local terrain and road access. Within that buffer zone, the army positioned tanks and troops in strategic locations and set up military checkpoints. Residents of a precinct located very close to the border (such as within 25 km of it) were either in immediate proximity of a military fortification or, at the very least, aware of its existence, making them especially cognizant of the threat of a Russian invasion, and therefore, more fearful of Russian influence.

In summary, living very close to the border may affect both the treatment and outcome variables and is, therefore, a potential confounding variable. (See the diagram below, which represents the causal relationships between the three variables of interest.)

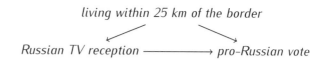

In the UA_survey dataset, the variable *within_25km* identifies whether a respondent lived in a precinct within 25 km of the border, and thus, measures our confounder. We can confirm that the confounding variable, *within_25km*, and the treatment variable, *russian_tv*, are related to each other by computing their correlation coefficient:

```
## compute correlation
cor(uas$within_25km, uas$russian_tv)
## [1] 0.8127747
```

Based on the output above, *within_25km* and *russian_tv* are highly correlated with each other. As we know, this does not necessarily mean that changes in one variable cause changes in the other. The positive correlation, however, does mean that a higher value of *within_25km* is associated with a higher value of *russian_tv*, on average. Since both variables are binary, *russian_tv* is more likely to equal 1 when *within_25km* also equals 1. To confirm this, we can create the two-way table of frequencies by running:

RECALL: table() creates a two-way frequency table when two variables are specified as required arguments. Example: table(*data$variable1, data$variable2*). In the output, the values of the variable specified as the first argument in the function are shown in the rows; the values of the second variable are shown in the columns.

```
## create two-way table of frequencies
table(uas$within_25km, uas$russian_tv)
##      0   1
## 0  139  14
## 1   19 186
```

As shown in the table above, among respondents living within 25 km of the border, about 91% are in a precinct that receives Russian TV ($186 \div (19+186) = 0.91$). In contrast, among respondents living more than 25 km away from the border, about 9% are in a precinct that receives Russian TV ($14 \div (139+14) = 0.09$). Compared to Ukrainians living farther away from the border, then, those living very close to it (i) are more likely to receive Russian TV and (ii) might have many different observed and unobserved characteristics that affect their propensity to vote for a pro-Russian party, including being more aware of the threat of a Russian invasion.

TIP: In this two-way table of frequencies, very few observations are in the off-diagonal (the diagonal running from the upper right to the lower left). There are only 14 respondents living more than 25 km away from the border who receive Russian TV, and there are only 19 respondents living within 25 km of the border who do not receive Russian TV. This suggests that *within_25km* is a strong confounder and that our estimate of the average treatment effect will rest on this small number of observations.

Once we have identified the potential confounders, the next step is to statistically control for them by fitting a multiple linear regression model. In contrast to simple linear regression models, **multiple linear regression models** have more than one X variable ("multi" means more than one). The multiple linear regression model is defined as:

Multiple linear regression models are linear models with more than one X variable.

$$Y_i = \alpha + \beta_1 X_{i1} + \cdots + \beta_p X_{ip} + \epsilon_i$$

where:

- Y_i is the outcome for observation i
- α is the intercept coefficient
- each β_j is the coefficient for variable X_j—we use j as a stand-in for all the different subscripts from 1 to p ($j=1,\ldots,p$)
- each X_{ij} is the observed value of the variable X_j for observation i ($j=1,\ldots,p$)
- p is the total number of X variables in the model
- ϵ_i is the error term for observation i.

Just as the simple linear model, this is a theoretical model that is assumed to reflect the true relationship between all the X variables and Y. Because we do not know the values of any of the coefficients (α, β_1, β_2, ..., β_p) or of the error terms (ϵ_i), we have to estimate them by fitting the model to the data.

In this case, the fitted model can be written as:

$$\widehat{Y}_i = \widehat{\alpha} + \widehat{\beta}_1 X_{i1} + \cdots + \widehat{\beta}_p X_{ip}$$

where:

- $\widehat{Y}_i$ is the predicted value of Y for observation i
- $\widehat{\alpha}$ is the estimated intercept coefficient
- each $\widehat{\beta}_j$ (pronounced beta hat sub j) is the estimated coefficient for variable X_j (j=1, ..., p)
- each X_{ij} is the observed value of the variable X_j for observation i (j=1, ..., p)
- p is the total number of X variables in the model.

Note that the simple regression linear model is a special case of the multiple linear regression model (the case in which p equals 1). When there is only one X variable, the fitted model is a line, and we are back in the simple linear regression model. For any p other than 1, the fitted model is not a line. If p equals 2, for instance, the fitted model is a plane in a three-dimensional space. (See example plane in the margin.)

Table 5.2 provides the mathematical definitions of each of the coefficients in the multiple linear regression model. As we can see there, the definitions of the coefficients in the simple linear regression model can be derived from those in the multiple linear regression model by setting the number of X variables to one.

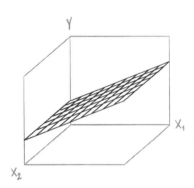

TABLE 5.2. Mathematical definition of coefficients in the multiple and simple linear regression models. (Note: The Latin expression *ceteris paribus* here means holding all other X variables constant.)

In the multiple linear regression model:
- the value of $\widehat{\alpha}$ equals the $\widehat{Y}$ when *all* X variables equal 0
- the value of each $\widehat{\beta}_j$ equals the $\triangle\widehat{Y}$ associated with $\triangle X_j$=1, while holding all other X variables constant.

multiple regression $\widehat{Y} = \widehat{\alpha} + \widehat{\beta}_1 X_1 + \cdots + \widehat{\beta}_p X_p$	simple regression $\widehat{Y} = \widehat{\alpha} + \widehat{\beta}X$
$\widehat{\alpha}$: $\widehat{Y}$ when all X_j=0 (j=1, ..., p)	$\widehat{\alpha}$: $\widehat{Y}$ when X=0
each $\widehat{\beta}_j$: $\triangle\widehat{Y}$ associated with $\triangle X_j$=1, while holding all other X variables constant or *ceteris paribus*	$\widehat{\beta}$: $\triangle\widehat{Y}$ associated with $\triangle X$=1

Let's look at the definition of each coefficient in turn:

- When there are multiple X variables, the value of $\widehat{\alpha}$ equals the predicted value of Y when *all* X variables equal zero. When there is only one X variable, the value of $\widehat{\alpha}$ equals the predicted value of Y when that one X variable equals zero.

- When there are multiple X variables, there will be multiple $\widehat{\beta}$ coefficients (one for each X variable). The value of each $\widehat{\beta}_j$ equals the predicted change in Y associated with a one-unit increase in X_j (the X variable affected by $\widehat{\beta}_j$), *while holding all other X variables constant.* When there is only one X variable, there will be only one $\widehat{\beta}$ coefficient. The value of $\widehat{\beta}$ equals the predicted change in Y associated with a one-unit increase in the one X variable included in the model. (Since there are no other X variables here, there is no need to hold them constant.)

How can the multiple linear regression model help us estimate average causal effects when confounders are present?

Let's assume the first X variable (X_1) is the treatment variable. The value of the corresponding estimated coefficient ($\widehat{\beta}_1$) equals the change in $\widehat{Y}$ *associated with* the presence of the treatment, while holding all the other X variables constant.

Now, if the model includes each potential confounding variable we are worried about as an additional X variable (that is, as a "control variable"), then the value of $\widehat{\beta}_1$ equals the change in $\widehat{Y}$ *caused by* the presence of the treatment, while holding the values of all confounding variables constant. In other words, now we can interpret $\widehat{\beta}_1$ using causal language because statistically controlling for all confounding variables in the estimation process makes the treatment and control groups comparable.

TIP: In this model, only the estimated coefficient that affects the treatment variable, $\widehat{\beta}_1$, can be interpreted using causal language; all others should continue to be interpreted using predictive language.

To better understand this, let's look at the diagram shown in figure 5.4, which represents the causal relationships between a confounding variable, Z, the treatment variable, X, and the outcome variable, Y. Intuitively, by adding Z as a control variable in the model, we statistically hold the values of Z constant, blocking the path shown with a gray dashed line, which links X and Y through Z. With this path blocked, no changes in Y can be attributed to changes in Z. Since the value of Z is being held constant, the only remaining source of change in Y is a change in X.

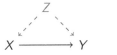

FIGURE 5.4. Representation of the causal relationships between a confounding variable, Z, the treatment variable, X, and the outcome variable, Y. The path blocked by adding Z as a control variable in the model is shown with a gray dashed line.

In other words, the difference in the average outcomes between the treatment and control groups that remains after holding all confounding variables constant can now be directly attributed to their difference with respect to the treatment (treated vs. untreated); no other differences between the two groups are in play.

Post-treatment variables are variables affected by the treatment:

$$X \rightarrow post\text{-}treatment\ variable$$

Example: if the treatment is attending a private school and private schools have smaller classes than public schools, then *small class* is a post-treatment variable because it is affected by the value of *private school*.

$$private\ school \rightarrow small\ class$$

FIGURE 5.5. Representation of the potential causal relationships between a post-treatment variable, *V*, the treatment variable, *X*, and the outcome variable, *Y*. The path blocked by adding *V* as a control variable in the model is shown with a gray dashed line.

Does this mean that we should add to the model as many control variables as possible? No. For example, we should make sure *not* to control for **post-treatment variables**, which are variables affected by the treatment. Adding a post-treatment variable to the model would render our causal estimates invalid because we would be controlling for a consequence of the treatment when trying to estimate its total effect.

To illustrate this, consider the causal diagram in figure 5.5. Suppose that we control for the post-treatment variable *V* when estimating the causal effect of *X* on *Y*. Doing so would block the causal path going from *X* to *Y* through *V*, which is one of the ways by which changes in *X* cause changes in *Y*, and therefore represents a portion of the total causal effect of *X* on *Y*.

In our current analysis, for example, we would not want to add to the model a variable capturing the average number of hours a respondent spent watching Russian TV each week. This is a post-treatment variable since it is causally affected by the treatment; its value directly depends on whether a respondent received Russian TV to begin with. Thus, controlling for this variable would soak up part of the causal effect we are interested in estimating.

> ESTIMATING AVERAGE CAUSAL EFFECTS USING OBSERVATIONAL DATA AND MULTIPLE LINEAR REGRESSION MODELS. If, in the multiple linear regression model where X_1 is the treatment variable, we control for *all* potential confounders by including them in the model as additional X variables, then we can interpret $\widehat{\beta}_1$ as a valid estimate of the average causal effect of X on Y.

Now that we know how to estimate an average treatment effect in the presence of confounders, let's return to our example. Given that our treatment variable is *russian_tv*, our outcome variable is *pro_russian_vote*, and our confounding variable is *within_25km*, the linear model we are interested in is:

$$pro\_russian\_vote_i = \alpha + \beta_1\ russian\_tv_i \\ + \beta_2\ within\_25km_i + \epsilon_i \quad (i=\text{respondents})$$

To fit a multiple linear regression model in R, we also use the lm() function. As you may recall, this function requires a formula of the type $Y \sim X$ when there is only one X variable. It requires a formula of the type $Y \sim X_1 + \cdots + X_p$ when there are multiple X variables. For example, to fit the linear model above, we run:

```
lm(pro_russian_vote ~ russian_tv + within_25km,
         data=uas) # fits linear model
##
## Call:
## lm(formula = pro_russian_vote ~ russian_tv +
##    within_25km, data=uas)
##
## Coefficients:
## (Intercept)    russian_tv    within_25km
##      0.1959        0.2876        -0.2081
```

> lm() fits a linear model. It requires a formula of the type $Y \sim X_1 + \cdots + X_p$. Note that when there is only one X variable, this formula becomes $Y \sim X$. To specify the object where the dataframe is stored, we can use the optional argument data or the $ character. Examples: lm(y_var ~ x_var1 + x_var2, data=data) or lm(data$y_var ~ data$x_var1 + data$x_var2).

Based on the output, the new fitted linear model is:

$$\widehat{pro\_russian\_vote} = 0.2 + 0.29 \ russian\_tv$$
$$-0.21 \ within\_25km$$

How should we interpret $\widehat{\beta_1}=0.29$? The value of $\widehat{\beta_1}$ equals the $\triangle \widehat{Y}$ associated with $\triangle X_1=1$, while holding all other variables constant. In addition, because the variable affecting this coefficient is the treatment variable, *russian_tv*, and the confounder we are worried about, *within_25*, is included in the model as a control variable, we can interpret $\widehat{\beta_1}$ using causal language. Thus, we interpret the value of $\widehat{\beta_1}$ as estimating that, when we hold living very close to the border constant, receiving Russian TV (as compared to not receiving it) increased a respondent's probability of voting for a pro-Russian party by 29 percentage points, on average. The validity of this causal interpretation depends on whether living very close to the border is the only confounding variable. If there are other confounders, this estimate of the average treatment effect would not be valid.

> TIP: The unit of measurement of $\widehat{\beta_1}$ in the multiple linear regression model follows the same rules as the unit of measurement of $\widehat{\beta}$ in the simple linear regression model. Here, since pro_russian_vote is binary, $\widehat{\beta_1}$ is measured in percentage points (after multiplying the output by 100).

5.4 THE EFFECT OF RUSSIAN TV ON UKRAINIAN ELECTORAL OUTCOMES

In the prior section, we found that Russian TV reception was estimated to increase a respondent's probability of voting for a pro-Russian party, suggesting that the propaganda aired by Russian TV in the months leading up to the 2014 Ukrainian parliamentary election may have helped parties with a pro-Russian agenda garner more votes. In this section, we examine whether we can find a similar causal relationship at the aggregate level. This analysis is particularly appropriate since the treatment variable itself (Russian TV reception) is measured at the precinct level.

> RECALL: In an individual-level analysis, the unit of observation is individuals. By contrast, in an aggregate-level analysis, the unit of observation is collections of individuals. For example, here our unit of observation is precincts, and therefore, each observation represents the residents of a particular precinct.

Here, we use aggregate-level data from all the precincts in three provinces in northeastern Ukraine: Chernihiv, Sumy, and Kharkiv. Among the Ukrainian provinces bordering Russia, only these three did not close their polling stations as a result of the ongoing conflict. These are the same provinces where the respondents to the survey analyzed above lived.

The dataset is provided in the file "UA_precincts.csv". Table 5.3 shows the names and descriptions of the variables included.

TABLE 5.3. Description of the variables in the UA_precincts dataset, where the unit of observation is precincts.

variable	description
russian_tv	identifies precincts that receive Russian TV: 1=there is reception or 0=there is no reception
pro_russian	vote share received in the precinct by pro-Russian parties in the 2014 Ukrainian parliamentary election (in percentages)
prior_pro_russian	vote share received in the precinct by pro-Russian parties in the 2012 Ukrainian parliamentary election (in percentages)
within_25km	identifies precincts that are within 25 kilometers of the Russian border: 1=it is within 25 kilometers of the border or 0=it is not within 25 kilometers of the border

RECALL: If the DSS folder is saved directly on your Desktop, to set the working directory, you must run setwd("~/Desktop/DSS") if you have a Mac and setwd("C:/user/Desktop/DSS") if you have a Windows computer (where *user* is your own username). If the DSS folder is saved elsewhere, please see subsection 1.7.1 for instructions on how to set the working directory.

As always, we start by reading and storing the data (assuming we have already set the working directory):

```
uap <- read.csv("UA_precincts.csv") # reads and stores data
```

To get a sense of the dataset, we look at the first few observations:

```
head(uap) # shows first observations
##   russian_tv pro_russian prior_pro_russian within_25km
## 1          0   2.7210884          25.14286           1
## 2          0   0.8928571          35.34483           0
## 3          1   1.6949153          20.53232           1
## 4          0  72.2689076          84.47761           1
## 5          0   1.2820513          28.99408           0
## 6          1   1.4285714          45.58824           0
```

Based on table 5.3 and the output of above, we learn that each observation in the dataset represents a precinct, and that the dataset contains four variables:

- *russian_tv* is a binary variable that identifies whether the precinct received Russian TV

- *pro_russian* and *prior_pro_russian* are the vote shares received by pro-Russian parties in the precinct in the parliamentary

elections of 2014 and 2012, respectively (both variables are measured in percentages)
- *within_25km* is a binary variable that identifies whether the precinct is within 25 km of the border.

We interpret the first observation as representing a precinct in Ukraine that does not receive Russian TV, where pro-Russian parties received about 3% and 25% of the votes in the parliamentary elections of 2014 and 2012, and that is within 25 km of the border with Russia.

To find the total number of observations in the dataset, we run:

```
dim(uap) # provides dimensions of dataframe: rows, columns
## [1] 3589    4
```

The dataset contains information about 3,589 precincts.

5.4.1 USING THE SIMPLE LINEAR MODEL TO COMPUTE THE DIFFERENCE-IN-MEANS ESTIMATOR

In this analysis, we are interested in estimating the effect that the intense, one-sided Russian TV coverage of Ukrainian politics had on the electoral performance of pro-Russian parties in the 2014 Ukrainian parliamentary election at the precinct level. Since the treatment took place between the 2012 and 2014 elections, we define our outcome variable as the change in the vote share received by pro-Russian parties between these two elections.

The causal link we are interested in is, then, between *russian_tv* and *pro_russian_change*, where *russian_tv* is the treatment variable and *pro_russian_change* is the outcome variable.

Russian TV reception $\rightarrow$ pro-Russian vote share change

Since we do not have our outcome variable of interest readily available in the dataset, we start the analysis by creating it. The change in the precinct-level vote share received by pro-Russian parties between 2012 and 2014 is defined as:

$$pro\_russian\_change = pro\_russian - prior\_pro\_russian$$

To create this variable, we run:

```
## create pro-russian change variable
uap$pro_russian_change <-
        uap$pro_russian - uap$prior_pro_russian
```

The new variable, *pro_russian_change*, is measured in percentage points because it is the difference between two percentages. For example, it equals -20 p.p. when a precinct's pro-Russian vote share dropped to 40% from 60% (40%−60%=-20 p.p.).

To get a sense of the contents of *pro_russian_change*, we can create its histogram by running:

```
## create histogram
hist(uap$pro_russian_change)
```

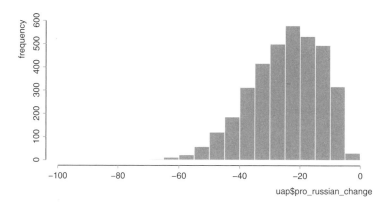

Note that all the values of *pro_russian_change* are negative, which means that in all the precincts under study, the vote share received by pro-Russian parties decreased between these two elections. As a result of the conflict leading up to the 2014 election, pro-Russian political parties lost support across the country, even in their traditional strongholds in eastern and southern Ukraine. Our question is, then, whether Russian TV reception caused the precinct-level vote share for pro-Russian parties to decline by a smaller amount.

To calculate the difference-in-means estimator, we can fit a simple linear model without any controls, just as we did in the previous section. The linear model we are interested in here is:

$$pro\_russian\_change_i = \alpha + \beta \ russian\_tv_i + \epsilon_i \quad (i=\text{precincts})$$

where:

- *pro_russian_change$_i$* is the percentage-point change in the vote share received by pro-Russian parties in precinct i between the 2012 and 2014 Ukrainian parliamentary elections
- *russian_tv$_i$* is the treatment variable, which indicates whether precinct i received Russian TV
- ϵ_i is the error term for precinct i.

To fit the linear model, we run:

```
lm(pro_russian_change ~ russian_tv,
      data=uap) # fits linear model
##
## Call:
## lm(formula = pro_russian_change ~ russian_tv, data=uap)
##
## Coefficients:
## (Intercept)        russian_tv
##    -25.146           1.783
```

Based on the output, the fitted linear model is:

$$\widehat{pro\_russian\_change} = -25.15 + 1.78 \ russian\_tv$$

How should we interpret $\widehat{\beta}$=1.78? The value of $\widehat{\beta}$ equals the $\triangle \widehat{Y}$ associated with $\triangle X$=1, and because *russian_tv* (the X variable in the model) is the treatment variable, $\widehat{\beta}$ is also equivalent to the difference-in-means estimator. As a result, we interpret the value of $\widehat{\beta}$ as estimating that receiving Russian TV (as compared to not receiving it) increased the change in the precinct-level vote share received by pro-Russian parties by 1.78 percentage points, on average. Note that the positive sign of $\widehat{\beta}$ is consistent with our expectation regarding the effect of Russian TV propaganda. It indicates that pro-Russian parties experienced smaller vote share losses in precincts with Russian TV reception. The validity of this causal effect estimate depends on whether the precincts that received Russian TV were comparable to the precincts that did not; that is, it depends on the absence of confounding variables.

RECALL: The estimated slope coefficient, $\widehat{\beta}$, is measured in:
- the same unit of measurement as Y, if Y is non-binary
- percentage points (after multiplying the output by 100), if Y is binary.

Here, since *pro_russian_change* is non-binary and measured in percentage points, $\widehat{\beta}$ is also measured in percentage points.

5.4.2 CONTROLLING FOR CONFOUNDERS USING A MULTIPLE LINEAR REGRESSION MODEL

A confounding variable we might worry about, again, is close proximity to the border. On the one hand, precincts very close to the border should be more likely to receive Russian TV ($Z \rightarrow X$). On the other hand, given the military deployments along the border, we might expect that pro-Russian parties experienced larger vote share losses in precincts very close to the border ($Z \rightarrow Y$).

Given that close proximity to the border (defined here as being within 25 km) affects both (i) the likelihood of receiving the treatment and (ii) the outcome, it constitutes a confounder.

located within 25 km of the border

Russian TV reception ⟶ *pro-Russian vote share change*

In the UA_precincts dataset, the variable *within_25km* captures whether a precinct is within 25 km of the border, and thus, measures our confounder. We can confirm that the confounding variable, *within_25km*, and the treatment variable, *russian_tv*, are related to each other by computing their correlation coefficient:

```
## compute correlation
cor(uap$within_25km, uap$russian_tv)
## [1] 0.5317845
```

Based on the output above, *within_25km* and *russian_tv* are moderately correlated with each other.

Now that we have identified the confounding variable, we are ready to fit a multiple linear regression model to estimate the average treatment effect. Here, since the treatment variable is *russian_tv* and the potential confounding variable is *within_25km*, the linear model we are interested in is:

$$pro\_russian\_change_i = \alpha + \beta_1\ russian\_tv_i$$
$$+\ \beta_2\ within\_25km_i + \epsilon_i \quad (i\text{=precincts})$$

To fit the multiple linear regression model above, we run:

```
lm(pro_russian_change ~ russian_tv + within_25km,
        data=uap) # fits linear model
##
## Call:
## lm(formula = pro_russian_change ~ russian_tv +
##    within_25km, data=uap)
##
## Coefficients:
##     (Intercept)      russian_tv      within_25km
##        -24.302           8.822          -14.614
```

Based on the output, the new fitted linear regression model is:

$$\widehat{pro\_russian\_change} = \text{-24.3} + 8.82\ russian\_tv$$
$$\text{-14.61}\ within\_25km$$

How should we interpret $\widehat{\beta_1}$=8.82? The value of $\widehat{\beta_1}$ equals the $\triangle\widehat{Y}$ associated with $\triangle X_1$=1, while holding all other variables constant. In addition, because the variable affecting this coefficient is the treatment variable, *russian_tv*, and the confounder we are worried about, *within_25*, is included in the model as a control variable, we can interpret $\widehat{\beta_1}$ using causal language. Thus, we interpret the value of $\widehat{\beta_1}$ as estimating that, when we hold close proximity to the border constant, receiving Russian TV (as compared to not receiving it) increased the change in the precinct-level vote share received by pro-Russian parties by 8.82 percentage points, on average. If the close proximity of the precincts to the border successfully captures the only confounding variable in the relationship between our two main variables of interest, then this is a valid estimate of the average treatment effect.

5.5 INTERNAL AND EXTERNAL VALIDITY

We have already learned how to estimate the average change in the outcome caused by the treatment. (In chapter 2, we saw how to estimate the average treatment effect using data from a randomized experiment, and in this chapter, we have seen how to estimate it using observational data.) There are more issues we must consider when conducting or evaluating a scientific causal study, including the following two properties: (i) internal validity and (ii) external validity.

The **internal validity** of a study refers to the extent to which the causal assumptions are satisfied. In other words, it reflects the confidence we have in our causal estimates. It asks, is the estimated causal effect valid for the sample of observations in the study? The answer depends on whether we have successfully eliminated or controlled for all potential confounders, that is, on whether the treatment and control groups used for the estimation can be considered comparable, after statistical controls are applied (if any are).

The **external validity** of a study refers to the extent to which the conclusions can be generalized. It asks, is the estimated causal effect valid beyond this particular study? The answer depends on (i) whether the sample of observations in the study is representative of the population to which we want to generalize the results, and (ii) whether the treatment used in the study is representative of the treatment for which we want to generalize the results.

The **internal validity** of a study refers to the extent to which its causal conclusions are valid for the sample of observations in the study. The **external validity** of a study refers to the extent to which its causal conclusions can be generalized.

RECALL: In a representative sample, characteristics appear at similar rates as in the population as a whole.

5.5.1 RANDOMIZED EXPERIMENTS VS. OBSERVATIONAL STUDIES

How do studies based on experimental data compare to those based on observational data along these two dimensions?

When it comes to internal validity, randomized experiments have a significant advantage over observational studies. In experiments, the use of random treatment assignment eliminates all potential confounding variables. By contrast, in observational studies, while we can statistically control for observed confounders, there is always the possibility that we fail to account for unobserved confounders.

When it comes to external validity, randomized experiments can suffer from limitations that put them at a disadvantage compared to observational studies. First, for ethical and logistical reasons, randomized experiments are often done using a convenient sample of subjects who are willing to participate in the study. (For example, you have probably seen ads recruiting subjects for experiments in exchange for money.) In some cases, then, volunteers come from a particular segment of the population; they may be low-income and/or underemployed. In such cases, the sample of individuals would likely be non-representative of the whole population of interest. By contrast, in observational studies, we can usually analyze data from either the entire population or a random selection of observations from that population.

Second, randomized experiments are often conducted in artificial environments such as laboratories, making the treatments less realistic, and therefore, less comparable to real-world treatments. For example, it is not the same to watch a TV program in a laboratory as in the comfort of your own home, where many other things compete for your attention (phone calls, visits to the fridge, and TV programs on other channels). By contrast, in observational studies, we usually observe the treatment in the environment in which we are interested.

In summary, an advantage in internal validity often comes with a compromise in external validity, and vice versa. Studies based on randomized experiments tend to have strong internal validity but relatively weak external validity. Observational studies tend to have relatively weak internal validity but strong external validity. This dynamic explains why scholars use both types of studies to estimate causal effects; they often have complementary strengths. Nonetheless, some studies based on experimental data have strong external validity, and some studies based on observational data have strong internal validity. We should pay attention to the study details when evaluating them.

5.5.2 THE ROLE OF RANDOMIZATION

The ideal research design for estimating average treatment effects would make use of the two kinds of randomization we have seen. It would not only randomly select its observations from the population, but it would also randomly assign treatment among those observations. (See figure 5.6 on the next page.)

Assuming that we were also able to make the treatment as realistic as possible, this design would create a study with strong external and internal validity. As discussed, random sampling is the best way to make the sample representative of the population and, thereby, ensure strong external validity (enabling us to generalize the results to the target population). Similarly, random treatment assignment is the best way to make treatment and control groups comparable and, thereby, ensure strong internal validity (enabling us to draw valid causal inferences).

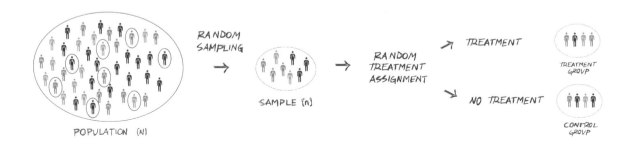

As discussed in chapter 2 and above, for ethical, logistical, and financial reasons, few studies include both types of randomization. It is useful, however, to know what the ideal research design would look like; it serves as a benchmark when designing or evaluating causal studies.

FIGURE 5.6. The ideal research design would make use of the two kinds of randomization we have seen: random sampling and random treatment assignment.

5.5.3 HOW GOOD ARE THE TWO CAUSAL ANALYSES IN THIS CHAPTER?

Let's evaluate the internal and external validity of the two data analyses in this chapter: (i) the individual-level analysis and (ii) the precinct-level analysis.

How strong is their internal validity? In both analyses, receipt of the treatment (Russian TV reception) was determined by factors outside of the control of the researchers, such as the terrain and distance of the precincts to the Russian TV transmitters. Neither study is, therefore, a randomized experiment. Despite the fact that we cannot rely on the randomization of treatment assignment to eliminate all potential confounders, we can argue that both analyses have relatively strong internal validity.

First, once we focus on areas close to the Ukraine-Russia border (as we do in both cases), the variation in the reception of Russian TV plausibly yields an "as-if-random" assignment of the treatment; it is influenced by terrain and other factors that are likely to be unrelated to the level of support for pro-Russian parties. Second, we arguably remove any remaining differences between the treatment and control groups by statistically controlling for potential confounders. In both instances, we control for being very close to the border. If this is the only confounding variable present, then the internal validity of the analyses is strong.

How strong is their external validity? In the individual-level analysis, we use data from a random sample of individuals living in the precincts in which we are interested. In the aggregate-level analysis, we use data from all the Ukrainian precincts in which we are interested. In addition, in both studies we observe the treatment (that is, Russian TV reception) in its real-world environment. As a result, if we were interested in generalizing our results to the region from which our observations come, then, the external validity of both studies is strong. If we were interested in generalizing the conclusions to a different type of one-sided televised coverage of a political event in a different region of the world, we would have to assess to what degree the treatment and the observations in the analyses here are representative of the actual treatment and population of interest.

5.5.4 HOW GOOD WAS THE CAUSAL ANALYSIS IN CHAPTER 2?

As you may recall, in chapter 2 we analyzed the STAR dataset to estimate the effects of attending a small class on student performance. The data came from a randomized experiment conducted in Tennessee, where students were randomly assigned to attend either a small class or a regular-size class.

How strong is its internal validity? Since the treatment was assigned at random, all potential confounding variables should have been eliminated, making the group of students who attended a small class similar in all aspects to the group of students who attended a regular-size class. Thanks to random treatment assignment, then, the causal assumption is satisfied, and we can be confident that the causal estimates we arrived at are valid for the group of students who participated in the experiment. We can conclude that this analysis has strong internal validity.

See Diane Whitmore Schanzenbach, "What Have Researchers Learned from Project STAR?" *Brookings Papers on Education Policy*, no. 9 (2006): 205–28.

How strong is its external validity? Given the characteristics of the study, only students from large schools in Tennessee were able to participate in the experiment. As a result, the sample of participating students was not perfectly representative of all students in Tennessee. The sample was also not representative of students in the United States. For example, according to Schanzenbach (2006), the proportion of African Americans was larger in the sample than in the state overall, and the proportion of Hispanics and Asians was smaller in the sample than in the country as a whole. Consequently, we can conclude that, although we do get to observe the treatment of interest in the real world, the analysis has relatively weak external validity, especially if one wishes to generalize the study's conclusions to all schools and students in Tennessee or in the entire United States.

5.5.5 THE COEFFICIENT OF DETERMINATION, R^2

Note that at no point during our evaluation of the causal analyses did we mention any of the models' coefficient of determination, or R^2. This statistic is of no direct relevance when estimating average treatment effects. A model with a small R^2 might do a fine job estimating a valid causal effect, especially when the effect is small and there are few (or no) confounders we need to control for statistically. Alternatively, a model with a large R^2 might estimate an invalid causal effect, especially if the confounders we control for explain a large variation of the outcome variable, yet controlling for them fails to make treatment and control groups comparable.

RECALL: R^2, also known as the coefficient of determination, ranges from 0 to 1 and measures the proportion of the variation of the outcome variable explained by the model. The higher the R^2, the better the model fits the data.

5.6 SUMMARY

In this chapter, we returned to estimating causal effects but, this time, using observational data. We learned about confounding variables and why their presence complicates the estimation of causal effects. We saw how to fit a simple linear model to compute the difference-in-means estimator and how to fit a multiple linear model to control for confounders. Finally, we discussed how to evaluate causal studies based on their internal and external validity.

The statistical method used in this chapter, fitting a linear regression model, is the same as the one we used in the previous chapter. (Although we did not see an example of it, social scientists often use multiple linear regression models to make predictions, and not just simple linear regression models.) The goals of the analyses, however, differ. In chapter 4, we aimed to *predict* a quantity of interest, while in this chapter we aimed to *explain* a quantity of interest (that is, to estimate a causal effect).

Even though the mathematical models are the same, the role the X variable plays in the research question, the substantive interpretations of the estimated coefficients, and what we pay attention to in the analysis depend on whether we are analyzing data to make predictions or to estimate causal effects.

For example, when fitting a simple linear regression model to make predictions:

- X is a predictor.
- We interpret $\widehat{\beta}$ as the change in $\widehat{Y}$ *associated* with a one-unit increase in X.
- Since the goal is to make predictions with the smallest possible errors, we seek predictors that are highly correlated with the outcome variable of interest. The stronger the linear association between X and Y, the higher the R^2 and the better the fitted linear model will usually be at predicting Y using X.

By contrast, when fitting a simple linear regression model to estimate causal effects:

- X is the treatment variable.
- We interpret $\widehat{\beta}$ as the change in $\widehat{Y}$ *caused by* the presence of the treatment X.
- Since the goal is to arrive at valid estimates of causal effects, we seek to find or create situations in which the treatment and control groups used in the analysis can be considered comparable, after statistical controls are applied (if any are). In other words, we seek to eliminate or control for all potential confounding variables.

Thus, whenever we conduct a regression analysis or evaluate one conducted by someone else, we should keep the goal in mind.

5.7 CHEATSHEETS

5.7.1 CONCEPTS AND NOTATION

concept/notation	description	example(s)
confounding variable or confounder (Z)	also known as an omitted variable or a control variable; variable that affects both (i) the likelihood of receiving the treatment X and (ii) the outcome Y 	*family wealth* is a confounder in the causal relationship between attending a *private school* and *test scores* 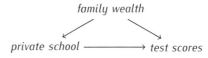
	confounders obscure the causal relationship between X and Y; just because we observe that two variables are highly correlated with each other does not automatically mean that one causes the other; there could be a third variable—a confounder—that affects both variables	students from wealthy families are more likely to attend a private school (*family wealth → private school*); students from wealthy families are more likely to receive after-school help such as one-on-one tutoring, which, in turn, will improve performance on tests (*family wealth → tutoring → test scores*)
	in the presence of confounding variables, correlation does not necessarily imply causation, and the difference-in-means estimator does *not* provide a valid estimate of the average treatment effect in randomized experiments, the randomization of treatment assignment eliminates all potential confounding variables	in the presence of the confounder, *family wealth*, we do not know what portion (if any) of the observed difference in average test performance between private and public school students is due to the schools the students attend and what portion is due to their differing levels of family wealth
fitted simple linear regression model where X is the treatment variable	if, in the fitted simple linear regression model, X is the treatment variable, $\widehat{\beta}$ is equivalent to the difference-in-means estimator, and thus, we interpret it using causal, not predictive, language this causal interpretation is valid if there are no confounding variables present	if X is the treatment variable and the fitted model is $\widehat{Y} = 2 - 3X$: we interpret $\widehat{\beta}$ as estimating that receiving the treatment decreases the outcome by 3 units, on average (in the same unit of measurement as the difference-in-means estimator)
multiple linear regression model	linear model with more than one X variable; theoretical model that we assume reflects the true relationship between Y and multiple X variables $$Y_i = \alpha + \beta_1 X_{i1} + \cdots + \beta_p X_{ip} + \epsilon_i$$ where: - Y_i is the outcome for observation i - α is the intercept coefficient - each β_j is the coefficient for variable X_j $(j=1,\ldots,p)$ - each X_{ij} is the observed value of the variable X_j for observation i $(j=1,\ldots,p)$ - p is the total number of X variables - ϵ_i is the error term for observation i	$$Y_i = 1 + 3X_{i1} + 5X_{i2} + \epsilon_i$$

continues on next page...

5.7.1 CONCEPTS AND NOTATION (CONTINUED)

concept/notation	description	example(s)
fitted multiple linear regression model	linear model fitted to the data to describe the relationship between Y and multiple X variables $$\widehat{Y}_i = \widehat{\alpha} + \widehat{\beta}_1 X_{i1} + \cdots + \widehat{\beta}_p X_{ip}$$ where: - $\widehat{Y}_i$ is the predicted outcome for observation i - $\widehat{\alpha}$ is the estimated intercept coefficient - each $\widehat{\beta}_j$ is the estimated coefficient for variable X_j ($j=1,\ldots,p$) - each X_{ij} is the observed value of the variable X_j for observation i ($j=1,\ldots,p$) interpretation of $\widehat{\alpha}$: the $\widehat{Y}$ when all X variables equal 0 interpretation of each $\widehat{\beta}_j$: the $\triangle \widehat{Y}$ associated with $\triangle X_j=1$, while holding all other X variables constant	$$\widehat{Y}_i = 1 + 3X_{i1} - 5X_{i2}$$ in this fitted multiple linear regression model: $\widehat{\alpha}=1$; when both X_1 and X_2 equal 0, we predict that Y will equal 1 unit, on average $\widehat{\beta}_1=3$; when X_1 increases by 1 and X_2 remains constant, we predict an associated increase in Y of 3 units, on average $\widehat{\beta}_2=-5$; when X_2 increases by 1 and X_1 remains constant, we predict an associated decrease in Y of 5 units, on average
fitted multiple linear regression model where X_1 is the treatment variable	if, in the fitted multiple linear regression model where X_1 is the treatment variable, we control for *all* potential confounders by including them in the model as additional X variables (that is, as control variables), then we can interpret $\widehat{\beta}_1$ as a valid estimate of the average causal effect of X on Y	if X_1 is the treatment variable, X_2 is the only potential confounder, and the fitted model is $\widehat{Y} = 1 + 3X_1 + 5X_2$: we interpret $\widehat{\beta}_1$ as estimating that, while holding X_2 constant, receiving the treatment increases the outcome by 3 units, on average (in the same unit of measurement as the difference-in-means estimator)
post-treatment variables	variables affected by the treatment: $$X \rightarrow \textit{post-treatment variable}$$ post-treatment variables should not be added as control variables; adding a post-treatment variable to the regression model would render our causal estimates invalid because we would be controlling for a consequence of the treatment when trying to estimate its total effect	if the treatment is attending a private school and private schools have smaller classes than public schools, then *small class* is a post-treatment variable because it is affected by the value of *private school* $$\textit{private school} \rightarrow \textit{small class}$$ when estimating the causal effect of attending a *private school*, we should not control for class size
internal validity	refers to the extent to which the causal conclusions of a study are valid for the sample of observations in the study; it depends on whether the treatment and control groups used for the estimation can be considered comparable, after statistical controls are applied (if any are)	randomized experiments have strong internal validity because the randomization of the treatment assignment eliminates all potential confounders; observational studies may also have strong internal validity if the analysis controls for all potential confounders
external validity	refers to the extent to which the causal conclusions of a study can be generalized; it depends on (i) whether the sample of observations is representative of the population to which we want to generalize the results, and (ii) whether the treatment used in the study is representative of the treatment for which we want to generalize the results	observational studies typically have strong external validity because they often analyze the entire target population and observe the treatment in the environment in which we are interested; randomized experiments may also have strong external validity if they manage to use a representative sample of subjects and make the treatment comparable to the real-world one

5.7.2 R FUNCTIONS

function	description	required argument(s)	example(s)
lm()	fits a linear model	when there is only one X variable: $Y \sim X$; when there are multiple X variables: $Y \sim X_1 + \cdots + X_p$ optional argument data: specifies the object where the dataframe is stored; alternative to using $ for each variable	## both of these pieces of code fit the same simple linear regression model: lm($data\$y\_var \sim data\$x\_var$) lm($y\_var \sim x\_var$, data=$data$) ## both of these pieces of code fit the same multiple linear regression model: lm($data\$y\_var \sim data\$x\_var1 + data\$x\_var2$) lm($y\_var \sim x\_var1 + x\_var2$, data=$data$)

6. PROBABILITY

R symbols, operators, and functions introduced in this chapter: c(), sample(), rnorm(), pnorm(), for(i in 1:n){}, and print().

In the last four chapters, we have analyzed data for the purpose of (i) estimating causal effects with both randomized experiments and observational data, (ii) inferring population characteristics via survey research, and (iii) making predictions. Thus far, we have focused our attention on identifying systematic relationships and ignored the noise in the data. Real-world data, however, contain a nontrivial amount of noise, or irrelevant variation, which adds uncertainty to our conclusions. In the next chapter, we will learn how to quantify the degree of statistical uncertainty in our empirical findings. First, though, we need to learn about probability and how we can use it to model variation.

6.1 WHAT IS PROBABILITY?

There are two different ways of interpreting probability: frequentist and Bayesian.

According to the **frequentist** interpretation, probabilities represent proportions of specific events occurring over a large number of identical trials. Specifically, the probability of an event is the proportion of its occurrence among infinitely many identical trials.

According to the **frequentist** interpretation, probabilities represent proportions of specific events occurring over infinitely many identical trials.

RECALL: We define the proportion of observations that meet a criterion as:

$$\frac{\text{number of observations}}{\text{total number of observations}}$$
$$\text{that meet criterion}$$

To interpret a proportion as a percentage, we multiply the decimal value by 100.

Think of a coin flip, for example. What is the probability of getting heads when flipping a coin? Imagine flipping the coin a large number of times. The probability of getting a head can be approximated by the number of heads realized over the number of coin flips. If the coin is fair, as we increase the number of flips, the proportion of heads should approach 0.5, meaning that about 50% of the coin flips should result in heads.

According to the **Bayesian** interpretation, probabilities represent personal, subjective beliefs about the relative likelihood of events.

In contrast, according to the **Bayesian** interpretation, probabilities represent one's subjective beliefs about the relative likelihood of events. For example, when we state that the probability of rain today is about 80%, we are not describing the frequency of rain events over multiple days. We are simply describing how certain we are about the event occurring. A probability of 1, or 100%, indicates certainty that the event will occur. A probability of 0, or 0%, indicates certainty that the event will not occur.

Critics of the frequentist interpretation argue that it is impossible to conduct an infinite number of identical trials. (For example, when flipping a coin, it would be difficult to maintain the same launch angle and speed.) Critics of the Bayesian interpretation argue that personal, subjective beliefs should not play a role when analyzing data. Fortunately, despite their differences, the two interpretations rely on the same mathematical rules. For the rest of the chapter, we focus on these common rules.

6.2 AXIOMS OF PROBABILITY

Probability axioms are the basic rules upon which the entire probability theory rests. Before we learn about the axioms of probability, we need to define some concepts:

- A **trial** is an action or set of actions that produces outcomes of interest. For example, rolling a die can be considered a trial.

- An **outcome** is the result of a trial. Rolling a die produces one of six possible outcomes: 1, 2, 3, 4, 5, or 6.

- An **event** is a set of outcomes. In the example at hand, one possible event is *rolling a number less than 3*, which includes two possible outcomes, 1 and 2. Note that events may include any number of outcomes. For example, another possible event is *rolling a 3*, which includes only one outcome, 3.

- **Mutually exclusive events** are events that do not share any outcomes. The two events defined above, *rolling a number less than 3* and *rolling a 3*, for example, are mutually exclusive events since they have no outcomes in common.

- The **sample space**, denoted as Ω (the Greek letter Omega), is the set of all possible outcomes produced by a trial. Since it is a set of outcomes, the sample space is also considered an event. In the case of rolling a die, $\Omega = \{1, 2, 3, 4, 5, 6\}$.

- An **event** is said to **occur** if any one of the possible outcomes included in the event is realized. For example, if we roll a 1, we would consider that the event *rolling a number less than 3* has occurred and so has the event defined by the sample space.

A **trial** is an action or set of actions that produces outcomes of interest. An **outcome** is the result of a trial. An **event** is a set of outcomes. **Mutually exclusive events** are events that do not share any outcomes. The **sample space** is the set of all possible outcomes produced by a trial. An **event** is said to **occur** if any one of the possible outcomes included in the event is realized.

There are three axioms of probability. Remarkably, we can derive the entire probability theory from these three basic rules.

1. The first axiom states that the probability of any event A is non-negative. In mathematical notation, we can write this axiom as:

$$P(A) \geq 0$$

where P stands for "the probability of" and A represents the event.

This means that probabilities can be either zero or positive. For example, the probability of *rolling a 3* cannot be negative.

2. The second axiom states that the probability of the sample space is always 1. In mathematical notation:

$$P(\Omega) = 1$$

where Ω represents the sample space, that is, the set of all possible outcomes produced by a trial.

For example, when rolling a die, the sample space, Ω, is $\{1, 2, 3, 4, 5, 6\}$. Recall that an event is said to occur if any one of the possible outcomes included in the event occurs. In this case, $P(\Omega)$ represents the probability that any one of the six possible outcomes occurs. In mathematical notation:

$$P(\Omega) = (1 \text{ or } 2 \text{ or } 3 \text{ or } 4 \text{ or } 5 \text{ or } 6) = 1$$

3. The third axiom states that, if events A and B are mutually exclusive (that is, they cannot occur at the same time), then the probability that either A or B occurs equals the probability that A occurs plus the probability that B occurs. In mathematical notation:

$$P(A \text{ or } B) = P(A) + P(B)$$

if A and B are mutually exclusive events

For example, the probability of either *rolling a number less than 3* or *rolling a 3* equals the probability of *rolling a number less than 3* plus the probability of *rolling a 3*, since the two events are mutually exclusive.

These axioms together imply that probabilities range from 0 to 1 and that the probabilities of all possible outcomes produced by a trial must add up to 1.

Consider flipping a coin once. This trial can result in two possible outcomes: *getting a head* or *getting a tail*. The sample space in this case is, then: $\Omega = \{head, tail\}$.

The probability of *getting a head* and the probability of *getting a tail* must both be between 0 and 1, and together they must add up to 1 since they constitute the sample space (that is, no other outcome is possible).

Let's see how we arrive at this conclusion using mathematical notation. We can start with axiom 2:

$$P(head \text{ or } tail) = 1$$

Since *getting a head* and *getting a tail* are two mutually exclusive events, according to axiom 3:

$$P(head \text{ or } tail) = P(head) + P(tail) = 1$$

Therefore, the probabilities of the two possible outcomes produced by flipping a coin must add up to 1.

6.3 EVENTS, RANDOM VARIABLES, AND PROBABILITY DISTRIBUTIONS

We can categorize most things that occur in our lives as **events**. The fact that you are reading this book is an event, and so is your height, the color of your eyes, your political party preference, and your choice to attend or not to attend college.

As soon as we assign a number to an event, we create what is known as a **random variable**. A random variable assigns a numeric value to each mutually exclusive event produced by a trial. In fact, we have been dealing with random variables throughout this book. We have just been calling them variables.

For example, if we assign a 1 to the event of attending college and a 0 to the event of not attending college, then the binary random variable *college*, as defined below, would capture these events.

An **event** is a set of outcomes that occur with a particular probability. A **random variable** assigns a numeric value to each mutually exclusive event produced by a trial. The **probability distribution** of a random variable characterizes the likelihood of each possible value the random variable can take.

POSSIBLE EVENTS PRODUCED BY A TRIAL	RANDOM VARIABLE *college*	PROBABILITY DISTRIBUTION OF *college*
- attending college - not attending college	- $college_i = 1$ if individual i attends college - $college_i = 0$ if individual i does not attend college	- $P(college=1)$ - $P(college=0)$

Each random variable has a **probability distribution**, which characterizes the likelihood of each value the variable can take. By definition, all probabilities in a distribution must add up to 1.

In mathematical notation, we can write the probability that the random variable X takes the value x as:

$$P(X=x) = p$$

where:

- X is the random variable
- x is the fixed value the random variable X may take
- p is the probability that X takes the value x.

For example, the distribution of the random variable *college* above represents the probability of attending college, $P(college=1)$, and the probability of not attending college, $P(college=0)$, since those are the only two possible values the variable can take.

6.4 PROBABILITY DISTRIBUTIONS

In this book, we focus on two types of probability distributions: (i) the Bernoulli distribution, which is the probability distribution of a binary variable; and (ii) the normal distribution, which is the probability distribution we commonly use as a good approximation for many non-binary variables. Within the normal distribution, we will pay special attention to the standard normal distribution.

As we saw in chapter 3, functions such as mean, median, standard deviation, and variance can be used to summarize numerically the main traits of the probability distribution of a random variable. In this section, we focus on (i) the center of the distributions as measured by the mean, and (ii) the spread of the distributions as measured by the variance (which, as you may recall, is equivalent to the standard deviation squared).

6.4.1 THE BERNOULLI DISTRIBUTION

The **Bernoulli distribution** is the probability distribution of a binary variable. Since binary variables can take only two values (1 or 0), the Bernoulli distribution characterizes two probabilities: the probability that the variable equals 1 and the probability that the variable equals 0.

The **Bernoulli distribution** is the probability distribution of a binary variable. It is characterized by one parameter, p, which is the probability that the binary random variable takes the value of 1. Consequently, $1-p$ is the probability that the binary random variable takes the value of 0. The mean of a Bernoulli distribution is p and the variance is $p(1-p)$.

By definition, the sum of all probabilities in a Bernoulli distribution must equal 1. If we use p to denote the probability that the binary variable equals 1, the probability that the binary variable equals 0 is $1-p$ (notice that $p+(1-p)=1$).

Consider again the flip of a coin. The action of flipping a coin can result in only one of two possible events: heads or tails. If we assign 1 to heads and 0 to tails, we can create a binary random variable with the results. The distribution of this random variable—a Bernoulli distribution—represents the probability that we get heads as well as the probability that we get tails. The definition of this binary random variable and its distribution are:

$$flip_i = \begin{cases} 1 \text{ if coin flip } i \text{ lands on heads;} & P(flip=1) = p \\ 0 \text{ if coin flip } i \text{ lands on tails;} & P(flip=0) = 1-p \end{cases}$$

The mean of a Bernoulli distribution is equal to p, that is, the probability that the binary variable equals 1, and the variance of a Bernoulli distribution is equal to $p(1-p)$. (We will see examples shortly.)

RECALL: As we saw in chapter 1, the mean of a binary variable is equivalent to the proportion of the observations that have the characteristic identified by the variable. In other words, the mean of a binary variable is the probability that the variable equals 1, denoted as p.

To approximate the value of p, we could flip the coin many times and calculate the proportion of heads among the multiple flips. For illustration purposes, see the example below, where we hypothetically flip a coin 12 times and calculate the corresponding proportions.

REALIZED EVENTS	REALIZED VALUES OF A RANDOM VARIABLE	APPROXIMATE PROBABILITY DISTRIBUTION

$$flip = \{1, 0, 1, 0,$$
$$1, 1, 1, 1,$$
$$1, 0, 1, 0\}$$

$$P(flip=1) \approx \frac{\text{number of heads}}{\text{number of flips}}$$
$$\approx 8/12 = 0.67$$

$$P(flip=0) \approx \frac{\text{number of tails}}{\text{number of flips}}$$
$$\approx 4/12 = 0.33$$

In the example above, the proportion of heads is 67%, and the proportion of tails 33%. These proportions are far from 50% because we flipped the coin only 12 times. As we increase the number of flips, if the coin is fair, the proportion of heads, p, and the proportion of tails, $1-p$, should approach 50%.

TIP: In mathematical notation, the symbol $\approx$ stands for "approximately equal to."

To get a better sense of this, we can use R to simulate flipping a fair coin 1 million times and then calculate the proportions of heads and tails. We start by listing the two possible values that might result from each coin flip using the function c(), which stands for "combine values into a vector." The following code creates an object named *possible_values* with a vector containing a 1 and a 0, where 1 stands for heads and 0 for tails:

c() combines values into a vector (a collection of elements, each identified by an index). The values to be combined should be specified inside the parentheses and separated by commas. Example: c(1, 2, 3).

```
## create a vector with possible values
possible_values <- c(1, 0) # 1 for heads, 0 for tails
```

TIP: The code used in this chapter can be found in the "Probability.R" file.

Now we can ask R to choose one of these two values at random 1 million times, where the probability of choosing 1 and the probability of choosing 0 are each 0.5. To accomplish this, we can use

TIP: When writing code, do not use
a comma to indicate thousands or millions. Commas in R are reserved for
separating arguments. Example: write
size=1000000, not size=1,000,000.

RECALL: prop.table() converts a frequency table into a table of proportions. The only required argument
is the output of the function table()
with the code identifying the variable inside the parentheses. Example:
prop.table(table(data$variable)).

RECALL: mean() calculates the mean of
a variable, and var() calculates the variance. Examples: mean(data$variable)
and var(data$variable).

the function sample(), which stands for "randomly sample from a
set of values." Inside the parentheses, we first specify a vector
with the set of values from which we want to sample. In this case,
we use *possible_values* for this vector. Then, we specify that (i)
we want 1 million draws by setting the argument size to equal
1000000, (ii) the draws should be with replacement—meaning
that we allow the same value to be sampled more than once—by
setting the argument replace to TRUE, and (iii) the probabilities
of selecting each value are both 0.5 by setting the argument prob
to equal the vector c(0.5, 0.5), where the first number identifies
the probability of selecting a 1 (the first value in *possible_values*)
and the second number identifies the probability of selecting a 0
(the second value in *possible_values*).

```
## randomly sample from possible_values
flip  <- sample(possible_values,  # vector to draw from
                size=1000000, # 1 million times
                replace=TRUE, # with replacement
                prob=c(0.5, 0.5)) # from a fair coin
```

The variable *flip* contains the results of simulating 1 million flips
of a fair coin. (It contains 1 million observations of 1s and 0s.) To
calculate the proportion of 1s (heads) and 0s (tails), we can use
the function prop.table() in conjunction with the function table().

```
prop.table(table(flip)) # creates table of proportions
## flip
##        0        1
## 0.499933 0.500067
```

As we can see in the output above, once we simulate flipping a fair
coin 1 million times, the proportion of heads (*p*) and the proportion of tails (1−*p*) both approximate 0.5. (Note that the values
you will see in your console after running the code above will
likely not be the exact values shown here. Because we created
flip via a random process, it will contain slightly different values
each time it is created. In fact, all computations in this chapter
rely on random processes, and therefore, you should expect slight
differences throughout between the outputs we show and what
you see in your console.)

Now we can calculate the mean and variance of *flip* by running:

```
mean(flip)  # calculates the mean
## [1] 0.500067
```

```
var(flip)  # calculates the variance
## [1] 0.2500002
```

The mean of *flip* is about 0.5, which is what we expected given
that the mean of a Bernoulli distribution is equivalent to *p*, the
probability that the binary random variable equals 1 (here *p*=0.5).

We can interpret the mean of *flip*, then, as indicating that the probability of the coin landing on heads is 50% (0.5×100=50%).

Finally, the variance of *flip* is 0.25, which is also what we expected given that the variance of a Bernoulli distribution is equal to $p(1-p)$ (in this case: $0.5(1-0.5)=0.25$).

6.4.2 THE NORMAL DISTRIBUTION

The **normal distribution** is a well-known symmetric, bell-shaped distribution, commonly used as an approximation for the distribution of many non-binary variables.

For an illustration, let's return to the dataset we analyzed in chapter 2 and create the density histogram of the reading test scores from Project STAR:

```
star <- read.csv("STAR.csv") # reads and stores data

hist(star$reading, freq=FALSE) # creates density histogram
```

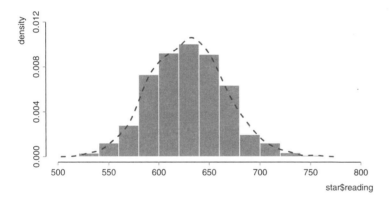

If we focus on the shape of the histogram demarcated by the height of the bins (shown by the dashed line we added to the density histogram above), we can see that the probability distribution of *reading* is more or less symmetric and bell-shaped. We can approximate the distribution of this non-binary variable using a normal distribution.

The theoretical normal distribution is a family of probability distributions that (i) characterize random variables that can take any value on the real line (from negative infinity to infinity), and (ii) follow a symmetric bell curve that has a very specific shape determined by the formula given in detail below. We refer to random variables that follow a normal distribution as normal random variables.

The **normal distribution** is the distribution of a normal random variable. It is characterized by two parameters: mean (μ, pronounced mu) and variance (σ^2, pronounced sigma-squared). In mathematical notation, we write a normal random variable X as:

$$X \sim N(\mu, \sigma^2)$$

RECALL: Before loading the dataset, we need to set the working directory. If the DSS folder is saved directly on your Desktop, to set the working directory, you must run setwd("~/Desktop/DSS") if you have a Mac and setwd("C:/*user*/Desktop/DSS") if you have a Windows computer (where *user* is your own username). If the DSS folder is saved elsewhere, please see subsection 1.7.1 for instructions on how to set the working directory.

RECALL: A density histogram provides a visualization of the (probability) distribution of a (random) variable. The relative height of the bins implies the relative likelihood of the values. The areas of all the bins in a density histogram must add up to 1. In R, the function hist() creates a density histogram when we set the optional argument freq to FALSE. Example: hist(*data$variable*, freq=FALSE).

The probability density function of the normal probability distribution is determined by the following formula:

$$\frac{1}{\sigma\sqrt{2\pi}}\, e^{-(x-\mu)^2/2\sigma^2}$$

where:

- μ is the mean of the random variable

- σ is the standard deviation and σ^2 is the variance of the random variable

- x is any value on the real line (from negative infinity to infinity) that the random variable may take

- π is the constant pi, which is approximately 3.1416

- e is the constant known as Euler's number, which is approximately 2.7183.

The **probability density function** of the normal distribution represents the likelihood of each possible value the normal random variable can take (from negative infinity to infinity). The relative height of the curve provides the relative likelihood of the values. The total area underneath the curve of a probability density function equals 1.

FIGURE 6.1. Probability density function of a normal random variable:

$$X \sim N(\mu, \sigma^2)$$

RECALL: The variance of a variable is the square of the variable's standard deviation. If σ is the standard deviation, then σ^2 is the variance.

The **probability density function** of the normal distribution (the formula in detail above) provides the height of the density curve for each value of x. (See figure 6.1.)

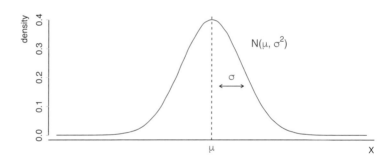

The shape of the curve of the probability density function depends on the values of two parameters:

- μ (the Greek letter mu), which stands for the mean of the random variable and determines the center of the distribution

- σ^2 (the Greek letter sigma, squared), which stands for the variance of the random variable and determines the spread of the distribution.

In mathematical notation, if a random variable X follows a normal distribution, we write:

$$X \sim N(\mu, \sigma^2)$$

where:

- X is the name of the random variable
- the symbol $\sim$ stands for "distributed according to"
- N stands for "normal distribution"
- μ is the mean and σ^2 is the variance of the variable.

For example, to state that X is distributed according to a normal distribution with mean 3 and variance 4, we write: $X \sim N(3, 4)$

To visualize the shape of the probability density function of $N(3, 4)$, we can use the formula in detail above. Alternatively and more conveniently, we can ask R to simulate it for us.

Using R, we can randomly draw 1 million observations from the normal distribution we are interested in. Then, we can create the density histogram of the drawn observations. A sample of 1 million observations is large enough that its distribution should approximate the distribution from which the observations are drawn.

We can start by using the function rnorm(), which stands for "randomly sample from a <u>norm</u>al distribution." The one required argument is the number of observations we want to sample. By default, this function samples from the normal distribution with mean 0 and variance 1. If we want to sample from another normal distribution, we can specify a different mean with the optional argument mean, and a different standard deviation with the optional argument sd. (Note that we need to specify the standard deviation, σ, not the variance, σ^2, of the normal distribution we want to sample from.) For example, to draw 1 million observations from $N(3, 4)$ and save them as a variable named X, we run:

```
## randomly sample from distribution N(3, 4)
X <- rnorm(1000000, # sample size
           mean=3, # mean
           sd=2) # standard deviation
```

> rnorm() randomly samples from a normal distribution. The only required argument is the number of observations we want to sample. By default, this function samples from the normal distribution with mean 0 and variance 1 (known as the standard normal distribution). To sample from a different normal distribution, we can specify a different mean with the optional argument mean, and a different standard deviation with the optional argument sd. Examples: rnorm(100) and rnorm(100, mean=3, sd=2).

Now, to visualize the probability distribution of X, we can create its density histogram.

```
hist(X, freq=FALSE) # creates density histogram
```

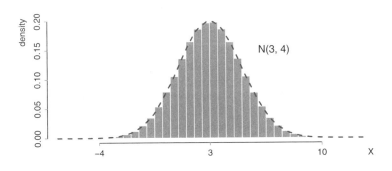

The shape of the probability density function of $N(3, 4)$ is demarcated by the height of the bins of the density histogram (shown by the dashed line we added to the histogram above).

To find out the mean and variance of X, we run:

```
mean(X) # calculates the mean
## [1] 2.998545

var(X) # calculates the variance
## [1] 3.998968
```

Based on the outputs above, the distribution of X is centered at about 3 with variance of about 4. This confirms that the sample of 1 million observations approximately follows the same distribution as the one from which the observations were drawn.

Now, we can follow the same procedure a few times to get a better sense of how the shape of normal distributions varies when the two defining parameters change. For example, figure 6.2 shows the probability density functions of three different normal distributions: $N(0, 1)$, $N(2, 1)$, and $N(0, 4)$.

FIGURE 6.2. Probability density functions of three normal distributions: $N(0, 1)$, $N(2, 1)$, and $N(0, 4)$.

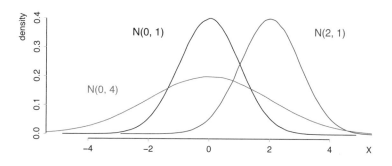

As shown above, both $N(0, 1)$ and $N(0, 4)$ are centered at 0, but $N(0, 4)$ is flatter and more spread out than $N(0, 1)$ because of its larger variance. The spread and height of $N(0, 1)$ and $N(2, 1)$ are the same because they have the same variance, but $N(2, 1)$ is centered at 2, whereas $N(0, 1)$ is centered at 0.

TIP: The area under the probability density function from negative infinity to x equals the cumulative probability that the normal random variable takes a value less than or equal to x: $P(X \leq x)$. The function that produces this probability is known as the cumulative distribution function.

How can we use a probability density function to compute probabilities? We can use the area underneath the curve of the probability density function to compute what are often referred to as *cumulative* probabilities, that is, the probability that a normal random variable takes a value *within a given range*. For example, the area under the curve between x_1 and x_2 equals the probability that the normal random variable takes a value between x_1 and x_2. (Since all probabilities in a distribution must add up to 1, the total area underneath the curve of a probability density function equals 1.)

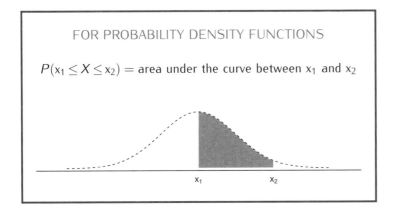

FOR PROBABILITY DENSITY FUNCTIONS

$$P(x_1 \leq X \leq x_2) = \text{area under the curve between } x_1 \text{ and } x_2$$

TIP: The height of the density curve for a particular value of x is not equivalent to the probability of x. There are infinitely many values a normal random variable, X, can take, and the probability that X takes a value *equal to* any specific value, x, is zero. As discussed here, however, we can use the area under the curve of a probability density function to compute the probability that X takes a value within a specific range.

This property of probability density functions enables us to figure out relative probabilities. For example, take a look at the probability density function of X shown in figure 6.3.

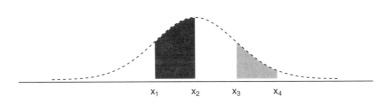

FIGURE 6.3. Probability density function of X where the area under the curve between x_1 and x_2 (shaded in red) is greater than the area under the curve between x_3 and x_4 (shaded in gray). Therefore, the probability that X takes a value between x_1 and x_2 is greater than the probability that X takes a value between x_3 and x_4.

The area under the curve between x_1 and x_2 (shaded in red) is larger than the area under the curve between x_3 and x_4 (shaded in gray). This means that the probability that X takes a value between x_1 and x_2 is greater than the probability that X takes a value between x_3 and x_4. In mathematical notation, we can state:

$$P(x_1 \leq X \leq x_2) > P(x_3 \leq X \leq x_4)$$

6.4.3 THE STANDARD NORMAL DISTRIBUTION

The **standard normal distribution** is the normal distribution with mean 0 ($\mu=0$) and variance 1 ($\sigma^2=1$). Since the square root of 1 is 1, the standard deviation of the standard normal distribution is also 1 ($\sigma=1$).

In mathematical notation, we usually refer to the standard normal random variable as Z and write it as:

$$Z \sim N(0, 1)$$

(Note that Z here has nothing to do with the Z we used to denote confounding variables in chapter 5.)

The **standard normal distribution** is the normal distribution with mean 0 and variance 1. In mathematical notation, we refer to the standard normal random variable as Z and write it as:

$$Z \sim N(0, 1)$$

Two properties of the standard normal distribution are particularly useful. First, because the distribution is symmetric and centered at 0, the probability that Z takes a value less than or equal to -z is the same as the probability that Z takes a value greater than or equal to z (where z is defined as $z \geq 0$). This is true because the area under the curve between negative infinity and -z is the same as the area under the curve between z and infinity.

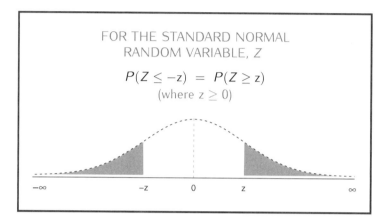

FOR THE STANDARD NORMAL
RANDOM VARIABLE, Z

$$P(Z \leq -z) \ = \ P(Z \geq z)$$
(where $z \geq 0$)

RECALL: As we mentioned in chapter 3, one of the distinct characteristics of normal distributions is that about 95% of the observations fall within two standard deviations from the mean (that is, are between the mean minus two standard deviations and the mean plus two standard deviations). Here, since the standard deviation equals 1, about 95% of the observations are between -2 and 2 (or more precisely, between -1.96 and 1.96).

Second, in the standard normal distribution, about 95% of the observations are between -2 and 2, or more precisely, between -1.96 and 1.96.

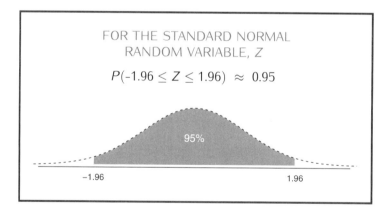

FOR THE STANDARD NORMAL
RANDOM VARIABLE, Z

$$P(-1.96 \leq Z \leq 1.96) \ \approx \ 0.95$$

95%

-1.96   1.96

Let's learn how to calculate probabilities of normal random variables in R so that we can better understand these two properties.

To calculate probabilities of normal random variables, we can use the function pnorm(), which stands for "the cumulative probability of a <u>n</u>ormal random variable from negative infinity to x." By default, this function calculates the probability that the standard normal random variable takes a value *less than or equal to* the number specified inside the parentheses. (See figure in the margin.) For example, to calculate the probability that Z takes a value less than or equal to -1.96, we run:

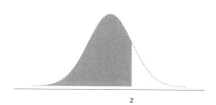

z

```
## probability of Z less than or equal to -1.96
pnorm(-1.96)
## [1] 0.0249979
```

Based on the output, we can state that the probability that Z takes a value less than or equal to -1.96 is about 2.5% (0.025×100=2.5%).

If we are interested in the probability that Z takes a value *greater than or equal to* a value, z, we can calculate the probability that Z takes a value *less than or equal to* z and then compute 1 minus the resulting probability. (This is true for all normal random variables because all probabilities in a distribution must add up to 1.)

pnorm() calculates the probability that the standard normal random variable, Z, takes a value *less than or equal to* the number specified inside the parentheses. To calculate probabilities of a different normal random variable, we can specify a different mean with the optional argument mean and a different standard deviation with the optional argument sd. Examples: pnorm(0) and pnorm(0, mean=3, sd=2).

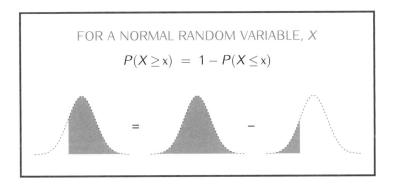

FOR A NORMAL RANDOM VARIABLE, X

$$P(X \geq x) = 1 - P(X \leq x)$$

TIP: For a normal random variable, X:
$$P(X=x) = 0$$

Therefore:
$$P(X \geq x) = P(X > x)$$
$$P(X \leq x) = P(X < x)$$

For example, if we want to calculate the probability that Z takes a value greater than or equal to 1.96, we run:

```
## probability of Z greater than or equal to 1.96
1 - pnorm(1.96)
## [1] 0.0249979
```

Based on the output, we can state that the probability that Z takes a value greater than or equal to 1.96 is also about 2.5%. This confirms that the probability that Z takes a value less than or equal to -1.96 is the same as the probability that Z takes a value greater than or equal to 1.96.

Now, if we are interested in the probability that Z takes a value between z_1 and z_2, we can calculate the probability that Z takes a value less than or equal to z_2 minus the probability that Z takes a value less than or equal to z_1. (This is also true for all normal random variables because, again, all probabilities in a distribution must add up to 1.)

TIP: For a normal random variable, X:
$$P(X=x) = 0$$
Therefore:
$$P(x_1 \leq X \leq x_2) = P(x_1 < X < x_2)$$
$$P(X \leq x) = P(X < x)$$

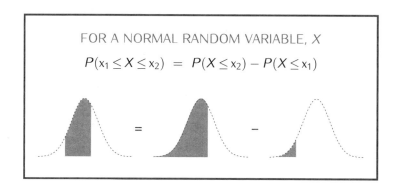

FOR A NORMAL RANDOM VARIABLE, X

$$P(x_1 \leq X \leq x_2) = P(X \leq x_2) - P(X \leq x_1)$$

For example, if we are interested in the probability that Z takes a value between –1.96 and 1.96, we can compute:

$$P(-1.96 \leq Z \leq 1.96) = P(Z \leq 1.96) - P(Z \leq -1.96)$$

So, to calculate the probability that Z takes a value between –1.96 and 1.96, we can run in R:

```
## probability of Z between -1.96 and 1.96
pnorm(1.96) - pnorm(-1.96)
## [1] 0.9500042
```

This output confirms that in the standard normal distribution, about 95% of the observations are between –1.96 and 1.96.

As we will soon see, it is helpful to know these two properties of the standard normal distribution because we can transform any normal random variable into the standard normal random variable. All we need to do is standardize it, that is, subtract the mean from the original normal random variable, and then divide the result by the standard deviation. Graphically, this transformation shifts the center and adjusts the spread of the distribution.

FORMULA 6.1. Formula to transform a normal random variable, X, into the standard normal random variable, Z.

HOW TO TRANSFORM
A NORMAL RANDOM VARIABLE INTO
THE STANDARD NORMAL RANDOM VARIABLE

$$\text{if } X \sim N(\mu, \sigma^2), \quad \frac{X - \mu}{\sigma} \sim N(0, 1)$$

where:
- μ is the mean of X
- σ^2 is the variance of X
- σ is the standard deviation of X $(\sigma = \sqrt{\sigma^2})$.

The resulting standardized variable is commonly referred to as the z-scores of the original random variable. (These are the same z-scores as the ones we used in chapter 3 when computing the correlation coefficient between two variables.)

Take, for example, the normal random variable, X, we created in the subsection above. The variable X has mean 3 and variance 4. Given formula 6.1, $(X-3)/2$ should follow the standard normal distribution. (Note that to standardize a normal random variable, we use the standard deviation, σ, not the variance, σ^2, in the denominator. To compute the standard deviation, we take the square root of the variance. In this case, the variance is 4, and therefore the standard deviation is 2.)

$$\text{if } X \sim N(3,\ 4), \quad \frac{X-3}{2} \sim N(0,\ 1)$$

To confirm this, we can ask R to create a new random variable, Z, equivalent to the variable X standardized:

```
## create new random variable
Z <- (X - 3) / 2 # standardized X
```

Then, we can create the density histogram of Z to visualize its probability distribution:

```
hist (Z, freq=FALSE) # creates density histogram
```

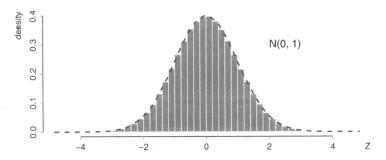

As we can see in the density histogram above, Z closely follows the standard normal distribution (centered at 0 and with a variance of 1). To verify this, we calculate the mean and variance of Z by running:

```
mean(Z) # calculates the mean
## [1] -0.0007277148
```

```
var(Z) # calculates the variance
## [1] 0.999742
```

As we expected, the distribution of Z is centered at more or less 0, and its variance is approximately 1.

To summarize, while X was a random variable distributed as $N(3, 4)$, after standardization (subtracting the mean and then dividing the result by the standard deviation), the resulting random variable is distributed as $N(0, 1)$. (See figure 6.4, which shows the probability density functions of both X and Z.)

FIGURE 6.4. Probability density functions of X and Z, where Z is equivalent to standardized X.

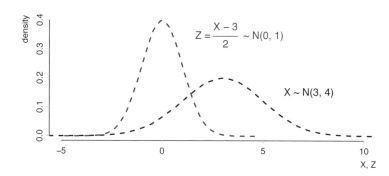

Why is the transformation of a normal random variable into the standard normal random variable helpful? Because we can use the properties of the standard normal distribution to compute probabilities for all the other types of normal distributions.

Imagine we want to know the range of values that contains 95% of the observations of the normal random variable X above, which again follows a $N(3, 4)$ distribution. Now that we know how to transform X into the standard normal distribution, we can use as our starting point the fact that in the standard normal distribution, about 95% of the observations are between -1.96 and 1.96.

$$P(\text{-}1.96 \leq Z \leq 1.96) \approx 0.95$$
$$P\left(\text{-}1.96 \leq \frac{X-3}{2} \leq 1.96\right) \approx 0.95 \quad \text{(since } Z = \frac{X-3}{2}\text{)}$$
$$P(\text{-}0.92 \leq X \leq 6.92) \approx 0.95 \quad \text{(after multiplying by 2 and adding 3 to each term)}$$

After substituting Z and isolating X, we arrive at the conclusion that 95% of the observations of X are between -0.92 and 6.92.

RECALL: To calculate probabilities of a different normal distribution than the standard normal with pnorm(), we specify the optional arguments mean and sd. Example: pnorm(0, mean=3, sd=2).

To confirm this result, we can calculate the probability that $N(3, 4)$ takes a value between -0.92 and 6.92, by running:

```
## probability of N(3, 4) between -0.92 and 6.92
pnorm(6.92, mean=3, sd=2) -
    pnorm(-0.92, mean=3, sd=2)
## [1] 0.9500042
```

Based on the output above, 95% of the observations of $X \sim N(3, 4)$ are indeed between -0.92 and 6.92.

6.4.4 RECAP

In this book, we focus on two types of random variables: binary and normal. Their probability distributions are summarized below.

IF X IS A BINARY RANDOM VARIABLE

X has a Bernoulli distribution, characterized by one parameter: p

mean $= p$
variance $= p(1-p)$

IF X IS A NORMAL RANDOM VARIABLE

X has a normal distribution, characterized by two parameters: μ and σ^2

mean $= \mu$
variance $= \sigma^2$

Now that we are familiar with what probability is and the probability distributions of binary and normal random variables, let's clarify the distinction between population parameters and sample statistics.

6.5 POPULATION PARAMETERS VS. SAMPLE STATISTICS

When analyzing data, we are usually interested in the value of a parameter at the population level. For example, we might be interested in the level of support for a particular political candidate among the population of all voters in a country. Typically, however, we have access to statistics from only a small sample of observations drawn from the target population. For example, we may know only the proportion of supporters among the voters who responded to a survey. In this section, we see how to use sample statistics to learn about the corresponding population parameters.

TIP: Parameters are unknown quantities of interest (often at the population level). Statistics are based on the sample of data observed; that is, they are sample-specific.

POPULATION PARAMETERS OF RANDOM VARIABLE X

mean $= \mathbb{E}(X)$
(expectation of X)

variance $= \mathbb{V}(X)$
(population variance of X)

SAMPLE STATISTICS OF n OBSERVATIONS OF X

mean $= \overline{X}$
(sample mean of X)

variance $= var(X)$
(sample variance of X)

The **sample mean of** X, $\overline{X}$, refers to the average value of X in a particular sample, while the **expectation of** X, $\mathbb{E}(X)$, refers to the population mean of the random variable X. The **sample variance of** X, $var(X)$, refers to the variance of X in a particular sample, while the **population variance of** X, $\mathbb{V}(X)$, refers to the population variance of the random variable X.

To distinguish the sample statistics from the corresponding parameters at the population level, we use different terms to refer to them. The **sample mean of** X, denoted as $\overline{X}$, refers to the average value of X in a particular sample, while the **expectation of** X, denoted as $\mathbb{E}(X)$, refers to the population mean of the random variable X. The **sample variance of** X, denoted as $var(X)$, refers to the variance of X in a particular sample, while the **population variance of** X, denoted as $\mathbb{V}(X)$, refers to the population variance of the random variable X.

RECALL: The mean of a binary variable is equivalent to the proportion of observations that have the characteristic identified by the variable.

In the current example, we can define *support* as a binary variable that identifies whether individual i supports the candidate of interest (1=support, 0=no support). The sample mean of *support* would be the proportion of supporters among survey respondents, and the expectation of *support* would be the proportion of supporters among all the individuals in the target population.

Are the population-level parameters identical to the sample-level statistics? They are generally not the same unless the sample is the entire population.

Sampling variability refers to the fact that the value of a statistic varies from one sample to another because each sample contains a different set of observations drawn from the target population. Smaller sample size generally leads to greater sampling variability.

The sample statistics differ from the population parameters because the sample contains noise. The noise comes from **sampling variability**. If we randomly draw multiple samples from the same population, each sample will contain different observations. As a result, each sample will yield different values of sample statistics, even if all the observations are drawn using random sampling. In the running example, different surveys will show varying levels of support for the candidate because they contain different respondents. This will be true even when the surveys use exactly the same method to select their respondents.

Smaller sample size generally leads to greater sampling variability. Conversely, as sample size increases, sampling variability decreases. This is why when we get to extremely large sample sizes, such as 1 million observations, the sample statistics approximate the population parameters well. In the survey example, as the sample size increases, we expect the sample proportion of supporters to approach the population proportion of supporters.

When drawing conclusions about the population from a sample, we need to take into consideration the noise in the data introduced by sampling variability. The two large sample theorems we discuss in this section—the law of large numbers and the central limit theorem—help us do just that by clarifying the relationship between population parameters and sample statistics.

6.5.1 THE LAW OF LARGE NUMBERS

The **law of large numbers** states that as sample size increases, the sample mean of X approximates the population mean of X.

The **law of large numbers** states that as the sample size increases, the sample mean of X approximates the population mean of X, also known as the expectation of X.

THE LAW OF LARGE NUMBERS

as n increases, $\overline{X} = \dfrac{\sum_{i=1}^{n} X_i}{n} \approx \mathbb{E}(X)$

where:

- n is the sample size
- X is the original random variable
- $\overline{X}$ is the sample mean of X
- $\mathbb{E}(X)$ is the population mean of X.

To illustrate the law of large numbers, we can use R to draw random samples of different sizes from the same distribution and compare the sample means to the population mean. To show the general applicability of this theorem, we will do this exercise twice, once with an original random variable that is binary and once with an original random variable that is normal.

EXAMPLE WITH A BINARY RANDOM VARIABLE

Suppose we are interested in the binary variable *support* as defined above (1=support, 0=no support). Since this is a binary variable, it has a Bernoulli distribution.

Further suppose that 60% of the voters in the country support the political candidate of interest. The probability that *support* equals 1, then, is 0.60 (p=0.60), which is equal to the population mean of *support* ($\mathbb{E}(support)$=0.60). (As we saw earlier, the mean of a Bernoulli distribution is equivalent to the probability that the binary variable equals 1, denoted as p.)

Now we can use the function sample() to draw three random samples from this particular binary variable, each of a different size. Note that in this case, we set the argument prob to equal c(0.6, 0.4) because the probability of 1 is 0.6 (p=0.60) and the probability of 0 is 0.4 (1−p=1−0.6=0.4).

```
## draw random samples from binary variable
support_sample_1 <- sample(c(1, 0), # possible values
                 size=10, # n=10
                 replace=TRUE, # with replacement
                 prob=c(0.6, 0.4)) # probabilities

support_sample_2 <- sample(c(1, 0),
                 size=1000, # n=1,000
                 replace=TRUE,
                 prob=c(0.6, 0.4))
```

RECALL: sample() randomly samples from a set of values. The only required argument is a vector with the set of values to draw from. By default, this function samples values without replacement. To specify the number of draws, we use the argument size. To draw with replacement, which allows the same value to be sampled more than once, we set the argument replace to TRUE. To specify the probabilities of selecting each value, we set the argument prob to equal a vector containing the probabilities of each value. Examples: sample(c(1, 2, 3)) and sample(c(0, 1), size=1000000, replace=TRUE, prob=c(0.2, 0.8)).

```
support_sample_3 <- sample(c(1, 0),
                    size=1000000, # n=1,000,000
                    replace=TRUE,
                    prob=c(0.6, 0.4))
```

As we can see in the code above, the first sample contains 10 observations, the second contains 1,000 observations, and the third contains 1 million observations. To calculate the mean for each of the three samples, we run:

```
## calculate sample means
mean(support_sample_1) # in n=10 sample
## [1] 0.8

mean(support_sample_2) # in n=1,000 sample
## [1] 0.62

mean(support_sample_3) # in n=1,000,000 sample
## [1] 0.599957
```

RECALL: The mean of a binary variable is interpreted as the proportion of observations that have the characteristic identified by the variable (after multiplying the number by 100).

The proportion of support among respondents varies across the three samples. In the first sample, 80% of respondents support the candidate; in the second, 62% of respondents support the candidate; and in the third, close to 60% of respondents support the candidate. The sample with the largest number of observations, sample 3 with 1 million observations, produces the proportion of support that is closest to the true proportion of support in the population. This finding is consistent with the fact that as the sample size increases, the sample mean tends to be closer to the population mean, which in this case is 60%.

EXAMPLE WITH A NORMAL RANDOM VARIABLE

Now suppose we are interested in the height, measured in inches, of each person in a population. We assume that the corresponding random variable, *height*, follows a normal distribution. Further suppose that we know that the mean of this normal distribution is 67 inches and the variance is 14 inches.

RECALL: rnorm() randomly samples from a normal distribution. The only required argument is the number of observations we want to sample. By default, this function draws observations from the standard normal distribution (mean=0 and sd=1). To sample from a different normal distribution, we can specify a different mean with the optional argument mean and a different standard deviation with the optional argument sd. Examples: rnorm(100) and rnorm(100, mean=1, sd=2).

We can use the function rnorm() to draw three random samples from this normal random variable, each of a different size:

```
## draw random samples from normal distribution
height_sample_1 <- rnorm(10, # n=10
                    mean=67, # population mean=67
                    sd=sqrt(14)) # population variance=14

height_sample_2 <- rnorm(1000, # n=1,000
                    mean=67,
                    sd=sqrt(14))
```

```
height_sample_3 <- rnorm(1000000, # n=1,000,000
                         mean=67,
                         sd=sqrt(14))
```

RECALL: When using the function rnorm(), to change the spread of the normal distribution, we need to specify the standard deviation, not the variance. Here, given that the variance is 14, the standard deviation is sqrt(14).

As in the previous example, the first sample contains 10 observations, the second contains 1,000 observations, and the third contains 1 million observations. To calculate the sample mean for each of the samples, we run:

```
## calculate sample means
mean(height_sample_1) # in n=10 sample
## [1] 65.21607

mean(height_sample_2) # in n=1,000 sample
## [1] 66.81554

mean(height_sample_3) # in n=1,000,000 sample
## [1] 66.99905
```

The average height varies across the three samples. It is about 65.22 inches in the first sample, 66.82 inches in the second, and 67 inches in the third. Here, too, as the sample size increases, the sample mean tends to approach the population mean of the original random variable, which in this case is 67 inches.

6.5.2 THE CENTRAL LIMIT THEOREM

The **central limit theorem** states that as the sample size increases, the standardized sample mean of X can be approximated by the standard normal distribution.

The **central limit theorem** states that as the sample size increases, the standardized sample mean of X can be approximated by the standard normal distribution.

THE CENTRAL LIMIT THEOREM

as n increases, $\dfrac{\overline{X} - \mathbb{E}(X)}{\sqrt{\mathbb{V}(X)/n}} \overset{\text{approx.}}{\sim} N(0, 1)$

where:
- n is the sample size
- X is the original random variable, and $\overline{X}$ is the sample mean, a random variable containing the sample means from multiple large samples of X
- $\mathbb{E}(X)$ is the population mean of X, and $\mathbb{V}(X)$ is the population variance of X
- $\overset{\text{approx.}}{\sim}$ stands for "approximately distributed according to," and $N(0, 1)$ is the standard normal distribution.

Let's see how we arrive at this theorem so that we can understand it better.

First, we can think of the sample mean of X as a random variable because it varies from one sample to another. As is the case with all random variables, the sample mean of X has its own distribution.

Second, the central limit theorem implies that as the sample size increases, the distribution of the sample mean of X approaches the normal distribution.

as n increases, $\overline{X}$ is approximately distributed as normal

Third, as you may recall, the normal distribution is characterized by two parameters: mean and variance. To figure out the mean and variance of the sample mean of X, we need to rely on the properties of expectations and variances. (See the formulas in detail below.)

FORMULA IN DETAIL

Some properties of expectations:

- $\mathbb{E}(aX) = a\,\mathbb{E}(X)$ where a is a constant and X is a random variable
- $\mathbb{E}(X_1 + X_2) = \mathbb{E}(X_1) + \mathbb{E}(X_2)$ where X_1 and X_2 are random variables.

Given the properties above, what is the population mean or expectation of the sample mean of X, $\mathbb{E}(\overline{X})$?

$$\mathbb{E}(\overline{X}) = \mathbb{E}\left(\frac{\sum_{i=1}^{n} X_i}{n}\right) \quad \text{because } \overline{X} = \frac{\sum_{i=1}^{n} X_i}{n}$$

$$= \frac{1}{n}\mathbb{E}\left(\sum_{i=1}^{n} X_i\right) \quad \text{because } \mathbb{E}(aX) = a\,\mathbb{E}(X)$$

$$= \frac{1}{n}\sum_{i=1}^{n}\mathbb{E}(X_i) \quad \begin{array}{l}\text{because}\\ \mathbb{E}(X_1 + X_2) = \mathbb{E}(X_1) + \mathbb{E}(X_2)\end{array}$$

$$= \frac{1}{n} \times n\,\mathbb{E}(X) \quad \text{because } \sum_{i=1}^{n}\mathbb{E}(X_i) = n\,\mathbb{E}(X)$$

$$= \mathbb{E}(X)$$

Some properties of variances:

- $\mathbb{V}(aX) = a^2\,\mathbb{V}(X)$ where a is a constant and X is a random variable
- $\mathbb{V}(X_1 + X_2) = \mathbb{V}(X_1) + \mathbb{V}(X_2)$ where X_1 and X_2 are random variables that are independent of each other (that is, the values of one variable cannot be used to infer the values of the other).

Given the properties above, what is the population variance of the sample mean of X, $\mathbb{V}(\overline{X})$?

$$\mathbb{V}(\overline{X}) = \mathbb{V}\left(\frac{\sum_{i=1}^{n} X_i}{n}\right) \qquad \text{because } \overline{X} = \frac{\sum_{i=1}^{n} X_i}{n}$$

$$= \left(\frac{1}{n}\right)^2 \mathbb{V}\left(\sum_{i=1}^{n} X_i\right) \qquad \text{because } \mathbb{V}(aX) = a^2\,\mathbb{V}(X)$$

$$= \left(\frac{1}{n}\right)^2 \sum_{i=1}^{n} \mathbb{V}(X_i) \qquad \begin{array}{l}\text{because}\\ \mathbb{V}(X_1 + X_2) = \mathbb{V}(X_1) + \mathbb{V}(X_2)\end{array}$$

$$= \frac{1}{n^2} \times n\,\mathbb{V}(X) \qquad \text{because } \sum_{i=1}^{n} \mathbb{V}(X_i) = n\,\mathbb{V}(X)$$

$$= \frac{\mathbb{V}(X)}{n}$$

As shown in detail above:

- the population mean of the sample mean of X equals the population mean of X:

$$\mathbb{E}(\overline{X}) = \mathbb{E}(X)$$

- the population variance of the sample mean of X equals the population variance of X divided by the sample size:

$$\mathbb{V}(\overline{X}) = \frac{\mathbb{V}(X)}{n}$$

Fourth, now that we know the population mean and variance of the sample mean, we can standardize the sample mean of X by subtracting the population mean and dividing the result by the population standard deviation (see formula 6.1). The standardized sample mean is then:

$$\frac{\overline{X} - \mathbb{E}(X)}{\sqrt{\mathbb{V}(X)/n}}$$

According to the central limit theorem, as the sample size increases, the standardized sample mean of X (as defined above) can be approximated by the standard normal distribution:

$$\text{as } n \text{ increases,} \quad \frac{\overline{X} - \mathbb{E}(X)}{\sqrt{\mathbb{V}(X)/n}} \overset{\text{approx.}}{\sim} N(0, 1)$$

Remarkably, this theorem holds when the original random variable X follows a Bernoulli distribution. In fact, it holds when the original random variable follows almost any of the distributions we use in statistics. This is important because we rarely know the probability distribution that generates the data of interest.

To illustrate this theorem, we can use R to (i) draw multiple, large random samples from the same distribution, (ii) compute the mean of each sample, (iii) standardize the mean of each sample applying formula 6.1 using the population mean and population variance of the sample mean, (iv) save the standardized sample means as a new variable, and (v) examine the distribution of the standardized sample means. If the samples are large enough, the standardized sample means should approximately follow the standard normal distribution.

Here we go over only one example, one in which the original random variable is binary. If the original random variable is normal, we do not need the central limit theorem. In this case, the standardized sample mean follows *exactly* the standard normal distribution, which makes the large sample approximation unnecessary.

EXAMPLE WITH A BINARY RANDOM VARIABLE

Let's return to the binary random variable *support*, which, as we discussed above, follows a Bernoulli distribution.

We continue to suppose that 60% of the voters in the country support the political candidate of interest. So, in this case: $p=0.60$.

Given the properties of Bernoulli distributions, the original random variable, *support*, should be centered at 0.60 and have a variance of 0.24.

$$\mathbb{E}(support) = p = 0.60$$
$$\mathbb{V}(support) = p(1-p) = 0.6 \times (1-0.6) = 0.24$$

c() combines values into a vector. If no main argument is provided, this function creates an empty vector that can be used to store outputs. Example: c().

To start the simulation, we need to create an empty vector where we will store the standardized means of the samples from the random variable *support*. For this purpose, we can use the function c(), which creates an empty vector when no arguments are specified inside.

```
## create an empty vector to store standardized sample means
sd_sample_means <- c()
```

Now, we can use R to draw 10,000 random samples from *support*, each one containing 1,000 observations, and save the standardized mean of each sample in the vector we have just created. Because we do not want to write the code to draw a random sample 10,000 times, we can use what is known as a for loop. A for loop executes a given code repeatedly, for as many times as indicated. (For a more detailed explanation on how for loops work, please see the appendix near the end of this chapter.)

For example, by running the code below, we are asking R, for each *i* in the sequence from *i*=1 until *i*=10,000 (so, 10,000 times in total), to:

- draw a random sample of 1,000 observations from a binary random variable with *p*=0.6

- calculate the standardized sample mean, which in this case is:

$$\frac{\overline{support}_i - \mathbb{E}(support)}{\sqrt{\mathbb{V}(support)/n}} = \frac{\overline{support}_i - 0.60}{\sqrt{0.24/1000}}$$

- store the standardized sample mean in observation *i* of the empty vector *sd_sample_means*.

```
## for loop with 10,000 iterations
for (i in 1:10000){
  ## draw a random sample of 1,000 observations
  ## from binary random variable with p=0.6
  support_sample <- sample(c(1, 0), # possible values
                  size=1000, # n=1,000
                  replace=TRUE, # with replacement
                  prob=c(0.6, 0.4)) # probabilities
  ## calculate and store the standardized sample mean
  sd_sample_means[i] <-
    (mean(support_sample)-0.60) / sqrt(0.24 / 1000)
}
```

After running the code above, *sd_sample_means* will contain the standardized sample means of 10,000 samples from the binary random variable we are interested in (that is, *p*=0.6).

Now we can visualize the distribution of the standardized sample means by creating the density histogram:

```
## create density histogram
hist (sd_sample_means, freq=FALSE)
```

for(i in 1:n){} is the basic syntax of a for loop. A for loop executes a given code repeatedly, for each *i* in the sequence from 1 to *n* (meaning for *i*={1,...,*n*}, using one *i* at a time, starting with *i*=1 and ending with *i*=*n*). The code to be executed repeatedly should be specified inside the curly brackets. Example: for(i in 1:3){print(i)} displays the value of i from i=1 until i=3.

TIP: Here *i* is not representing the position of the observation but rather the number of the iteration of the for loop. In the first iteration, *i*=1. In the last iteration, *i*=*n* (10,000 in this case).

[] is the operator used to extract a selection of observations from a vector. To its left, we specify the vector we want to subset. Inside the square brackets, we specify the criterion of selection. For example, we can specify the position of the observation *i* to be extracted. Example: vector[i].

TIP: Make sure to run this piece of code all at once, starting with for(i in 1:n){ and all the way until }. Otherwise, R will not be able to execute it and will give you an error message.

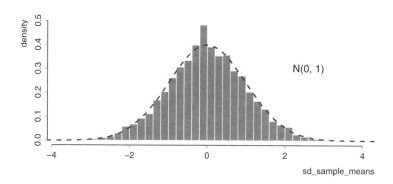

As we expected, even though the samples were drawn from a binary random variable, the standardized sample means approximately follow the standard normal distribution.

6.5.3 SAMPLING DISTRIBUTION OF THE SAMPLE MEAN

Thanks to the central limit theorem, we know that if we drew multiple large samples of a random variable X, with mean $\mathbb{E}(X)$ and variance $\mathbb{V}(X)$, the sample means would approximately follow a normal distribution with mean $\mathbb{E}(X)$ and variance $\mathbb{V}(X)/n$.

TIP: The central limit theorem states:

$$\frac{\overline{X} - \mathbb{E}(X)}{\sqrt{\mathbb{V}(X)/n}} \overset{\text{approx.}}{\sim} N(0,1)$$

Using formula 6.1 in the opposite direction, we can conclude:

$$\overline{X} \overset{\text{approx.}}{\sim} N\left(\mathbb{E}(X), \frac{\mathbb{V}(X)}{n}\right)$$

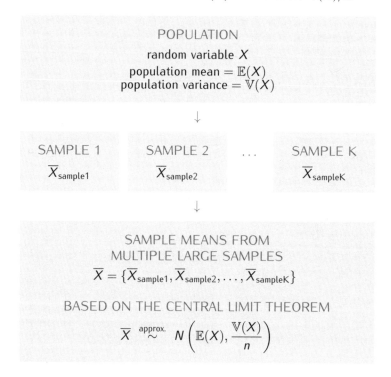

The **sampling distribution of the sample mean** characterizes how much the sample means vary from one sample to another due to sampling variability.

The distribution above is known as the **sampling distribution of the sample mean**. It characterizes how much the sample means vary from one sample to another due to sampling variability.

6.6 SUMMARY

This chapter introduced us to probability. First, we learned about the frequentist and Bayesian interpretations of probability and the axioms of probability. Next, we saw the probability distributions of two types of random variables, binary and normal, paying special attention to the standard normal distribution. Then, we learned two large sample theorems—the law of large numbers and the central limit theorem—and specifically how they help us understand the relationship between population parameters and sample statistics. Finally, we ended the chapter by using the central limit theorem to derive the sampling distribution of the sample mean. In the next chapter, we will learn how to use this knowledge to quantify the level of uncertainty in our population-level conclusions.

6.7 APPENDIX: FOR LOOPS

Let's start by looking at a simple example to understand how for loops work in R. Go ahead and run the following code:

```
for(i in 1:3){
  print(i) # print the value of i
}

## [1] 1
## [1] 2
## [1] 3
```

The first line of code, for(i in 1:3){, can be interpreted as: "For each *i* in the sequence from 1 to 3 (meaning for *i*={1, 2, 3}, using one *i* at a time, starting with *i*=1 and ending with *i*=3), execute the following code."

The second line is the code that will be executed repeatedly, in sequence, from *i*=1 until *i*=3. In this case, the code simply asks R to print the value of *i* using the function print().

Finally, the third line of code closes the parentheses we started in the first line, to indicate the end of the code to be executed repeatedly.

After running the three lines of code all together, R provides us three outputs, one for each *i* between 1 and 3. The first output is 1, since that was the value of *i* in the first iteration and so on.

Now, let's modify the for loop above to change the code we want R to execute repeatedly. Go ahead and run:

```
## for loop with 3 iterations
for(i in 1:3){
  ## draw a random sample of 1,000 observations
  ## from binary variable with p=0.5
  flip <- sample(c(1, 0), # possible values
                 size=1000, # n=1,000
                 replace=TRUE, # with replacement
                 prob=c(0.5, 0.5)) # probabilities
  ## print sample mean
  print(mean(flip))
}

## [1] 0.495
## [1] 0.505
## [1] 0.502
```

Because we didn't modify the first line of code, the for loop includes only three iterations. Hence, running the code produces three outputs. Each is the sample mean of simulating 1,000 flips from a fair coin (where 1 stands for heads and 0 stands for tails). Notice that each sample mean is slightly different. As we discussed earlier, these differences are due to sampling variability.

Now, we can modify the for loop so that instead of printing the sample means, R stores them into a vector. We start by creating an empty vector to store the sample means:

```
## create an empty vector to store sample means
sample_means <- c()
```

RECALL: c() combines values into a vector. If no main argument is provided, this function creates an empty vector that can be used to store outputs. Example: c().

Then, we need to modify the code to be executed repeatedly. Instead of print(mean(flip)), we write sample_means[i] <- mean(flip). This code saves each sample mean as a new observation in the vector *sample_means*. The [i] following the name of the vector on the left hand side of the assignment operator subsets the vector to the observation *i*. As a result, the first sample mean is saved as the first observation of the vector, and so on.

RECALL: [] is the operator used to extract a selection of observations from a vector. To its left, we specify the vector we want to subset. Inside the square brackets, we specify the criterion of selection. For example, we can specify the position of the observation to be extracted. Example: vector[i].

```
## for loop with 3 iterations
for (i in 1:3){
    ## draw a random sample of 1,000 observations
    ## from binary variable with p=0.5
    flip <- sample(c(1, 0),  # possible values
                   size=1000,  # n=1,000
                   replace=TRUE,  # with replacement
                   prob=c(0.5, 0.5))  # probabilities
    ## store sample mean
    sample_means[i] <- mean(flip)
}
```

After running the code above, *sample_means* should contain the sample means of three random samples. To confirm this, run the name of the object so that R provides its contents:

```
sample_means # shows contents of object
## [1] 0.481 0.531 0.485
```

Finally, if we wanted to draw 10,000 samples instead of three, we would modify the first line of the for loop. Instead of for(i in 1:3), we would write for(i in 1:10000).

```
## for loop with 10,000 iterations
for (i in 1:10000){
    ## draw a random sample of 1,000 observations
    ## from binary variable with p=0.5
    flip <- sample(c(1, 0),  # possible values
                   size=1000,  # n=1,000
                   replace=TRUE,  # with replacement
                   prob=c(0.5, 0.5))  # probabilities
    ## store sample mean
    sample_means[i] <- mean(flip)
}
```

6.8 CHEATSHEETS

6.8.1 CONCEPTS AND NOTATION

concept/notation	description	example(s)
frequentist interpretation of probabilities	probabilities represent proportions of specific events occurring over infinitely many identical trials	when flipping a coin, the probability of heads is the proportion of heads observed over infinitely many identical flips
Bayesian interpretation of probabilities	probabilities represent personal, subjective beliefs about the relative likelihood of events; a probability of 1, or 100%, indicates certainty that the event will occur; a probability of 0, or 0%, indicates certainty that the event will not occur	when stating that the probability of rain today is 80%, we are describing how certain we are about the rain event occurring; we are not describing the frequency of rain events over multiple days
trial	action or set of actions that produces outcomes of interest	rolling a die
outcome	the result of a trial	rolling a die produces one of six possible outcomes: 1, 2, 3, 4, 5, or 6
event	a set of outcomes; an event is said to occur if any one of the possible outcomes included in the event is realized	*rolling a number less than 3* is one of the potential events that may occur when rolling a die; if we roll a 1, we would consider that the event *rolling a number less than 3* has occurred
mutually exclusive events	events that do not share any outcomes	*rolling a number less than 3* and *rolling a 3* are mutually exclusive events when rolling a die
sample space (Ω)	denoted by the Greek letter Omega; the set of all possible outcomes produced by a trial; considered an event in itself	in the case of rolling a die: $$\Omega = \{1, 2, 3, 4, 5, 6\}$$
random variable	assigns a numeric value to each mutually exclusive event produced by a trial	we can create a random variable, *flip*, to capture the results of flipping coins, where 1s mean heads and 0s mean tails: $$flip_i = \begin{cases} 1 \text{ if coin flip } i \text{ lands on heads} \\ 0 \text{ if coin flip } i \text{ lands on tails} \end{cases}$$
probability distribution	characterizes the likelihood of each possible value a random variable can take; all probabilities in a distribution must add up to 1	the probability distribution of the random variable *flip* above could be: $$P(flip=1) = p = 0.67$$ $$P(flip=0) = 1-p = 1-0.67 = 0.33$$
Bernoulli distribution	probability distribution of a binary variable it is characterized by one parameter, p, which is the probability that the binary random variable takes the value of 1; consequently, $1-p$ is the probability that the binary random variable takes the value of 0 the mean of a Bernoulli distribution is p and the variance is $p(1-p)$	flipping a coin can result in only one of two possible events: heads or tails; if we assign 1 to heads and 0 to tails, we can create a binary random variable with the results of multiple coin flips; this binary random variable will follow a Bernoulli distribution $$P(flip=1) = p$$ $$P(flip=0) = 1-p$$

continues on next page...

6.8.1 CONCEPTS AND NOTATION (CONTINUED)

concept/notation	description	example(s)
normal distribution	distribution of a normal random variable we write a normal random variable X as: $$X \sim N(\mu, \sigma^2)$$ it is characterized by two parameters: - μ (the Greek letter mu), which stands for the mean of X - σ^2 (the Greek letter sigma, squared), which stands for the variance of X two useful properties of X: - $P(X \geq x) = 1 - P(X \leq x)$ - $P(x_1 \leq X \leq x_2) = P(X \leq x_2) - P(X \leq x_1)$	the density histogram of the normal random variable, X, with mean 3 and variance 4 is:
probability density function of the normal distribution	determined by the following formula: $$\frac{1}{\sigma\sqrt{2\pi}} e^{-(x-\mu)^2/2\sigma^2}$$ represents the likelihood of each possible value the normal random variable can take (from negative infinity to infinity); the relative height of the curve provides the relative likelihood of the values the area under the curve between x_1 and x_2 equals the probability that the normal random variable takes a value between x_1 and x_2; the total area underneath the curve equals 1	the shape of the probability density function is demarcated by the height of the bins of the density histogram; below is the density histogram of $X \sim N(3, 4)$ with the probability density function shown as a dashed line: the area under the curve between –4 and 1 is smaller than the area under the curve between 1 and 5; therefore, the probability that X takes a value between –4 and 1 is lower than the probability that X takes a value between 1 and 5
standard normal distribution	normal distribution with mean 0 and variance 1 in mathematical notation, we refer to the standard normal random variable as Z and write it as: $$Z \sim N(0, 1)$$ two useful properties of Z: - $P(Z \leq -z) = P(Z \geq z)$ (where $z \geq 0$) - $P(-1.96 \leq Z \leq 1.96) \approx 0.95$ to transform a normal random variable X into the standard normal random variable Z, we subtract the mean and then divide the result by the standard deviation: if $X \sim N(\mu, \sigma^2)$, $\dfrac{X - \mu}{\sigma} \sim N(0, 1)$	the probability density function of Z is: if $X \sim N(3, 4)$, then: $$\frac{X - 3}{2} \sim N(0, 1)$$

continues on next page...

6.8.1 CONCEPTS AND NOTATION (CONTINUED)

concept/notation	description	example(s)
expectation of X or expected value of X or $\mathbb{E}(X)$	mean of the random variable X at the population level	if the true support for a candidate at the population level is 40% and *support* is a binary variable that identifies the support for this candidate, then: $$\mathbb{E}(\text{support})=p=0.40$$
sample mean of X or $\overline{X}$	average value of X in a particular sample	if the support for a candidate among a sample of individuals from the population above is 35%, then: $$\overline{\text{support}}=0.35$$
population variance of X or $\mathbb{V}(X)$	variance of the random variable X at the population level	in the example above, because *support* is a binary variable, the population variance of *support* is: $$\mathbb{V}(\text{support})=p(1-p)=0.4(1-0.4)=0.24$$
sample variance of X or $var(X)$	variance of a sample of observations of X	in the example above, the variance of the variable *support* in the sample is: $$var(\text{support})=0.35(1-0.35)=0.23$$
sampling variability	refers to the fact that the value of a statistic varies from one sample to another because each sample contains a different set of observations drawn from the target population; smaller sample size generally leads to greater sampling variability	if we conduct 100 surveys, each containing a representative sample of 1,000 individuals from a population of millions, the results will differ from one survey to another because of sampling variability
law of large numbers	states that as the sample size increases, the sample mean of X approximates the population mean of X	the mean of a sample of 100,000 observations of X is likely to be closer to the population mean of X than the mean of a sample of 100 observations of X
central limit theorem	states that as the sample size increases, the standardized sample mean of X can be approximated by the standard normal distribution	if we were to draw multiple large samples of X, the standardized sample means will follow the standard normal distribution, regardless of how X is distributed
sampling distribution of the sample mean	characterizes how much the sample means vary from one sample to another due to sampling variability $$\overline{X} \overset{\text{approx.}}{\sim} N\left(\mathbb{E}(X), \frac{\mathbb{V}(X)}{n}\right)$$	if we drew multiple samples of 1,000 observations of a random variable X, with mean 2 and variance 4, the sample means would approximately follow a normal distribution with mean 2 and variance 0.004 (4/1000=0.004)

6.8.2 R SYMBOLS AND OPERATORS

code	description	example(s)
for(i in 1:n){}	basic syntax of a for loop; a for loop executes a given code repeatedly, for each i in the sequence from 1 to n, meaning for $i=\{1,\ldots,n\}$, using one i at a time, starting with $i=1$ and ending with $i=n$; the code to be executed repeatedly should be specified inside the curly brackets	for(i in 1:3){ print(i) } # displays the value of i from i=1 until i=3

6.8.3 R FUNCTIONS

function	description	required argument(s)	example(s)
c()	combines values into a vector (a collection of elements, each identified by an index)	values to be combined, separated by commas; if no main argument is provided, this function creates an empty vector that can be used to store outputs	c(1, 2, 3) c() # creates an empty vector

sample()	randomly samples from a set of values; by default, it samples without replacement	the vector with the set of values to draw from
		
		optional argument size: specifies the number of draws
		
		optional argument replace: if set to TRUE, the function draws with replacement (allowing the same value to be drawn more than once)
		
		optional argument prob: specifies the probabilities of selecting each value in the vector; we set this argument to equal a vector containing the probabilities of each value
			sample(c(1, 2, 3))
			  # randomly draws one observation at a time from the vector c(1, 2, 3), without replacement
			
			sample(c(0, 1),
			    size=1000,
			    replace=TRUE,
			    prob=c(0.2, 0.8))
			  # randomly draws 1,000 observations of 0s and 1s, with replacement, where the probability of a 0 is 20% and the probability of a 1 is 80%

rnorm()	randomly samples from a normal distribution; by default, this function samples from the standard normal distribution	the number of observations we want to sample
		
		optional argument mean: specifies the mean of the normal distribution to sample from (if different than the default of 0)
		
		optional argument sd: specifies the standard deviation of the normal distribution to sample from (if different than the default of 1)
			rnorm(100)
			  # randomly draws 100 observations from the standard normal distribution
			
			rnorm(100, mean=3, sd=2)
			  # randomly draws 100 observations from the normal distribution with mean 3 and standard deviation 2

pnorm()	calculates the probability that a normal random variable takes a value *less than or equal to* the number specified inside the parentheses; by default, it calculates probabilities of the standard normal random variable	the number for which we want to calculate the probability
		
		optional argument mean: specifies the mean of the normal random variable we want to compute probabilities of (if different than the default of 0)
		
		optional argument sd: specifies the standard deviation of the normal random variable we want to compute probabilities of (if different than the default of 1)
			pnorm(0)
			  # computes the probability that the standard normal random variable takes a value less than or equal to 0
			
			pnorm(0, mean=3, sd=2)
			  # computes the probability that the normal random variable with mean 3 and standard deviation 2 takes a value less than or equal to 0

print()	displays in the R console the specified argument	what we want to have displayed in the R console	print("this")

7. QUANTIFYING UNCERTAINTY

R symbols, operators, and functions introduced in this chapter: nrow(), predict(), abs(), and summary()$coef.

In the previous chapters, we analyzed data to estimate different quantities of interest. For example, in chapter 2, we analyzed data from Project STAR to estimate the average causal effect of attending a small class on students' reading test scores. In chapter 3, we analyzed data from the BES survey to estimate the proportion of UK voters in favor of Brexit. In chapter 4, we analyzed data from 170 countries to predict GDP growth using night-time light emissions. Finally, in chapter 5, we analyzed data from a survey of Ukrainians to estimate the average causal effect of receiving Russian TV on respondents' voting behavior. The results we arrived at in each of these analyses are, at best, applicable only to the sample of observations we analyzed. In most instances, however, we want to generalize our conclusions to the population from which the sample of observations was drawn. To do so, we need to account for sampling variability, which introduces uncertainty and makes the sample-level estimates different from the population-level quantities of interest. In this chapter, we learn how to quantify the degree of uncertainty in our estimates. As illustrations, we revisit each of the aforementioned analyses.

7.1 ESTIMATORS AND THEIR SAMPLING DISTRIBUTIONS

As we saw in chapter 6, when analyzing data, we are usually interested in a quantity at the population level, yet we typically have access to only a sample of observations. For example, in chapter 3, we were interested in the level of support for Brexit among all UK voters, but we knew only the proportion of supporters among BES survey respondents.

A **parameter** is an unknown quantity of interest. An **estimate** is a sample-level statistic that estimates a parameter. An **estimator** is a function of observed data that is used to produce an estimate of a parameter.

We call the unknown quantity of interest the **parameter**. (Parameters can be sample-level quantities, but we focus on population-level parameters.) We call the statistic that we compute using the sample data the **estimate**, and the formula that produces it, an **estimator**. Formally, an estimator is a function of observed data used to produce an estimate of a parameter.

In this book, we have seen how to use four estimators:

- In chapter 2, we used the difference-in-means estimator to estimate average treatment effects with a randomized experiment.
- In chapter 3, we used the sample mean to estimate population-level averages and proportions.
- In chapter 4, we used a fitted linear model to predict outcomes.
- In chapter 5, we used the coefficients of a fitted linear model to estimate average treatment effects with observational data.

In each of these analyses, we used an estimator to produce an estimate of the corresponding parameter. These estimates, however, are not necessarily identical to the parameters we are interested in. As we saw in the previous chapter, sample statistics differ from population-level parameters because each sample is only a subset of the target population, and sample statistics vary from one sample to another. In the case of the BES survey, the respondents account for only a tiny fraction of all UK voters. As a result, the sample proportion of survey respondents in favor of Brexit is not necessarily the same as the population proportion of *all* UK voters in favor of Brexit. In technical terms, our estimates have some uncertainty due to sampling variability.

Our goal, then, is to quantify the uncertainty in our estimates so that we can draw conclusions about the parameter. Since the value of an estimator varies from one sample to another, we can think of an estimator as a random variable.

POPULATION

parameter = unknown quantity of interest

↓

SAMPLE 1

using the estimator, we compute estimate$_1$

SAMPLE 2

using the estimator, we compute estimate$_2$

. . .

SAMPLE K

using the estimator, we compute estimate$_K$

↓

RANDOM VARIABLE

estimator = {estimate$_1$, estimate$_2$, . . . , estimate$_K$}

The **sampling distribution** of an estimator characterizes the degree to which the estimator varies from one sample to another due to sampling variability. The **standard error** of an estimator is the estimated standard deviation of the sampling distribution of the estimator.

The **sampling distribution** of this random variable characterizes the variability of the estimator from one sample to another, and in relation to the population-level parameter. To quantify the amount of uncertainty in our estimates, then, we need to characterize this sampling distribution.

At the end of the previous chapter, we used the central limit theorem to derive the sampling distribution of the sample mean. We can do the same for the other estimators.

One implication of the central limit theorem is that all the estimators covered in this book have a sampling distribution that is approximately normal and centered at the population-level parameter. (Note that we always assume that the samples are large enough that we can reliably use the central limit theorem.)

To quantify the variation around the population-level parameter, we need to measure the spread of the sampling distribution of the estimator. As we saw in chapter 3, we can use the standard deviation of a random variable to measure the spread of its distribution. Unfortunately, in most cases we cannot compute the standard deviation of the sampling distribution of an estimator directly. Doing so would require drawing multiple samples from the target population, but we rarely have access to more than one sample. Instead, we estimate the standard deviation based on the one sample we draw. We refer to the estimated standard deviation of the sampling distribution of an estimator as the **standard error** of the estimator. (The formula for the standard error is different for each estimator; some of these formulas are quite complicated and beyond the scope of this book.)

Figure 7.1 depicts the sampling distribution of an estimator. As we can see, the standard error quantifies the degree of uncertainty of the estimator due to sampling variability. It measures the amount of variation of the estimator around the true value of the population-level parameter.

FIGURE 7.1. Sampling distribution of an estimator. All the estimators covered in this book have a sampling distribution that is approximately normal and centered at the true value of the population-level parameter. The standard error of an estimator quantifies the spread of its sampling distribution, which is a measure of the degree of uncertainty of the estimator.

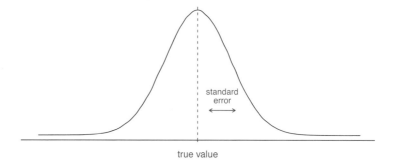

Note that since we usually draw only one sample from the population, we can compute only one value of the estimator. This one estimate might be close to the true value of the parameter (as is, for example, the value of estimate$_1$ in the figure in the margin), or it might be quite far away (as is the value of estimate$_2$). When working with only one sample of data, we never know how far our estimate is from the true value since the true value is unknown.

The difference between the estimate and the true value is called the **estimation error**:

$$estimation\ error_i = \text{estimate}_i - \text{true value}$$

where:

- *estimation error$_i$* is the estimation error for sample *i*
- estimate$_i$ is the estimate for sample *i*
- true value is the true value of the population-level parameter.

In the hypothetical cases above, the estimation errors would be (estimate$_1$−true value) and (estimate$_2$−true value).

While we can never compute the estimation error of a particular estimate, we can calculate two helpful statistics about the estimation error using the central limit theorem.

First, we can derive the **average estimation error**, also known as bias, over multiple hypothetical samples.

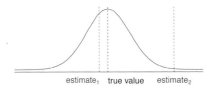

estimate$_1$ true value   estimate$_2$

The **estimation error** is the difference between the estimate and the true value of the parameter. The **average estimation error**, also known as bias, is the average difference between the estimate and the true value of the parameter over multiple hypothetical samples. An estimator is said to be **unbiased** if the average estimation error over multiple hypothetical samples is zero. The **standard error** is an estimate of the average size of the estimation error over multiple hypothetical samples.

FORMULA IN DETAIL

In mathematical notation, the average estimation error is:

$$average\ estimation\ error = \mathbb{E}(\text{estimate}_i - \text{true value})$$

where:

- $\mathbb{E}$ is the population mean
- estimate$_i$ is the estimate for sample *i*
- true value is the true value of the population-level parameter, which equals the population mean of the sampling distribution of the estimator.

An estimator is said to be **unbiased** if the average estimation error over multiple hypothetical samples is zero. While the details are beyond the scope of this book, it is worth noting that all the estimators covered here are unbiased estimators of their corresponding parameters. They provide, on average, accurate estimates. This is consistent with the fact that our estimators all have a sampling distribution that is centered at the true value of the population-level parameter.

Second, we can derive the average *size* of the estimation error over multiple hypothetical samples. This is actually what the **standard error** of the estimator measures. (As we saw in chapter 3, the standard deviation of a random variable measures the average distance of the observations to the mean; here, this average distance is equivalent to the average size of the estimation error.)

FORMULA IN DETAIL

In mathematical notation, the standard error of the estimator is:

$$standard\ error = \sqrt{\mathbb{V}(estimator)} \qquad \text{because standard deviation} = \sqrt{\mathbb{V}(X)}$$

$$= \sqrt{\mathbb{E}[(\text{estimate}_i - \mathbb{E}(estimator))^2]} \qquad \text{because } \mathbb{V}(X) = \mathbb{E}[(X - \mathbb{E}(X))^2]$$

$$= \sqrt{\mathbb{E}[(\text{estimate}_i - \text{true value})^2]} \qquad \text{because } \mathbb{E}(estimator) = \text{true value}$$

where:
- $\mathbb{V}$ is the population variance, and $\mathbb{E}$ is the population mean
- *estimator* is a random variable across multiple hypothetical samples, and estimate$_i$ is the estimate for sample i
- true value is the true value of the population-level parameter, which equals the population mean of the sampling distribution of the estimator.

Note the difference between the average estimation error and the standard error. In the formula for the average estimation error, positive errors cancel out negative errors. By contrast, in the formula for the standard error, positive errors do not cancel out negative errors. (The errors are squared so that they are all positive. Then, after computing the average squared error, we take the square root to return to the initial unit of measurement.) As a result, these two statistics generally differ from each other. While the estimators we use have average estimation errors that equal zero, their standard errors usually do not equal zero.

Putting it all together, if we were to draw multiple samples from the target population and calculate the estimate for each sample, the random variable *estimator* would be approximately distributed as follows:

$$estimator \overset{\text{approx.}}{\sim} N\left(\text{true value},\ (\text{standard error})^2\right)$$

where:
- *estimator* is a random variable containing the estimates from multiple hypothetical samples
- $\overset{\text{approx.}}{\sim}$ stands for "approximately distributed according to"
- N stands for "normal distribution," the first number inside the parentheses denotes the mean of the normal distribution, and the second number denotes the variance

- true value is the true value of the population-level parameter
- standard error is the estimated standard deviation of the estimator across multiple samples, so (standard error)^2 is the estimated variance of the estimator across multiple samples.

Since the sampling distributions of all the estimators in this book can be approximated with the normal distribution, we can standardize the estimators using formula 6.1.

For each of the estimators, then, if we drew multiple samples from the same target population and computed the standardized estimate for each sample, the resulting statistic would approximately follow the standard normal distribution. (See formula 7.1.)

THE STANDARDIZED ESTIMATOR

$$\frac{estimator - \text{true value}}{\text{standard error}} \overset{\text{approx.}}{\sim} N(0, 1)$$

where:

- *estimator* is a random variable across multiple hypothetical samples
- true value is the true value of the population-level parameter
- standard error is the estimated standard deviation of the estimator across multiple samples.

FORMULA 7.1. Formula of the standardized estimator and its distribution across multiple hypothetical samples.

As we will see in detail below, we can use this distribution to draw conclusions about a population-level parameter. In particular, we can use it for two purposes:

First, we can use the sampling distribution to compute confidence intervals. The confidence interval of an estimator provides the range of values that is likely to include the true value of the parameter. In section 7.2, we learn how to construct confidence intervals for the sample mean, the difference-in-means estimator, and the predicted value of an outcome.

Second, we can use the sampling distribution for hypothesis testing. Through hypothesis testing, we determine whether the true value of a parameter is likely to equal a particular value. For example, we may want to determine whether an average treatment effect is different from zero at the population level. In section 7.3, we learn to use hypothesis testing with the difference-in-means estimator as well as with estimated regression coefficients.

7.2 CONFIDENCE INTERVALS

A **confidence interval** provides the range of values that is likely to include the true value of the parameter.

A **confidence interval** provides the range of values that is likely to include the true value of the parameter.

Three levels of confidence are conventionally used in the social sciences to construct confidence intervals: 90%, 95%, and 99%. The level of confidence indicates the probability, over multiple samples, that the true value lies within the interval. With higher levels of confidence, the degree of uncertainty decreases, but the width of the confidence interval increases. The most commonly used level of confidence is 95%, so that is what we use here.

To construct a 95% confidence interval, we start with one of the properties of the standard normal distribution. As we saw in chapter 6, about 95% of the observations in the standard normal random variable fall between -1.96 and 1.96. In mathematical notation, if Z is the standard normal random variable, then:

$$P(-1.96 \leq Z \leq 1.96) \approx 0.95$$

TIP: We focus on this property of the standard normal distribution because we want to construct the 95% confidence interval. If we wanted to construct the 99% confidence interval instead, for example, we would start with the fact that in the standard normal distribution, about 99% of the observations are between -2.58 and 2.58. The resulting confidence interval would be much wider.

Since the standardized estimator approximately follows the standard normal distribution (see formula 7.1), over multiple samples, 95% of the standardized estimators fall between -1.96 and 1.96.

$$P\left(-1.96 \leq \frac{estimator - \text{true value}}{\text{standard error}} \leq 1.96\right) \approx 0.95$$

After moving terms around to isolate the true value, we arrive at:

$$P(\,estimator - 1.96 \times \text{standard error}$$
$$\leq \text{true value} \leq$$
$$estimator + 1.96 \times \text{standard error}\,) \approx 0.95$$

Given the probability above, we can define the 95% confidence interval of an estimator as shown in formula 7.2.

FORMULA 7.2. Formula to construct the 95% confidence interval, the 95% CI for short. In 95% of the samples, the 95% confidence interval constructed using this formula will contain the true value of the parameter.

95% CONFIDENCE INTERVAL

95% CI = [*estimator* − 1.96 × standard error,
estimator + 1.96 × standard error]

where:

- *estimator* is a random variable across multiple hypothetical samples
- standard error is the estimated standard deviation of the estimator across multiple hypothetical samples.

This confidence interval provides bounds on where the true value of the parameter is likely to be. Since the confidence level of the interval is 95%, if we were to draw multiple samples from the same population, 95% of the intervals constructed using this formula should contain the true value of the parameter. In other words, the confidence level of the interval refers to the probability that the interval contains the true value *over multiple samples*.

In reality, as we have already discussed, we usually draw only one sample. As a result, we can construct only one confidence interval. This one confidence interval may or may not contain the true value. Discerning whether it does or not is impossible since we do not know the true value.

Thanks to the central limit theorem, we know that in 5% of the samples, the 95% confidence interval will *not* contain the true value of the parameter. Unfortunately, we have no way of knowing whether we happen to be analyzing one of those fringe samples. This is why it is so important to replicate social scientific studies, that is, to arrive at similar conclusions when analyzing a different sample of data from the same target population. While getting one unlucky sample occurs 5% of the time, getting two unlucky independent samples in a row occurs only 0.25% of the time.

It is important to replicate social scientific studies to confirm that we arrive at similar conclusions when analyzing a different sample from the same target population.

Now that we know the general formula for constructing confidence intervals, let's see how we can use it to construct the confidence interval for the following three estimators: (i) the sample mean, (ii) the difference-in-means estimator, and (iii) predicted outcomes from a fitted linear model.

7.2.1 CONFIDENCE INTERVAL FOR THE SAMPLE MEAN

Let's return to the analysis of chapter 3. There, we analyzed data from the BES survey conducted before the 2016 Brexit referendum to measure public opinion among the entire UK population.

TIP: The code for this chapter's analysis can be found in the "Uncertainty.R" file.

By running the following code, we (i) read and store the dataset in an object named *bes*, (ii) eliminate observations with missing data (including observations from respondents who were either undecided or did not intend to vote) and store the new dataset in an object named *bes1*, (iii) show the number of observations and the number of variables in the *bes1* dataset, and (iv) show the first six observations. (Remember to first set the working directory so that R knows where to find the CSV file.)

RECALL: If the DSS folder is saved directly on your Desktop, to set the working directory, you must run setwd("~/Desktop/DSS") if you have a Mac and setwd("C:/*user*/Desktop/DSS") if you have a Windows computer (where *user* is your own username). If the DSS folder is saved elsewhere, please see subsection 1.7.1 for instructions on how to set the working directory.

```
bes <- read.csv("BES.csv") # reads and stores data

bes1 <- na.omit(bes) # eliminates observations with NAs

dim(bes1) # provides dimensions of dataframe: rows, columns
## [1] 25097    4
```

```
head(bes1) # shows first observations
##    vote leave education age
## 1 leave    1         3  60
## 3 stay     0         5  73
## 4 leave    1         4  64
## 6 stay     0         4  85
## 7 leave    1         3  78
## 8 leave    1         2  51
```

As you may recall, *leave* is a binary variable that identifies Brexit supporters, that is, respondents who intended to vote "leave".

If we want to know the proportion of BES respondents who were in favor of Brexit, we can calculate the mean of *leave*, since the mean of a binary variable is equivalent to the proportion of the observations that have the characteristic identified by the variable. The mean of *leave* can be calculated by running:

```
mean(bes1$leave) # calculates the mean
## [1] 0.4718891
```

Based on the output, we can state that 47.19% of BES respondents were in favor of Brexit ($0.4719 \times 100 = 47.19\%$).

Can we infer from this that about 47% of *all* UK voters were in favor of Brexit? We cannot. This is a sample-level result. To draw conclusions at the population level, we need to take into consideration the noise introduced by sampling variability.

We can construct a measure of uncertainty for the sample mean. In particular, we can derive the 95% confidence interval by substituting in formula 7.2 the sample mean and its standard error. This results in the following 95% confidence interval:

95% CONFIDENCE INTERVAL FOR THE SAMPLE MEAN

$$\left[\ \overline{Y} \ - \ 1.96 \times \sqrt{\frac{var(Y)}{n}}, \quad \overline{Y} \ + \ 1.96 \times \sqrt{\frac{var(Y)}{n}} \ \right]$$

where:

- $\overline{Y}$ is the sample mean of Y
- $\sqrt{var(Y)/n}$ is the standard error of the sample mean
- $var(Y)$ is the sample variance of Y
- n is the number of observations in the sample.

This interval provides the range of values that is likely to contain the true value of the population mean of Y, or $\mathbb{E}(Y)$.

In the running example, to compute the confidence interval for the sample mean of *leave*, we start by computing and storing the sample size, n, into an object so that we can more easily operate with its value.

To compute the sample size of a dataframe, we can use the function nrow(), which stands for "number of rows." The only required argument is the name of the object where the dataset is stored. Here, to compute and store the sample size in an object named n, we run:

nrow() computes the number of rows of a dataframe. The only required argument is the name of the object where the dataframe is stored. Example: nrow(*data*).

```
n <- nrow(bes1) # computes and stores n
```

Now we can compute the lower limit of the interval by running:

```
## calculate lower limit of the 95% CI for sample mean
mean(bes1$leave) - 1.96 * sqrt(var(bes1$leave) / n)
## [1] 0.4657127
```

And, we can compute the upper limit by running:

```
## calculate upper limit of the 95% CI for sample mean
mean(bes1$leave) + 1.96 * sqrt(var(bes1$leave) / n)
## [1] 0.4780655
```

Based on the outputs above, we conclude that the true proportion of support for Brexit among *all* UK voters was likely to be between 46.57% and 47.81%.

There is an alternative way of expressing confidence intervals, which is popular in the world of polling. It involves using what is known as the **margin of error**, defined as half the width of the confidence interval. Using this term, we can express the confidence interval as:

The **margin of error** of an estimator is defined as half the width of the estimator's confidence interval. As a result, we can express the confidence interval as:

estimator $\pm$ margin of error

$$estimator \pm \text{margin of error}$$

In this case, the margin of error equals 0.62 percentage points. (The width of the confidence interval is 47.81%−46.57%=1.24 p.p.; half of that is 0.62 p.p.) Thus, we can state that the likely proportion of support for Brexit among all UK voters was 47.19% with a margin of error of 0.62 percentage points.

RECALL: The difference between two percentages is measured in percentage points (%−%=p.p.).

TIP: Here, the 95% confidence interval can be expressed as either [46.57%, 47.81%] or 47.19% $\pm$ 0.62 p.p.

The margin of error here is small because, as we computed earlier, the BES survey has a large sample size of 25,097 observations. Most polls have a much smaller sample size, of about 1,000 observations, and as a result their margins of error are much larger. (As the sample size, n, decreases, the width of the confidence interval increases.) In general, the degree of uncertainty of our estimates will be larger with smaller sample sizes.

RECALL: If the DSS folder is saved directly on your Desktop, to set the working directory, you must run setwd("~/Desktop/DSS") if you have a Mac and setwd("C:/*user*/Desktop/DSS") if you have a Windows computer (where *user* is your own username). If the DSS folder is saved elsewhere, please see subsection 1.7.1 for instructions on how to set the working directory.

7.2.2 CONFIDENCE INTERVAL FOR THE DIFFERENCE-IN-MEANS ESTIMATOR

We can use a similar procedure to construct the confidence interval for the difference-in-means estimator. Let's return to the analysis of chapter 2. There, we analyzed data from Project STAR, an experiment in which students were randomly assigned to attend either a small class or a regular-size class.

By running the following code, we (i) read and store the dataset in an object named *star*, (ii) show the number of observations and the number of variables in the dataset, (iii) show the first six observations, and (iv) create a new binary variable named *small* identifying the students who were assigned to attend a small class. (Remember to first set the working directory.)

```
star <- read.csv("STAR.csv") # reads and stores data

dim(star) # provides dimensions of dataframe: rows, columns
## [1] 1274    4

head(star) # shows first observations
##    classtype reading math graduated
## 1      small     578  610         1
## 2    regular     612  612         1
## 3    regular     583  606         1
## 4      small     661  648         1
## 5      small     614  636         1
## 6    regular     610  603         0

star$small <- ifelse(star$classtype=="small",
                     1, 0) # creates the treatment variable
```

As you may recall, the purpose of the analysis was to estimate the average causal effect of attending a small class on three measures of student performance: third-grade reading test scores, third-grade math test scores, and the probability of graduating from high school. We focus here on the causal effect on the reading scores.

Because the treatment was randomly assigned, we can assume that students who attended a small class were comparable before schooling to students who attended a regular-size class. As a result, we can use the difference-in-means estimator to estimate the average treatment effect.

To calculate the difference-in-means estimator for reading, we run the following piece of code:

```
## compute the difference-in-means estimator for reading
mean(star$reading[star$small==1]) -
  mean(star$reading[star$small==0])
## [1] 7.210547
```

Based on the output, we can state that among the students who participated in Project STAR, attending a small class increased performance on the third-grade reading test by an estimated 7.21 points, on average. This value is the estimated average treatment effect for the sample of 1,274 students who participated in the experiment. How about at the population level? What would have been the average causal effect of attending a small class on the entire population of students from which the sample was drawn?

We can construct a measure of uncertainty for the difference-in-means estimator. We can derive the 95% confidence interval by substituting in formula 7.2 the difference-in-means estimator and its standard error:

95% CONFIDENCE INTERVAL
FOR THE DIFFERENCE-IN-MEANS ESTIMATOR

LOWER LIMIT:

$$\overline{Y}_{\substack{\text{treatment} \\ \text{group}}} - \overline{Y}_{\substack{\text{control} \\ \text{group}}} \; - \; 1.96 \times \sqrt{\frac{var(Y_{\text{treatment}})}{n_{\text{treatment group}}} + \frac{var(Y_{\text{control}})}{n_{\text{control group}}}}$$

UPPER LIMIT:

$$\overline{Y}_{\substack{\text{treatment} \\ \text{group}}} - \overline{Y}_{\substack{\text{control} \\ \text{group}}} \; + \; 1.96 \times \sqrt{\frac{var(Y_{\text{treatment}})}{n_{\text{treatment group}}} + \frac{var(Y_{\text{control}})}{n_{\text{control group}}}}$$

where:

- $\overline{Y}_{\substack{\text{treatment} \\ \text{group}}} - \overline{Y}_{\substack{\text{control} \\ \text{group}}}$ is the difference-in-means estimator
- $\sqrt{var(Y_{\text{treatment}})/n_{\text{treatment group}} + var(Y_{\text{control}})/n_{\text{control group}}}$ is the standard error of the difference-in-means estimator
- $var(Y_{\text{treatment}})$ and $var(Y_{\text{control}})$ are the sample variances of Y under the treatment and control conditions
- $n_{\text{treatment group}}$ and $n_{\text{control group}}$ are the number of observations in the treatment and the control groups in the sample.

To compute the confidence interval for the difference-in-means estimator, we start by creating two separate dataframes, one for the treatment group and one for the control group. This will help

[] is the operator used to extract a selection of observations from a dataframe. To its left, we specify the dataframe we want to subset. Inside the square brackets, we specify the criterion of selection. Since a dataframe is composed of two dimensions, rows and columns, we can specify a criterion of selection on one or both dimensions. First, we specify the criterion of selection of the rows, and then the criterion of selection of the columns (separated by a comma). If the first criterion is left blank, all rows are extracted, and if the second criterion is left blank, all columns are extracted. Example: *data[data$var1==1,]* extracts the observations that have a value of 1 in *var1* as well as their corresponding values in all the other variables in the dataframe *data*.

simplify our computations. To subset the original dataframe, we can use the [] operator. To its left, we specify the dataframe we want to subset, star in this case. Inside the square brackets we specify (1) the criterion of selection of the rows, and (2) the criterion of selection of the columns (in this order and separated by a comma). To extract the observations that refer to the treatment group, we use star$small==1 as the criterion of selection of rows. To extract the observations that refer to the control group, we use star$small==0 as the criterion of selection of rows. (As you may recall, we can use the relational operator == to specify a logical test.) In both cases, we leave the criterion of selection of columns blank, indicating that we want to extract all variables. To subset and store as new objects the two dataframes, then, we run:

```
## create separate dataframes for each group
treatment <- star[star$small==1, ] # for the treatment group
control   <- star[star$small==0, ] # for the control group
```

Next, we can compute and store as a new object the sample size of each of the two dataframes by running:

```
## compute and store sample sizes for each group
n_t <- nrow(treatment) # for the treatment group
n_c <- nrow(control) # for the control group
```

Now, to compute the lower limit of the 95% confidence interval for the difference-in-means estimator, we run:

```
## calculate lower limit of 95% CI for diffs-in-means
mean(treatment$reading) - mean(control$reading) -
  1.96 * sqrt(var(treatment$reading) / n_t
            + var(control$reading) / n_c)
## [1] 3.167621
```

And, to compute the upper limit, we run:

```
## calculate upper limit of 95% CI for diffs-in-means
mean(treatment$reading) - mean(control$reading) +
  1.96 * sqrt(var(treatment$reading) / n_t
            + var(control$reading) / n_c)
## [1] 11.25347
```

Based on the outputs above, we conclude that the average causal effect of attending a small class on third-grade reading test scores among *all* students in the target population was likely an increase of between 3.17 and 11.25 points or, expressed differently, an increase of 7.21 ± 4.04 points. (The width of the confidence interval here is 11.25−3.17=8.08 points, and so the margin of error is 4.04 points.)

7.2.3 CONFIDENCE INTERVAL FOR PREDICTED OUTCOMES

Finally, we can use a similar procedure to construct confidence intervals for predicted outcomes. Let's return to the analysis of chapter 4, where we fitted a linear model to predict GDP growth using changes in night-time light emissions.

By running the following code, we (i) read and store the dataset in an object named *co*, (ii) show the number of observations and variables in the dataset, (iii) show the first six observations, and (iv) create our two variables of interest. (Remember to first set the working directory.)

RECALL: If the DSS folder is saved directly on your Desktop, to set the working directory, you must run setwd("~/Desktop/DSS") if you have a Mac and setwd("C:/*user*/Desktop/DSS") if you have a Windows computer (where *user* is your own username). If the DSS folder is saved elsewhere, please see subsection 1.7.1 for instructions on how to set the working directory.

```
co <- read.csv("countries.csv")  # reads and stores data

dim(co)  # provides dimensions of dataframe: rows, columns
## [1] 170   5

head(co)  # shows first observations
##    country     gdp  prior_gdp    light  prior_light
## 1      USA  11.107      7.373    4.227        4.482
## 2    Japan 543.017    464.168   11.926       11.808
## 3  Germany   2.152      1.793   10.573        9.699
## 4    China  16.558      4.901    1.451        0.735
## 5       UK   1.098      0.754   11.856       13.392
## 6   France   1.582      1.208    8.513        6.909

## create GDP percentage change variable
co$gdp_change <-
   ((co$gdp - co$prior_gdp) / co$prior_gdp) * 100

## create light percentage change variable
co$light_change <-
   ((co$light - co$prior_light) / co$prior_light) * 100
```

As you may recall, to predict GDP growth using the percentage change in night-time light emissions, we employed the following linear model:

$$\widehat{gdp\_change}_i = \widehat{\alpha} + \widehat{\beta}\ light\_change_i \quad (i=\text{countries})$$

where:

- $\widehat{gdp\_change}_i$ is the average predicted percentage change in GDP from 1992–1993 to 2005–2006 among countries in which the value of *light_change* equals *light_change$_i$*

- *light_change$_i$* is the percentage change in night-time light emissions experienced by country *i* from 1992–1993 to 2005–2006.

To fit the linear model and store it as an object, we run:

```
fit  <- lm(gdp_change ~ light_change,
              data=co) # fits and stores linear model

fit  # shows contents of object
##
## Call:
## lm(formula = gdp_change ~ light_change, data = co)
##
## Coefficients:
## (Intercept)   light_change
##      49.8202        0.2546
```

The fitted model is then:

$$\widehat{gdp\_change} = 49.82 + 0.25 \ light\_change$$

Now, we can use this model to make predictions. For example, in chapter 4, we found that a country in which night-time light emissions increased by 20% during a 13-year period is predicted to have experienced GDP growth of about 55% in the same time period, on average (49.82+0.25×20=54.82).

Because of potential noise in the data, there is some uncertainty around this prediction. As we did in the last two subsections, we can construct a 95% confidence interval to measure this uncertainty. In this case, the math is much more complicated, so we ask R to compute it for us.

To calculate the 95% confidence interval for a predicted outcome, we can use the function predict(), which makes predictions based on a fitted linear model. This function requires as its main argument the name of the object that contains the output of the lm() function. To specify the value of the predictor we want to use for the prediction, we use the optional argument newdata. This argument needs a dataframe, which we can create using the function data.frame(). Inside these parentheses, we specify the value of the predictor: light_change=20 in this case. Finally, if in addition to the prediction, we want R to provide the 95% confidence interval, we set the optional argument interval to equal "confidence". By default, this argument provides the interval using a level of confidence of 95%. (If we wanted a different level of confidence, we would specify the optional argument level.)

```
## compute 95% confidence interval for prediction
predict ( fit ,  # object with lm() output
       newdata=data.frame(light_change=20), # set value of X
        interval ="confidence") # provide 95% confidence interval
##        fit      lwr      upr
## 1 54.91233 48.77123 61.05343
```

---

predict() makes predictions based on a fitted linear model. The only required argument is the name of the object that contains the output of the lm() function. By default, this function produces a prediction for every observation in the dataset used to fit the linear model. To produce only one prediction based on a particular value of the predictor(s), we set the optional argument newdata to equal data.frame(), where inside the parentheses we specify the value of the predictor(s). To also produce the 95% confidence interval of that one prediction, we set the optional argument interval to equal "confidence". To change the level of confidence of the interval, we would specify the optional argument level. Example: fit <- lm(y_var ~ x_var, data=data) then predict(fit, newdata=data.frame(x_var=5), interval="confidence", level=0.99).

The first number R provides is the predicted outcome based on the specified (i) fitted linear model and (ii) value of the predictor. The next two numbers are the lower and upper limits of the 95% confidence interval. Based on the output above, then, we can state that the 95% confidence interval of our predicted outcome is [48.77, 61.05].

We can, therefore, conclude that a country in which night-time light emissions increased by 20% during a 13-year period would have likely experienced in the same time period an average GDP growth of between 48.77% and 61.05%, or 54.91% ± 6.14 p.p. (The width of the interval here is 61.05%−48.77%=12.28 p.p., and so the margin of error is 6.14 p.p.)

7.3 HYPOTHESIS TESTING

Hypothesis testing is a methodology that we use to determine whether a parameter is likely to equal a particular value. (There are other uses of hypothesis testing, but we focus on this specific application.) For example, we can use hypothesis testing to determine whether or not an average treatment effect is different from zero in the target population.

Hypothesis testing is based on the idea of proof by contradiction. We start by assuming the contrary of what we would like to prove and show how this assumption leads to a logical contradiction.

Specifically, we begin by defining what is known as the **null hypothesis**, denoted as H_0. This is the hypothesis we would like to eventually refute, that is, find sufficient evidence against. For example, if we are interested in whether a treatment affects an outcome, on average, at the population level, we would set the null hypothesis to state that the true value of the parameter—the average treatment effect at the population level, in this case— equals zero. This would mean that the outcome neither increases nor decreases, on average, as a result of the treatment.

In general, the null hypothesis can state that the true value equals any particular value, which we denote by θ (the Greek letter theta). In this book, however, we always set the null hypothesis to state that the true value of the parameter equals zero. In mathematical notation, the null hypothesis is:

H_0: true value $= \theta$ (in general)

H_0: true value $= 0$ (in this book)

Hypothesis testing is a methodology we use to determine whether a parameter is likely to equal a particular value. The **null hypothesis**, H_0, is the hypothesis we would like to eventually refute; in this book, H_0: true value$=0$. The **alternative hypothesis**, H_1, is the hypothesis we test the null hypothesis against; in this book, H_1: true value$\neq 0$.

Next, we set the **alternative hypothesis**, denoted as H_1. This is the hypothesis we test the null hypothesis against. In this book, we employ what is known as a two-sided alternative hypothesis, which states that the true value of the parameter is not θ, without restricting the parameter to being above or below θ. In particular, since we set θ to equal zero in our null hypothesis, our alternative hypothesis states that the true value of the parameter is not zero, without restricting the sign of the parameter to being positive or negative. In mathematical notation, the alternative hypothesis is:

H_1: true value $\neq \theta$ (in general)

H_1: true value $\neq 0$ (in this book)

Now, let's return to the distribution of our standardized estimator over multiple hypothetical samples (formula 7.1):

$$\frac{estimator - \text{true value}}{\text{standard error}} \overset{\text{approx.}}{\sim} N(0, 1)$$

If the null hypothesis is correct and the true value of the parameter equals θ, then we end up with:

$$\frac{estimator - \theta}{\text{standard error}} \overset{\text{approx.}}{\sim} N(0, 1) \quad (\text{if true value} = \theta)$$

A **test statistic** is a function of observed data that can be used to test the null hypothesis. Here we use a test statistic called the **z-statistic**, whose distribution under the null hypothesis is the standard normal distribution.

This random variable is known as the **z-statistic**. The z-statistic is an example of a **test statistic**, which is a function of observed data that can be used to test the null hypothesis.

In the case of our null hypothesis, in which the true value of the parameter is set to equal zero, the test statistic and its distribution across multiple hypothetical samples are:

FORMULA 7.3. Formula of the test statistic and its distribution under the null, when the null hypothesis states that the true value of the parameter equals zero.

TEST STATISTIC

$$\text{z-statistic} = \frac{estimator}{\text{standard error}} \overset{\text{approx.}}{\sim} N(0, 1)$$

where:

- *estimator* is a random variable across multiple hypothetical samples
- standard error is the estimated standard deviation of the estimator across multiple hypothetical samples.

Suppose we were to draw multiple samples from the same target population and compute the z-statistic for each sample. Then, thanks to the central limit theorem, we know that if the null hypothesis were true, the z-statistics would approximately follow the standard normal distribution. In reality, however, we usually draw only one sample. As a result, we can observe only one realization of the z-statistic. We denote the observed value of the z-statistic as z^{obs}.

Now we can gauge the degree of consistency between what we observe and the null hypothesis. Here is the general idea: If the observed value of the test statistic is extreme relative to the distribution of the test statistic under the null hypothesis (as is, for example, the value of z_1^{obs} in the figure in the margin), then what we observe would be highly unlikely if the null hypothesis were true. We would, thus, conclude that the null hypothesis is likely to be false. In statistical terms, we would *reject the null hypothesis*. Alternatively, if the observed value of the test statistic is typical under the null hypothesis (as is the value of z_2^{obs}), then what we observe would be likely if the null hypothesis were true. We would, in this case, not have enough evidence to claim that the null hypothesis is likely to be false. In statistical terms, we would *fail to reject the null hypothesis*. Let's add more details.

Because we know the distribution of the test statistic under the null hypothesis, we can compute the probability that we observe a value at least as extreme as the one we observed if indeed the null hypothesis is true. This probability is called the **p-value**. Here, because our alternative hypothesis is two-sided, we calculate what is known as the two-sided p-value.

The two-sided p-value computes the probability that we observe a test statistic as extreme as the one we observed in either direction of the real line. Here, it is equivalent to (i) the area under the curve of the standard normal distribution between negative infinity and $-|z^{obs}|$, plus (ii) the area under the curve of the standard normal distribution between $|z^{obs}|$ and infinity (where, again, z^{obs} is the observed value of the z-statistic). (See the shaded areas in figure 7.2.)

TIP: The distribution of the test statistic *under the null hypothesis* is the distribution the test statistic would approximately follow if the null hypothesis were true. Here, the distribution of the test statistic under the null hypothesis is the standard normal distribution, $N(0, 1)$.

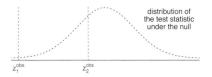

distribution of the test statistic under the null

z_1^{obs} z_2^{obs}

The **p-value** is the probability that we observe a value of the test statistic at least as extreme as the one we actually observed if the null hypothesis is true.

RECALL: The probability that Z takes a value between z_1 and z_2 is equivalent to the area under the curve of the standard normal distribution between z_1 and z_2.

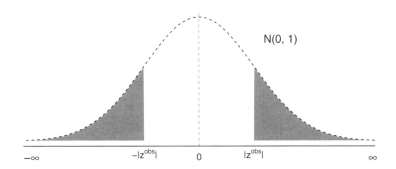

$N(0, 1)$

$-\infty$ $-|z^{obs}|$ 0 $|z^{obs}|$ ∞

FIGURE 7.2. The two-sided p-value is the probability of observing a test statistic below $-|z^{obs}|$ plus the probability of observing a test statistic above $|z^{obs}|$ in the standard normal distribution, which is the distribution of the test statistic if the null hypothesis is true.

In mathematical notation, the two-sided p-value is defined as:

$$\text{two-sided p-value} \; = \; P(Z \le \text{-}|z^{obs}|) \; + \; P(Z \ge |z^{obs}|)$$

Since the standard normal distribution is symmetric and centered at zero, the probability of a value below $\text{-}|z^{obs}|$ is the same as the probability of a value above $|z^{obs}|$. This property enables us to simplify the formula of the two-sided p-value:

$$\text{two-sided p-value} \; = \; 2 \times P(Z \le \text{-}|z^{obs}|)$$

When calculating the two-sided p-value, we add the two above-mentioned probabilities because we consider extreme values in either direction of the real line. We use this type of p-value whenever the alternative hypothesis is two-sided, that is, when it does not constrain the sign of the parameter. Had we stated as our alternative hypothesis that the parameter is positive (because we knew for sure that it could not be negative), then we could compute a one-sided p-value, which would equal the probability that we observe a test statistic as extreme as the one we observed only in the positive direction. (See figure in the margin.)

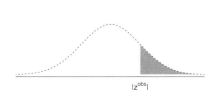

$|z^{obs}|$

In general, a smaller p-value provides stronger evidence against the null hypothesis. A very small p-value indicates that the observed value of the test statistic would be highly unlikely if the null hypothesis were true. Thus, when the p-value is very small, there are two possible scenarios: either (a) the null hypothesis is true and we observed something highly unlikely, or (b) the null hypothesis is not true. As the p-value decreases into extremely small magnitudes, we become increasingly confident that the null hypothesis is not true, and thus, we reject it.

The **significance level** determines the rejection threshold of the test and characterizes the probability of false rejection of the null hypothesis.

How small does the p-value need to be for us to reject the null hypothesis? We reject the null hypothesis when the p-value is equal to or smaller than what is known as the **significance level** (or just "level") of the test. Social scientists conventionally use one of three significance levels: 10%, 5%, and 1%. In this book, we use 5% as our significance level. Thus, we reject the null hypothesis when the p-value is equal to or smaller than 0.05 (or 5%), and we fail to reject the null hypothesis when the p-value is greater than 0.05 (or 5%).

RECALL: To interpret a proportion or a probability as a percentage, we multiply the decimal value by 100.

Note that through this procedure, we never *accept the null hypothesis*. Failing to reject the null hypothesis is not the same as accepting it. Just because we have not found evidence against the null hypothesis doesn't mean that we have proven it to be true. On the flip side, however, rejecting the null hypothesis *is* the same as accepting the alternative hypothesis, although we typically do not express it that way.

A result is said to be **statistically significant** at the 5% level when we can reject the null hypothesis using the 5% rejection threshold and conclude that the corresponding parameter is distinguishable from zero. Alternatively, a result is said to be **not statistically significant** at the 5% level when we fail to reject the null hypothesis using the 5% rejection threshold and conclude that the corresponding parameter is not distinguishable from zero.

When a result is statistically significant at the 5% level, do we know for sure that the true value of the corresponding parameter is not zero? No, we do not. A p-value of 5% does not rule out the possibility that the parameter is zero. In fact, thanks to the central limit theorem, we know that if the null hypothesis is true, in 5% of the samples drawn from the target population, we will wrongly reject the null when using a significance level of 5%. Indeed, the significance level of a test characterizes the probability of false rejection of the null hypothesis (known as *type I error*). The smaller the level used in the test, the less likely we are to falsely reject the null. The possibility of wrongly rejecting the null illustrates the importance of replicating social scientific studies to confirm their conclusions. While the probability of falsely rejecting the null hypothesis in any one sample is 5%, the probability of falsely rejecting the null twice in a row, when analyzing two independent samples of data drawn from the same target population, is only 0.25%.

The cut-off points of the test statistic used to determine whether to reject the null hypothesis are called **critical values**. If the distribution of the test statistic is well-approximated by the standard normal distribution and our alternative hypothesis is two-sided, the critical value for the 5% significance level is 1.96. This means that when we observe a z-statistic that in absolute value is greater than or equal to 1.96, we will reject the null at the 5% level, and when we observe a z-statistic that in absolute value is less than 1.96, we will fail to reject the null at the 5% level. (For an explanation, see the formula in detail below.)

A result is **statistically significant** at the 5% level when the corresponding parameter is distinguishable from zero using 5% as the rejection threshold. Conversely, a result is **not statistically significant** at the 5% level when the corresponding parameter is not distinguishable from zero using 5% as the rejection threshold.

A **critical value** is the cut-off point of the test statistic used to determine whether to reject the null hypothesis. If the distribution of the test statistic is well-approximated by the standard normal distribution and our alternative hypothesis is two-sided, the critical value for the 5% significance level is 1.96.

FORMULA IN DETAIL

First, recall that the two-sided p-value is:

$$\text{two-sided p-value} = P(Z \leq -|z^{obs}|) + P(Z \geq |z^{obs}|)$$

If $|z^{obs}|$ equals 1.96, the two-sided p-value will approximately equal 0.05 (or 5%):

$$\text{two-sided p-value} = P(Z \leq -1.96) + P(Z \geq 1.96) \approx 0.05$$

Here is the reasoning: As we saw in chapter 6, the probability that Z takes a value between -1.96 and 1.96 is approximately 95%. Therefore, the probability that Z takes a value less than or equal to -1.96 plus the probability that Z takes a value greater than or equal to 1.96 is approximately 5% $(1-0.95=0.05)$.

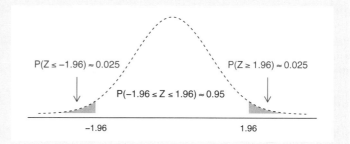

Second, note that as $|z^{obs}|$ increases, that is, moves farther into the tails of the distribution, the associated two-sided p-value decreases because the area under the curve that measures this probability becomes smaller. (As we move from left to right in the figure below, the values of $|z^{obs}|$ increase and the associated two-sided p-values decrease.)

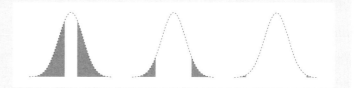

Taken together, if the absolute value of the z-statistic is greater than or equal to 1.96, the two-sided p-value will be less than or equal to 0.05 (or 5%), and so we will reject the null at the 5% significance level. Conversely, if the absolute value of the z-statistic is less than 1.96, the two-sided p-value will be greater than 0.05 (or 5%), and so we will fail to reject the null at the 5% significance level.

To summarize, below is the formal procedure for conducting hypothesis testing to determine whether a parameter is likely different than zero using the 5% significance level. Note, again, that you can compare either the absolute value of the observed z-statistic to 1.96 or the associated two-sided p-value to 0.05. These two procedures are mathematically equivalent and lead to the same conclusion.

HYPOTHESIS TESTING
WITH 5% SIGNIFICANCE LEVEL

1. Specify null and alternative hypotheses:

$$H_0: \text{true value} = 0$$
$$H_1: \text{true value} \neq 0$$

2a. Compute observed value of the test statistic:

$$z^{obs} = \frac{\text{estimator}}{\text{standard error}}$$

2b. Compute associated two-sided p-value:

$$\text{two-sided p-value} = 2 \times P(Z \leq -|z^{obs}|)$$

3. Conclude:

- If $|z^{obs}| \geq 1.96$ or p-value ≤ 0.05,
  reject the null hypothesis and conclude that the result
  is statistically significant at the 5% level.

- If $|z^{obs}| < 1.96$ or p-value > 0.05,
  fail to reject the null hypothesis and conclude that the
  result is not statistically significant at the 5% level.

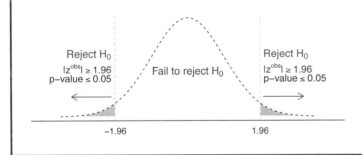

Now that we know the general procedure for conducting hypothesis testing, let's see how we can use it to determine whether a treatment affects an outcome, on average, at the population level. We start by learning how hypothesis testing works with the difference-in-means estimator. Then, we learn how it works with estimated regression coefficients.

7.3.1 HYPOTHESIS TESTING WITH THE DIFFERENCE-IN-MEANS ESTIMATOR

Let's return to our analysis of Project STAR. Since this was a randomized experiment, we can use the difference-in-means estimator to estimate average treatment effects.

To conduct hypothesis testing with the difference-in-means estimator, first we set the null hypothesis to state that the true value of the average treatment effect at the population level equals zero. In mathematical notation:

$$H_0: \mathbb{E}[Y_i(X_i=1) - Y_i(X_i=0)] = 0$$

where:

- $\mathbb{E}[Y_i(X_i=1) - Y_i(X_i=0)]$ is the average treatment effect at the population level, where $\mathbb{E}$ denotes the population mean
- $Y_i(X_i=1)$ and $Y_i(X_i=0)$ are the potential outcomes under the treatment and control conditions, respectively, for individual i.

Next, we set the alternative hypothesis to state that the treatment either increases or decreases the outcome, on average, at the population level. In mathematical notation:

$$H_1: \mathbb{E}[Y_i(X_i=1) - Y_i(X_i=0)] \neq 0$$

Then, using formula 7.3, we construct the following test statistic for the difference-in-means estimator:

TEST STATISTIC FOR THE DIFFERENCE-IN-MEANS ESTIMATOR

$$\text{z-statistic} = \frac{\overline{Y}_{\text{treatment group}} - \overline{Y}_{\text{control group}}}{\sqrt{\frac{var(Y_{\text{treatment}})}{n_{\text{treatment group}}} + \frac{var(Y_{\text{control}})}{n_{\text{control group}}}}}$$

where:

- $\overline{Y}_{\text{treatment group}} - \overline{Y}_{\text{control group}}$ is the difference-in-means estimator
- $\sqrt{\frac{var(Y_{\text{treatment}})}{n_{\text{treatment group}}} + \frac{var(Y_{\text{control}})}{n_{\text{control group}}}}$ is the standard error of the difference-in-means estimator
- $var(Y_{\text{treatment}})$ and $var(Y_{\text{control}})$ are the sample variances of Y under the treatment and control conditions
- $n_{\text{treatment group}}$ and $n_{\text{control group}}$ are the number of observations in the treatment and the control groups in the sample.

Now that we know what we need to compute to test the null hypothesis in this case, let's continue the analysis we started in subsection 7.2.2. To compute (and store) the observed value of the test statistic in the running example, we run:

```
## calculate and store observed value of test statistic
z_obs <- (mean(treatment$reading) -
                mean(control$reading)) /
            sqrt(var(treatment$reading) / n_t +
                var(control$reading) / n_c )

z_obs # shows contents of object
## [1] 3.495654
```

In the sample of data we are analyzing, the value of the test statistic is 3.5. Since its absolute value is greater than 1.96, we can already reject the null hypothesis and conclude that the effect is statistically significant at the 5% level.

Even so, let's continue to compute the associated p-value. Since the test statistic is 3.5, the two-sided p-value is the probability that in the standard normal distribution, we observe a value less than -3.5 or greater than 3.5. This is equivalent to two times the probability that we observe a value below -3.5.

To compute p-values in R, we can use the function pnorm() in conjunction with the function abs(), which stands for "absolute value." For example, to compute the p-value here, we run:

```
## calculate the associated two-sided p-value
2 * pnorm( -abs(z_obs))
## [1] 0.0004729011
```

Based on the output above, if the null hypothesis is true, the probability of observing a test statistic equal to or larger than 3.5 (in absolute value) is 0.05% ($0.0005\times100=0.05\%$). This is an extremely small probability.

Since the p-value is smaller than 5%, we reject the null hypothesis and conclude that the effect is statistically significant at the 5% level. In other words, we conclude that attending a small class is likely to have a non-zero average causal effect on reading scores for *all* students in the target population, and not only for those who participated in Project STAR.

Note that we could have arrived at the same conclusion using the 95% confidence interval for the difference-in-means estimator we computed in subsection 7.2.2. If the 95% confidence interval of an estimator does not include zero, we will reject the null hypothesis that the corresponding parameter equals zero at the 5% level. By the same logic, if it does include zero, we will fail to reject the null hypothesis.

TIP: If you are starting a new R session here, you need to re-run the lines of code that we wrote in subsection 7.2.2 that:
- set the working directory
- read and store the dataset
- create the treatment variable
- create two separate dataframes, one for the treatment group and one for the control group
- compute and store the sample sizes of each of the two dataframes.

RECALL: pnorm() calculates the probability that the standard normal random variable, Z, takes a value *less than or equal to* the number specified inside the parentheses. Example: pnorm(0).

abs() calculates the absolute value of the argument specified inside the parentheses. Example: abs(-2).

TIP: Computing confidence intervals and conducting hypothesis testing are equivalent procedures and will lead us to the same conclusions as long as the level of confidence of the interval equals 100 minus the significance level of the test.

> RELATIONSHIP BETWEEN CONFIDENCE INTERVALS AND HYPOTHESIS TESTING: If the 95% confidence interval of an estimator does not include zero, we will reject the null hypothesis that the corresponding parameter equals zero at the 5% level. By the same logic, if it does include zero, we will fail to reject the null hypothesis.

In the example at hand, the 95% confidence interval for the difference-in-means estimator was [3.17, 11.25]. Since the interval did not include zero, we could have already concluded that the effect is statistically significant at the 5% level.

7.3.2 HYPOTHESIS TESTING WITH ESTIMATED REGRESSION COEFFICIENTS

We have just learned how to use hypothesis testing to determine whether an average treatment effect is statistically significant based on the difference-in-means estimator. This procedure is useful for analyses of randomized experiments in which we do not have to worry about confounding variables.

As we saw in chapter 5, when analyzing observational data, we do worry about the presence of confounding variables obscuring the causal relationship between the treatment and the outcome. In this case, the difference-in-means estimator no longer provides a valid estimate of the average treatment effect. Instead, we can fit a multiple linear regression model in which X_1 is the treatment variable and all other X variables are the confounding variables. If the model includes all potential confounding variables as control variables, $\widehat{\beta}_1$ (the estimated coefficient affecting the treatment variable X_1) can be interpreted as a valid estimate of the average treatment effect. We can then use hypothesis testing to determine whether the effect, represented by $\widehat{\beta}_1$, is likely to be zero.

Let's return to the analysis in chapter 5 of the survey conducted after the 2014 election on a random sample of Ukrainians living in precincts within 50 kilometers of the Ukraine-Russia border.

RECALL: If the DSS folder is saved directly on your Desktop, to set the working directory, you must run setwd("~/Desktop/DSS") if you have a Mac and setwd("C:/*user*/Desktop/DSS") if you have a Windows computer (where *user* is your own username). If the DSS folder is saved elsewhere, please see subsection 1.7.1 for instructions on how to set the working directory.

By running the following code, we (i) read and store the dataset in an object named *uas*, (ii) show the number of observations and variables in the dataset, and (iii) show the first six observations. (Remember to first set the working directory.)

```
uas <- read.csv("UA_survey.csv") # reads and stores data

dim(uas) # provides dimensions of dataframe: rows, columns
## [1] 358   3
```

```
head(uas) # shows first observations
##   russian_tv pro_russian_vote within_25km
## 1            1               0            1
## 2            1               1            1
## 3            0               0            0
## 4            0               0            1
## 5            0               0            1
## 6            1               0            0
```

As you may recall, we were interested in estimating the effect that receiving Russian TV had on a respondent's probability of voting for a pro-Russian party in the 2014 parliamentary election. We were concerned that living in close proximity to the border was a confounding variable, given the existence of military fortifications along the border at the time.

The treatment variable was *russian_tv*, the outcome variable was *pro_russian_vote*, and the confounding variable was *within_25km*. To estimate the average treatment effect, we employed the following multiple linear regression model:

$$pro\_russian\_vote_i = \alpha + \beta_1 \ russian\_tv_i$$
$$+ \ \beta_2 \ within\_25km_i + \epsilon_i \quad (i=\text{respondents})$$

where:

- *pro_russian_vote$_i$* is the binary variable that identifies whether respondent *i* voted for a pro-Russian party in the 2014 Ukrainian parliamentary election
- *russian_tv$_i$* is the treatment variable, which indicates whether the precinct where respondent *i* lives received Russian TV
- *within_25km$_i$* is the confounding variable, which indicates whether the precinct where respondent *i* lives is within 25 kilometers of the border
- ϵ_i is the error term for respondent *i*.

To fit the linear model and store it as an object, we run:

```
fit <- lm(pro_russian_vote ~ russian_tv + within_25km,
          data=uas) # fits and stores linear model
```

```
fit # shows contents of object
##
## Call:
## lm(formula = pro_russian_vote ~ russian_tv
##          + within_25km, data=uas)
##
## Coefficients:
## (Intercept)    russian_tv   within_25km
##      0.1959        0.2876       -0.2081
```

Based on the value of $\widehat{\beta}_1$ above, we estimate that, when we hold living very close to the border constant, receiving Russian TV (as compared to not receiving it) increased a respondent's probability of voting for a pro-Russian party by 29 percentage points, on average.

Does this mean that the average treatment effect is different from zero at the population level (that is, across *all* Ukrainians who live near the border with Russia)? To decide whether we have statistically significant evidence to conclude one way or the other, we use hypothesis testing.

First, we set the null hypothesis to state that receiving Russian TV had an average causal effect on Ukrainians' voting behavior at the population level of zero. In other words, we set the true value of β_1 to equal zero. (Note that when we speak of the true regression coefficient, we do not use the "hat," because it is not an estimate. We are referring to the value one would obtain if the model were fitted to the population.) In mathematical notation:

$$H_0: \beta_1 = 0$$

Next, we set the alternative hypothesis to state that the true coefficient does not equal 0; that is, receiving Russian TV either increased or decreased Ukrainian's probability of voting for a pro-Russian party, on average, at the population level. In mathematical notation:

$$H_1: \beta_1 \neq 0$$

Then, using formula 7.3, we construct the following test statistic for the estimated regression coefficient $\widehat{\beta}_1$:

TEST STATISTIC FOR $\widehat{\beta}_1$

$$\text{z-statistic} = \frac{\widehat{\beta}_1}{\text{standard error of } \widehat{\beta}_1}$$

where:
- $\widehat{\beta}_1$ is the estimated regression coefficient
- standard error of $\widehat{\beta}_1$ is the estimated standard deviation of the estimated regression coefficients over multiple samples.

In this case, we do not go into the specifics of how to compute the standard error of $\widehat{\beta}_1$ because it is rather complicated. We focus instead on how to ask R to compute it.

For this purpose, we can use the function summary(), which computes several statistics related to a fitted linear model, including the standard errors of the estimated regression coefficients. To focus on the statistics we are interested in, we can ask R to show us only the element named coef of the output from the function summary() by running summary()$coef, where inside the parentheses we specify the name of the object that contains the output of the lm() function. (Recall that we use the $ character to access a variable inside a dataframe; in general, we can use it to access an element within an object.) For example, go ahead and run:

```
## show table with statistics related to fitted model
summary(fit)$coef
##                  Estimate  Std. Error  t value   Pr(>|t|)
##(Intercept)        0.19590   0.0345782  5.665602  3.0321e-08
##russian_tv         0.28759   0.0765243  3.758194  2.0002e-04
##within_25km       -0.20806   0.0768105 -2.708802  7.0798e-03
```

As shown above, R provides a table of statistics related to the fitted linear model. The first column shows the estimated coefficients: $\hat{\alpha}$, $\hat{\beta}_1$, and $\hat{\beta}_2$. The second column shows the standard errors of each of the coefficients. The third column shows the values of the test statistics for each of the coefficients. Finally, the fourth column shows the associated two-sided p-values.

Note that, by default, R does not assume that the sample size is large enough to use the central limit theorem. As a result, the distribution of the test statistic under the null hypothesis is no longer the standard normal distribution but rather a distribution called the t-distribution. Consequently, the name of the test statistic changes from z-statistic to t-statistic, although the formula remains the same. (Note that R refers to the observed value of the t-statistic as t-value.) Compared to the standard normal distribution, the t-distribution is also symmetric and bell-shaped but has fatter tails. The p-values computed by R here are slightly larger and, as a result, lead to somewhat more conservative inferences. As long as the sample is not very small, however, the difference is typically negligible. (In fact, as the sample size increases, the t-distribution converges to the standard normal distribution.) When drawing conclusions, then, we can ignore the differences and rely on the p-values provided by R in the table above.

The statistics we care about are those related to $\hat{\beta}_1$, the estimated coefficient that affects *russian_tv*, since that is the coefficient that can be interpreted as the average treatment effect in this case.

Based on the table of results above, the value of the test statistic associated with $\hat{\beta}_1$ is 3.76. This is indeed the result we arrive at if we divide $\hat{\beta}_1$ by its standard error (0.2876/0.0765=3.76).

summary()$coef provides a table with the following statistics related to a fitted linear model: estimated regression coefficients, standard errors, test statistics, and two-sided p-values. The one required argument is the output of the lm() function. Example: fit <- lm(y_var ~ x_var, data=data) and then summary(fit)$coef.

TIP: What does R mean by 2.0002e−04? (See p-value associated with $\hat{\beta}_1$.) It means 0.00020002, or 2.0002×10^{-4}. When a number is either too large or too small to be displayed compactly, R uses what is known as scientific notation, where e stands for "times ten raised to the power of." To get a better sense of how scientific notation works, see the examples below:

$$2e{+}04 = 2 \times 10^4 = 20{,}000$$
$$0e{+}00 = 0 \times 10^0 = 0$$
$$2e{-}04 = 2 \times 10^{-4} = 0.0002$$

TIP: Most studies that fit linear regression models to analyze data report the estimated coefficients and their standard errors in a table similar to one of the two below:

	Estimated Coefficients	Standard Errors
Russian TV	0.2876	(0.0765)
Within 25 km	−0.2080	(0.0768)
Intercept	0.1959	(0.0346)

Or, if multiple models are fitted:

	Model 1	Model 2
Russian TV	0.1191	0.2876
	(0.045)	(0.0765)
Within 25 km		−0.2080
		(0.0768)
Intercept	0.1709	0.1959
	(0.0336)	(0.0346)

Although the values of the test statistics are not provided, they can be easily computed by dividing the estimated coefficients by their standard errors, which are usually displayed in parentheses.

Because the absolute value of the test statistic is greater than 1.96 (the critical value for the 5% level), we already have enough evidence to reject the null hypothesis at the 5% significance level and determine that the effect is statistically significant.

Even so, let's take a look at the associated p-value. Based on the table above, the two-sided p-value associated with $\widehat{\beta}_1$ is 0.0002. Thus, if the null hypothesis is true, the probability of observing a test statistic equal to or larger than 3.76 (in absolute value) is 0.02% ($0.0002 \times 100 = 0.02\%$). Since the p-value is smaller than 5%, here too we reject the null hypothesis and determine that the effect is statistically significant at the 5% level.

We conclude, then, that receiving Russian TV likely had a non-zero average causal effect on the probability of voting for a pro-Russian party in the 2014 parliamentary election for *all* Ukrainians living close to the border with Russia, not just for those who participated in the survey.

7.4 STATISTICAL VS. SCIENTIFIC SIGNIFICANCE

A result is **scientifically significant** when it is large enough to be consequential.

A common misconception is that statistical significance is equivalent to scientific significance. As we have just seen, an effect is statistically significant when it is not likely to be zero. In contrast, an effect is **scientifically significant** when its size is large enough to be consequential. Therefore, results that are statistically significant are not necessarily scientifically significant, and vice versa.

Suppose that we found that reducing class sizes had a tiny, albeit statistically distinguishable from zero, effect on test performance. This effect would be statistically significant but not scientifically significant. Based on this study, we would not recommend redirecting educational resources toward extra teachers and classroom space to implement a policy of class-size reduction.

By comparison, imagine that we found that attending a remediation program doubled the probability of graduating from high school, although the effect was found to be not distinguishable from zero due to the small size of the program. This effect would be scientifically significant but not statistically significant. Based on this study, we would at the very least recommend expanding the study by involving a larger number of students.

Typically, we aim to find results that are both statistically and scientifically significant.

7.5 SUMMARY

In this chapter, we learned to make inferences about unknown population-level quantities of interest using sample data. First, we learned to compute confidence intervals, which identify the range of values that is likely to include the true value of our quantity of interest. Then, we learned to conduct hypothesis testing to figure out whether an average causal effect is likely to be different than zero at the population level. Finally, we discussed the difference between statistical and scientific significance. Along the way, we completed some of the analyses from chapters 2 through 5. In particular, we quantified the degree of uncertainty in our estimates so that we could draw conclusions regarding all the observations in the target population and not just those in the sample of data analyzed.

With this chapter, we complete our friendly introduction to data analysis for the social sciences. We hope we have piqued your interest in data science and how it can be used to answer important questions about the real world.

7.6 CHEATSHEETS

7.6.1 CONCEPTS AND NOTATION

concept/notation	description	example(s)
parameter	unknown quantity of interest; it can be a sample-level quantity, but we focus on population-level parameters	the level of support for Brexit among all UK voters is a population-level parameter
estimate	sample-level statistic that estimates a parameter	the proportion of supporters among BES survey respondents is an estimate of the level of support for Brexit among all UK voters
estimator	function of observed data that is used to produce an estimate of a parameter	the sample mean is the estimator used to produce the estimate above
sampling distribution of an estimator	characterizes the degree to which the estimator varies from one sample to another due to sampling variability; it enables us to quantify the amount of uncertainty in our estimates; for all the estimators we use in this book: $$estimator \overset{approx.}{\sim} N\left(\text{true value}, (\text{s.e.})^2\right)$$ where true value is the true value of the population-level parameter and s.e. is the standard error of the estimator	thanks to the central limit theorem, we know that if we drew multiple large samples of a random variable X, with mean $\mathbb{E}(X)$ and variance $\mathbb{V}(X)$, the sample means would approximately follow a normal distribution with mean $\mathbb{E}(X)$ and variance $\mathbb{V}(X)/n$; the sample distribution of the sample mean is thus: $$\overline{X} \overset{approx.}{\sim} N\left(\mathbb{E}(X), \frac{\mathbb{V}(X)}{n}\right)$$
standard error of an estimator	estimated standard deviation of the sampling distribution of the estimator; estimate of the average size of the estimation error over multiple hypothetical samples	the formula for the standard error is different for each estimator; given the sampling distribution of the sample mean above, the standard error of the sample mean is: $$\sqrt{\frac{\mathbb{V}(X)}{n}}$$ (recall that the standard deviation equals the square root of the variance)
estimation error	difference between the estimate and the true value of the parameter	since the true value of the parameter is unknown, we can never compute the estimation error for any one sample, but thanks to the central limit theorem, we can derive (i) the average size of the estimation error over multiple hypothetical samples (see standard error above), and (ii) the average estimation error over multiple hypothetical samples
average estimation error	also known as bias; average difference between the estimate and the true value of a parameter over multiple hypothetical samples	all the estimators covered in this book have an average estimation error equal to zero
unbiased estimator	estimator for which the average estimation error over multiple samples is zero; estimator that provides, on average, accurate results	all the estimators covered in this book are unbiased estimators of their corresponding parameters; their sampling distributions are centered at the true value of the parameter

continues on next page...

7.6.1 CONCEPTS AND NOTATION (CONTINUED)

concept/notation	description	example(s)
confidence interval	provides the range of values that is likely to include the true value of the parameter three levels of confidence are conventionally used in the social sciences to construct confidence intervals: 90%, 95%, and 99%; the level of confidence refers to the probability that the interval contains the true value of the parameter over multiple samples; the formula to construct the 95% confidence interval is: 95% CI = [*estimator*−1.96×standard error, *estimator*+1.96×standard error]	the 95% confidence interval for the sample mean of *leave* in the BES survey is: [0.4657, 0.4781] we conclude, then, that the true proportion of support for Brexit among *all* UK voters was likely to be between 46.57% and 47.81%
margin of error	defined as half the width of the estimator's confidence interval; as a result, we can express the confidence interval as: *estimator* ± margin of error	in the example above, the margin of error equals 0.62 percentage points, which is half the width of the confidence interval; we can state that the likely proportion of support for Brexit among *all* UK voters was 47.19% with a margin of error of 0.62 percentage points
hypothesis testing	methodology we use to determine whether a parameter is likely to equal a particular value	we can use hypothesis testing to determine whether or not an average treatment effect is different from zero in the target population
null hypothesis or H_0	hypothesis we would like to eventually refute; it states that the true value of the parameter equals a particular value, θ (the Greek letter theta) H_0: true value = θ in this book, our null hypothesis states that the true value of the parameter is zero H_0: true value = 0	in our analysis of the survey of Ukrainians, $\widehat{\beta_1}$ is the estimator we use to estimate the average causal effect of receiving Russian TV on Ukrainians' probability of voting for a pro-Russian party in the 2014 parliamentary election; our null hypothesis states that Russian TV reception had zero average causal effect on Ukrainians voting behavior; in other words, it states that β_1 (the true value of the coefficient affecting the treatment variable) equals zero H_0: $\beta_1 = 0$
alternative hypothesis or H_1	hypothesis we test the null hypothesis against; the two-sided alternative hypothesis states that the true value of the parameter is not θ, without restricting the parameter to being above or below θ H_1: true value $\neq \theta$ in this book, our alternative hypothesis states that the true value of the parameter is not zero H_1: true value $\neq 0$	in our analysis of the survey of Ukrainians, our alternative hypothesis is that receiving Russian TV had either a positive or a negative causal effect on Ukrainians' voting behavior; in other words, it states that β_1 does not equal zero H_1: $\beta_1 \neq 0$
test statistic	function of observed data that can be used to test the null hypothesis	the z-statistic is an example of a test statistic

continues on next page...

7.6.1 CONCEPTS AND NOTATION (CONTINUED)

concept/notation	description	example(s)
z-statistic	test statistic whose distribution under the null hypothesis is the standard normal distribution; in general: $$z\text{-}statistic = \frac{estimator - \theta}{standard\ error} \sim N(0, 1)$$ in this book, since H_0: true value $= 0$: $$z\text{-}statistic = \frac{estimator}{standard\ error}$$ we denote the observed value of the z-statistic as z^{obs}	when the estimator is $\widehat{\beta}_1$, the formula of the test statistic is: $$z\text{-}statistic = \frac{\widehat{\beta}_1}{standard\ error\ of\ \widehat{\beta}_1}$$ in our analysis of the survey of Ukrainians, the observed value of the test statistic is: $$z^{obs} = \frac{0.2876}{0.0765} = 3.76$$
p-value	probability that we observe a value of the test statistic at least as extreme as the one we actually observed if the null hypothesis is true; when the null hypothesis is two-sided, we compute the two-sided p-value, which conveys the probability that we observe a test statistic as extreme as the one we observed in either direction of the real line: $$\text{two-sided p-value} = 2 \times P(Z \le -|z^{obs}|)$$	in our analysis of the survey of Ukrainians, the two-sided p-value is: $$\text{p-value} = 2 \times P(Z \le -|3.76|) \approx 0.0002$$ if the null hypothesis is true, the probability of observing a test statistic equal to or larger than 3.76 (in absolute value) is 0.02% ($0.0002 \times 100 = 0.02\%$)
significance level	determines the rejection threshold of the test and characterizes the probability of false rejection of the null hypothesis; social scientists conventionally use one of three significance levels: 10%, 5%, and 1%	if we use 5% as our significance level: we will reject the null hypothesis when the p-value is equal to or smaller than 0.05 (or 5%), and we will fail to reject the null hypothesis when the p-value is greater than 0.05 (or 5%) we will wrongly reject the null hypothesis in 5% of the samples drawn from the target population
statistical significance	a result is statistically significant at the 5% level when it is distinguishable from zero using 5% as the rejection threshold specifically, if $|z^{obs}| \ge 1.96$ or the two-sided p-value ≤ 0.05, we will reject the null hypothesis and conclude that the result is statistically significant at the 5% level conversely, a result is not statistically significant at the 5% level when it is not distinguishable from zero using 5% as the rejection threshold	in our analysis of the survey of Ukrainians: $$|z^{obs}| = 3.76 \quad \text{and} \quad \text{p-value} \approx 0.0002$$ thus, we reject the null hypothesis and conclude that receiving Russian TV was likely to have a non-zero average causal effect on the probability of voting for a pro-Russian party in the 2014 parliamentary election for all Ukrainians, not just for those in the sample we observed
critical value	cut-off point of the test statistic used to determine whether to reject the null hypothesis	if the distribution of the test statistic is well-approximated by the standard normal distribution and our alternative hypothesis is two-sided, the critical value for the 5% significance level is 1.96; if $|z^{obs}| \ge 1.96$, we will reject the null hypothesis; conversely, if $|z^{obs}| < 1.96$, we will fail to reject the null hypothesis
scientific significance	a result is scientifically significant when it is large enough to be consequential	a result might be statistically significant but be so small as to not be scientifically significant

7.6.2 R SYMBOLS AND OPERATORS

code	description	example(s)
[]	operator used to extract a selection of observations from a dataframe; to its left, we specify the dataframe we want to subset; inside the square brackets, we specify the criterion of selection; since a dataframe is composed of two dimensions, rows and columns, we can specify a criterion of selection on one or both dimensions; first, we specify the criterion of selection of the rows, and then the criterion of selection of the columns (separated by a comma); if the first criterion is left blank, all rows are extracted, and if the second criterion is left blank, all columns are extracted; (for other uses, see pages 50, 61, and 187)	$data[data\$var1==1,]$ # extracts the observations that have a value of 1 in *var1* as well as their corresponding values in all the other variables in the dataframe *data*

7.6.3 R FUNCTIONS

function	description	required argument(s)	example(s)
nrow()	computes the number of rows of a dataframe	name of the object where the dataframe is stored	nrow(*data*)
predict()	makes predictions based on a fitted linear model	the name of the object that contains the output of the lm() function by default, this function produces a prediction for every observation in the dataset used to fit the linear model; to produce only one prediction based on a particular value of the predictor(s), we set the optional argument newdata to equal data.frame(), where inside the parentheses we specify the value of the predictor(s) to also produce the 95% confidence interval of one prediction, we set the optional argument interval to equal "confidence"; to change the confidence level of the interval to a probability different than 95%, we would specify the optional argument level	fit <- lm(*y_var* ~ *x_var*, data=*data*) # stores fitted model into an object named fit predict(fit, newdata=data.frame(*x_var*=5), interval="confidence", level=0.99) # produces the predicted average value of *y_var* when *x_var*=5 as well as the 99% confidence interval for the given predicted outcome
abs()	calculates the absolute value	what we want to compute the absolute value of	abs(-2)
summary() $coef	provides a table with the following statistics related to a fitted linear model: estimated regression coefficients, standard errors, test statistics, and two-sided p-values	the name of the object containing the output of the lm() function	fit <- lm(*y_var* ~ *x_var*, data=*data*) # stores fitted model into an object named fit summary(fit)$coef # provides table with results

Index of Concepts

Index of Mathematical Notation

Index of R and RStudio